BY ROGER L. SIMON

Books

Heir
The Mama Tass Manifesto
The Big Fix
Wild Turkey
Peking Duck
California Roll
The Straight Man
Raising the Dead
The Lost Coast
Director's Cut
Turning Right at Hollywood and Vine
I Know Best

Screenplays

The Big Fix
Bustin' Loose (story by Richard Pryor)
My Man Adam
Enemies, A Love Story (with Paul Mazursky)
Scenes from a Mall (with Paul Mazursky)
Prague Duet (with Sheryl Longin)
A Better Life (story)

I Know Best

How Moral Narcissism Is Destroying
Our Republic, If It Hasn't Already

Roger L. Simon

ENCOUNTER BOOKS
New York • London

First American edition published in 2016 by Encounter Books, an activity of Encounter for Culture and Education, Inc., a nonprofit, tax exempt corporation.
Encounter Books website address: www.encounterbooks.com

Manufactured in the United States and printed on acid-free paper. The paper used in this publication meets the minimum requirements of ANSI/NISO Z39.48-1992 (R 1997) (*Permanence of Paper*).

FIRST AMERICAN EDITION

LIBRARY OF CONGRESS CATALOGING-IN-PUBLICATION DATA
Names: Simon, Roger L. (Roger Lichtenberg), 1943– author.
Title: I know best : how moral narcissism is destroying our republic, if it hasn't already / Roger L. Simon.
Description: New York : Encounter Books, [2016]
Identifiers: LCCN 2015028553| ISBN 9781594038051 (hardcover : alk. paper) | ISBN 9781594038068 (ebook)
Subjects: LCSH: Political culture—United States. | Political psychology—United States. | United States—Moral conditions. | United States—Politics and government—2009–
Classification: LCC JK1726 .S56 2016 | DDC 306.20973—dc23
LC record available at http://lccn.loc.gov/2015028553

Interior page design and composition by: BooksByBruce.com

There's nothing so bad for a woman as a man who thinks he's good.

—Oscar Hammerstein

AN ANNOTATED TABLE OF CONTENTS

I
Why This?. 1
In which the author explains why he's bothering—once again—to examine why half of America doesn't talk to the other half and why neither side changes its opinion about anything almost ever.

II
What the Least Great Generation Hath Wrought. 5
Why the author's generation, those born during and just before World War II, like John Lennon, Gloria Steinem, and imitators like Bill Clinton (not the boomers), are responsible for just about everything that has gone wrong with our culture and are the original, postwar "moral narcissists."

III
Qu'est-ce Que C'est "Moral Narcissism"?. 11
What exactly is this form of narcissism that is destroying—if it hasn't already destroyed—our families, friendships, workplace atmosphere, and democratic republic?

IV
Who Was the King of All Moral Narcissists?. 15
Jeopardy question: "bearded writers." He wrote his most famous works in the library of the British Museum.

V
Good versus Bad Narcissism: Henrik Ibsen
versus Jonathan Gruber. 21
Which works better and will last longer—A Doll's House or Obamacare?

VI
The Weather. 25
Grandmother always said, "In polite society, when you don't know people, just talk about something neutral, like the weather." That was then, this is now.

VII

For the Birds. 35
*Rachel Carson and how "environmentalism" came to replace Christianity,
Judaism, and even Hare Krishna (well, not so much) as our new religion.*

VIII

Wonderful Copenhagen. 39
*What I discovered to be the true motivations behind the snowbound UN
Climate Change Conference in Copenhagen.*

IX

Nostalgia for Racism. 49
*How and why moral narcissism helped bring back racism and the disastrous
racial violence across America at the very time it was starting to diminish.*

X

Booker T. Washington Really Did Know Best. 67
*The great African American educator knew long ago that the Sharptons of
the world were the real racists.*

XI

Selfies from Raqqa. 73
How moral narcissists fight the War on Terror to lose.

XII

Islam Denialism. 81
If you think all religions are equal, you can skip this chapter.

XIII

The Moral Narcissist Sleep Room. 89
*Oh, les beaux jours when we were all at the barricades, pulling up the
pavement in Paris!*

XIV

Nostalgia for Marxism 101
*"I want a revolution where everyone can drink cappuccino at the Café
Royal."—Daniel Cohn-Bendit of the Nanterre Six, during the Paris "events"
of May 1968.*

XV

Luxurious Leftism 109
The irresistible rise of the "red bourgeoisie."

XVI

Anatomy of the American Nomemklatura 119
And why it's stronger and more pervasive than even the Soviet original.

XVII

The Media Is the (Moral Narcissist's) Message 127
Who is really raping whom?

XVIII

Nostalgia for Class Consciousness 145
Nostalgia for Marxism's junior partner.

XIX

Bang! Bang! You're Not Dead! 153
How I learned to love the Second Amendment by outliving my mother.

XX

Narcissus in the Time of Atheism 157
Our society has a gaping hole.

XXI

The Mother's Milk of Moral Narcissism 161
Alternative title "The Soros and the Pity" (with apologies to Marcel Ophüls).

XXII

Unwinding—The Merry Month of May 2015 171
Moral narcissism reaches its height in that 2015 month . . . until the next one.

XXIII

Change 181
How do we get out of this? And can we?

XXIV

The Devil in Disguise 185
Seeing the devil in morally narcissistic clothes.

XXV

Envoi: Confessions of a Libertarian Neocon 191
   Living an oxymoron.

Acknowledgments (actually a dedication in the back) 193
Notes 195
Index 201

I

Why This?

In which the author explains why he's bothering—once again—to examine why half of America doesn't talk to the other half and why neither side changes its opinion about anything almost ever.

I was already well into writing this book before I realized why I was writing it. It shouldn't have taken that long. As the French say, the more it changes, the more it's the same thing. For the last seven or eight years I have been obsessed with one question above all, Why do so *few* people permanently change their views about political and social issues even in the face of literally earthshaking world events?

A corollary question is, Why do so many people return to their original views so determinedly, even if they have altered them for a short while? What is this pull that makes people go back to where they were, wrapping themselves in what they always thought as if it were a childhood security blanket?

Immediately after the terror murders in Paris in January 2015 at the office of the satirical magazine *Charlie Hebdo* and the kosher market Hypercacher, historian Jeffrey Herf wrote this to inaugurate his blog for the *Times of Israel*:

> I remember well that in the few months following 9/11, the American intellectual world, especially that of liberals and left-leaning people, was in a state of welcome confusion. The familiar denunciations of American "imperialism" and the habits of sympathy for "national

1

liberation movements" that had emerged in the protest against the war in Vietnam in the 1960s did not fit the realities of September 11, 2001. ... Sadly, the new thinking did not last long, or rather, it lasted but was supplanted by experts who told stories about a "moderate" Muslim Brotherhood and about the need to avoid inflaming Muslims with public discussion of Islamism. Many decades of investment in the cultural capital of the conventional habits of left and right were proving too powerful to overcome.[1]

How does this happen? Is it merely "human nature"? If so, what is it about human nature that makes us behave that way? What is the provenance of these "conventional habits" Herf speaks of, habits that lock us into tired ideologies and world views that preclude progress and change even as many adopt terminology that pretends to the opposite, proclaiming that they are the future, that they are "progressive"?

This is the enigma that has fascinated me for the better part of the last decade, after having undergone a political change of my own that began in the 1990s and accelerated after 9/11. This is not just an academic exercise because—at the tail end of a presidency of a man who is, at best, ambivalent about American Exceptionalism—we are at yet another turning point in Western Civilization and the history of the United States. This is the same politician who, at a fundraiser in 2008, famously accused his adversaries of being "bitter people, clinging to their guns or religion or an antipathy to people who aren't like them." But perhaps there was an element of projection in that accusation, because if there was any "clinging" going on, much of it was being done by Barack Obama and his adoring San Francisco audience of the time. And what they were really expressing and reinforcing, that is, clinging to, was not primarily their criticism of their opponents—that was secondary—but their own collective feelings of superiority to them. *They were best.* What they were expressing is a large part, most likely the dominant part, of the answer to the aforementioned enigma of why so few are able to change their views over a lifetime, and it is the subject of this book: moral narcissism.

But a second enigma occurred to me as I was yet deeper into the book. Why moral narcissism? What was its function, really? This made the experience of writing oddly similar to those I have had before, writing a series of mystery novels. It wasn't until I came to the final chapters that I figured out why. As it so often did when I wrote detectives stories, the answer surprised me. Possibly it changed my life.

II

What the Least Great Generation Hath Wrought

Why the author's generation, those born during and just before World War II, like John Lennon, Gloria Steinem, and imitators like Bill Clinton (not the boomers), are responsible for just about everything that has gone wrong with our culture and are the original, postwar "moral narcissists."

I am of the generation that read *The Communist Manifesto* before we read the US Constitution.

Well, not exactly. I did the read the Constitution and the Federalist Papers, mostly in student outline versions, so I could get a decent grade in high school American history and get into a good college. But I *really* read *The Communist Manifesto*. It was my samizdat, my underground literature. I can still recall the experience now, well over fifty years later—the intense, almost breathless feeling as I pored over the dog-eared, slim, cheap blue paperback with the prematurely yellowing pages until the small hours of morning. I underlined phrases with my ball point, lapping up Marx and Engels's conception of history as class struggle in my bedroom in ultrabourgeois Scarsdale, New York. Not that I even then considered myself a Communist or anything close, but there was something about it, the sense of rebellion maybe, the need to separate myself from the common, not to mention from my forebears, that drove me to pay attention. It drove me to keep reading and to commit the short book's ideological theories to memory, later to spout those ideas to my friends and family as if I believed in them even when I didn't.

I was not alone. In the 1950s a small but ever-growing group of bright young men and women was acting similarly, evolving inexorably into a generation that would in turn shape generations to come, even to the present day. We did so more effectively, or at least more permanently, than our parents, the Greatest Generation of World War II. They should have been the ones to form the future but, as it happened, we were the ones. We overcame them to become the commissars of the American zeitgeist, the arbiters of all things cultural and consequently political. No one else has gotten in much of a word edgewise.

I am not talking here about what is commonly referred to as the boomer generation, born just after the war in an optimistic blast of baby making. We were *pre*-boomers. I, only a foot soldier in this cohort army, was born in November 1943, but look at the icons: John Lennon, born in 1940; Tom Hayden, in 1939; Abbie Hoffman, in 1936; Gloria Steinem, in 1934; Allen Ginsberg, 1926; and Timothy Leary—apostle of "turn on, tune in, drop out" and virtual patron saint of hippie culture—born in, wait for it, 1920. (He was a "war baby" all right—a World War I baby!) The game was already well established, the rules already made, long before the boomers arrived on the scene. They were just our younger brothers and sisters, trying to play catch-up. They lived in imitation of us, expanding on what we did, playing variations on a theme and commercializing "the Revolution" until it was virtually bred in the bone, the very essence of American and consequently modern European culture. All others were outliers.

So who were we if *not* the boomers? How would you name us? You could call us the Generation of 1968, because that was when we made our most-enduring mark, when the "whole world was watching," as the chant went from the Chicago Democratic National Convention of that year. It seemingly never stopped. But a better title for us than the Generation of 1968, what the French call *babacool*, is the *Least* Great Generation, because that's what we were. Maybe the Ungrateful Generation. We may have contributed significant amounts to the lifestyle—music, films, fashion, food—but as the years rolled on and centuries turned, it became ever clearer that we were callow, even selfish, inside. All our neo-Marxist declarations, recycled through hippiedom or not, were meaningless. We were just Eliot's "Hollow Men" in hipster attire. Worse than that, we had—consciously or unconsciously or both—worked to unwind everything our parents had built. And it had its result, although not all of us desired it—or were later surprised by what we wrought. These days the robust American Exceptionalism that defeated the Germans and the Japanese and then rebuilt those despotic societies as still-functioning democracies in a virtually unprecedented manner is a distant, almost forgotten, memory.

What has happened to that America and how did we get where we are now? Can this better past, imperfect as that too undoubtedly was, ever be recaptured? What was the overweening psychology of this Least Great Generation that impelled it to dismantle a once great country? The word "narcissism" gets bandied about a lot. We all have our definitions of it—something between a handsome Greek youth transfixed by his image in a reflecting pool and something more clinical and scientific. Psychoanalytic texts speak of grandiosity, an extreme self-centeredness to such an extent that there is a failure to distinguish between the self and the external world. Another simpler but reductive explanation might come from the old joke about actors, "Enough about me. What do you think about me?"

We were all actors.

Whatever the case, the popularity of narcissism as a descriptive term for the behavior of our society is not a new phenomenon. As far back as 1979, Christopher Lasch published a now famous book *The Culture of Narcissism* that described the American behavioral patterns as largely narcissistic. According to Lasch, our family structure had produced a personality type consistent with "pathological narcissism." We were constantly seeking attention from the outside world, making us a nation of insecure weaklings forever in search of validation to tell us we were alive, to give us a raison d'être. Lasch saw the radicals of the sixties, like the Weather Underground, as manifestations of this pathology. He also cited the "personal growth" movements of the seventies—est, Rolfing, Hare Krishna, various forms of Buddhism, organic food, vegetarianism, and so forth. These belief systems and quasi ideologies continued to gain adherents during the eighties and nineties and on into the current century with writers like David Brooks and Charles Murray documenting how what was once youthful rebellion became the norms of the contemporary bourgeoisie. The Generation of '68 and its followers had gone mainstream, transmogrifying radical symbols into specific forms of conspicuous consumption. Everything was smeared. A trip to Whole Foods in a Tesla became the equivalent of striking a blow against world hunger. A smug and increasingly uniform political correctness dominated the culture, as in Seattle when Columbus Day was replaced by Indigenous Peoples Day.

The election of Barack Obama was the apotheosis of this melding of lifestyle with political world view. That he celebrated his victory in front of Grecian columns was symbolic in more ways than one. Narcissus was in the house—both on stage and in the audience. The me generation had found its perfect leader. Hope and change were never specified, because we all knew what he meant. How could it be otherwise? He was speaking, as was said in an earlier era, to "our crowd." But our crowd had become everyone who saw themselves as politically correct, even if they weren't sure what that meant or implied. It sounded good. Whatever it was had to be true. Obama was cool and his adversaries were not. He was our image in the reflecting pool, preening in front of those Greek columns, nose slightly elevated. Not surprisingly, with the failure of his presidency, it became de rigueur for the Right to accuse Barack Obama of being narcissistic, or of having a narcissistic personality disorder. It is one of the key explanations for that failure, even though no sector of our society is immune. We are all narcissists. It's just a matter of degree. Narcissism is everywhere.

When something obtains that much popular acceptance, one is tempted to think it is nonsense, mere cant, or at least overstated. Not true. It's worse. Christopher Lasch, as the saying goes, didn't know the half of it. Narcissism has taken over our society to such an extent that we cannot see straight. It has disconnected us, or a great many of us, from reality, and is in the process of undermining what tiny bit of democracy we have left. Every even mildly unconventional thought has a "trigger warning" lest someone be offended. Narcissism is making us blind. It is the secret sauce destroying America from within. It is also the handmaiden of perpetual distraction, the misdirection that prevents us ever from solving anything.

But ignore for the moment Narcissus admiring his visage in the pool, or even endless Kardashians parading across television screens as "real" housewives metastasizing from city to city. That is not the form of narcissism that need concern us unduly. Whatever we think of the aesthetics, it is at best a minor contributing factor and essentially trivial. Another far more lethal form of narcissism dominates and leads the parade of self-regard that is destroying our culture, even gnawing away at the fabric of Western Civilization itself, which is on the verge of disintegration, excessive as that may sound.

That form is *moral* narcissism—a pathology that underlies the whole liberal Left ethic today and some of the Right as well.

III

Qu'est-Ce Que C'est "Moral Narcissism"?

What exactly is this form of narcissism that is destroying—if it hasn't already destroyed—our families, friendships, workplace atmosphere, and democratic republic?

What is moral narcissism anyway? The short form is this: What you believe, or claim to believe or *say* you believe—not what you do or how you act or what the results of your actions may be—defines you as a person and makes you "good." It is how your life will be judged by others and by yourself. In nineteenth-century France, Brillat-Savarin told us that "You are what you eat." In twenty-first-century America, almost all of us seem to have concluded that "You are what you say you are. You are what you proclaim your values to be, irrespective of their consequences." *That* is moral narcissism.

It is a narcissism that emanates from a *supposed* personal virtue augmented by a *supposed* intellectual clarity. It is what allows Hillary Clinton to go from undergraduate Alinskyite to Chappaqua plutocrat with a net worth in the tens of millions without missing a beat, or John Kerry to go from Vietnam War protestor likening his fellow soldiers to Genghis (pronounced Jenn-jiss) Khan to a billionaire with a yacht constructed in New Zealand that he houses in Rhode Island to avoid the taxes of his native Massachusetts.

This is not exactly the aforementioned narcissism we remember from school, with Narcissus staring endlessly at the reflection in that pool, although it is related. It is more a narcissism of political and social thought, a narcissism that evolved as religion declined, a narcissism of ideas and attitudes, a narcissism of "I know best," of "I believe therefore I am." It is our identity tied up inextricably to our belief system in a way that brooks no examination. It is a narcissism of groupthink that makes you assume you are better than you are because you have the same received and conventional ideas as your peers, a mutual reward system not unlike the French concept of BTBG—*bon type, bon genre*—but taken to a national extreme. There is only one way to be, one kind of idea and attitude to have. There are no others. Why even bother to look, consider, or try to understand them?

And those ideas and attitudes are "reflected" in the following narcissistic manner—if your intentions are good, if they conform to the general received values of your friends, family, and co-workers, what a person of your class and social milieu is *supposed* to think, everything is fine. You are that "good" person. You are ratified. You can do anything you wish. It doesn't matter in the slightest what the results of those ideas and beliefs are, or how society, the country, and in some cases, the world suffers from them. It doesn't matter that they misfire completely, cause terror attacks, illness, death, riots in the inner city, or national bankruptcy. You will be applauded and approved of. Like the 1960s song by the Animals, it's all okay "if your intentions are good." No one will even notice what happened. You'll be fine. In fact, better than that, your status will continue to rise as you continue to parrot the received wisdom. It's the Peter Principle gone ideational.

Moral narcissism is the reason so few people change their views about anything and need something as cataclysmic as Nazi Germany to do so. And even then many change tentatively, reluctantly, ready to revert to type at any time.

But deeper down, beneath this conformity, it's all about how you feel about yourself. Self-regard is all. In the world of moral narcissism, we are all the ladies of Code Pink, craving attention, fairly yearning to be dragged out of a congressional hearing, preening for television cameras, as we mouth the most clichéd of progressive slogans, oblivious to their impact in the real world or even, remotely, to their veracity.

Not only are we good. We are *the best* and therefore we can do anything we wish. We have permission. Moral narcissism is the ultimate "Get out of jail free" card in a real-life Monopoly game. No matter what you do, if you have the right opinions, if you say the right things to the right people, you're exempt from punishment. People will remember your pronouncements, not your actions.

Hollywood stars, media personalities, and many politicians are proto-types of this behavior, but we are all prey to it. Look behind almost every issue of our day—climate, environment, energy, gun control, defense, foreign affairs, terrorism, education, income inequality, immigration, race (especially), women's rights, gay rights, political correctness (the mother lode of moral narcissism), microaggressions and trigger warnings (moral narcissism as modern day opera bouffe), media bias, cultural and entertainment bias, not to mention the very size and scope of government itself—and you will find the profound influence of moral narcissism, almost always for the worse. It is the prime hidden motor for our society, pointing to our republic's demise because it makes people blind to reality and democracy moot.

Even so, it could be argued that in a free country it should be your privilege to follow your narcissism, to support any foolish, unexamined, self-aggrandizing belief you want, if that is your wish, at the ballot box and elsewhere. In many instances, it will coincide with your self-interest, at least in the short run. But within that narcissism is the root of the destruction of that very society that is giving you that freedom, because the narcissistic allure is not far from the allure of fascism—a refracted hero worship. If our politics is dictated by what makes us feel good about ourselves, our mirror will soon, perhaps inevitably, morph into mass movements in which mock gestapo salutes or pseudo-anarchist Guy Fawkes face masks, not to mention faded T-shirts emblazoned with mass murderers like Che and Mao, become the real thing and not just symbols of adolescent rebellion.

Many of the abovementioned issues are tilted to the left by moral narcissism, but several push right as well. As much of a pose as progres-sivism may be, conservatives and libertarians are not excused. They too are part of this inescapable zeitgeist. How could they not be? In recent years, moral narcissism weighed heavily in the neoconservative belief that America could nation build in the Middle East, transforming tribal cultures like Iraq and Afghanistan into democracies like Denmark. Remember the slogan "Democracy! Whisky! Sexy!" that dominated the Right side of the Internet at the beginning of Operation Iraqi Freedom in a grand display of self-congratulatory triumphalism and misplaced hipness? Even the *New York Times* was quoting it.[1] Everyone would be like us—living freedom, jazz, and kicks. In a world where only the "whisky" part of the triumvirate survives—and that more than likely on private Saudi jets headed from Riyadh to Paris—and the Islamic State runs rampant over the very territory we thought we democratized, how antique that slogan seems now. How sadly misguided.

Other examples of right-wing moral narcissism exist, particularly in areas where social conservatism bleeds over into a holier-than-thou attitude toward one's fellow citizens, telling them how to live even when they are, in many instances, already quietly and privately living that way. Here certain beliefs work at cross-purposes, as in the opposition to gay marriage when the impulse that gays have to formalize their union is often highly bourgeois and essentially conservative. Similarly, social conservatives, putatively strong adherents of small government, veer equally strongly to the side of government intervention where abortion is concerned, wanting it forbidden by the state. Again, this frequently works at cross-purposes, since the women whose abortions they wish to forbid are often already opposed to abortion themselves. They just want to make their own choice. The legal intervention of government into their personal zone of privacy naturally repels them and has, if anything, the opposite effect from what is desired by those same social conservatives.

Further, libertarianism, particularly in its more extreme forms, can be fertile ground for moral narcissism. That government is best that governs least morphs into that government is best which governs barely or not at all. This becomes a posture dizzyingly close to anarchism. Yet few really want no government at all—especially given its results—but a fair number like to say they do or pretend as much to themselves or others. Thus the libertarian can find himself inadvertently in the camp of an Occupy Wall Street protestor, dancing around in that Guy Fawkes mask and burning down what he might otherwise respect and support, an odd contradiction indeed. The advice about not letting the perfect be the enemy of the good is a cliché for a reason. Like those on the left, often people on the right seek a form of purity impossible in human affairs. For those people, moral narcissism is their friend.

IV

Who Was the King of All Moral Narcissists?

Jeopardy question: "bearded writers." He wrote his most famous works in the library of the British Museum.

While moral narcissism is frequently an ally of the Right, it is quite often the Left's best friend. Big government of the socialist or democratic socialist sort adores moral narcissism, for it is, in a sense, the *creator* of big government. Karl Marx himself was one of history's great moral narcissists—a man who definitely *knew best*, sitting by himself in the library of the British Museum, dictating to the human race at some length how it should order itself. "The ends justify the means" is almost the perfect catchphrase for all moral narcissism. If you have what you think are the correct ideas, you can do anything. In retrospect, it should be no surprise that the results of Marx's then untested ideas were catastrophic. The number of corpses traceable to them in the Soviet Union, China, Nazi Germany, Cambodia, Cuba, Vietnam, Korea, and elsewhere is finally uncountable, although low estimates for Stalin—twenty million deaths—and Mao—forty million—should be sufficient to make the case even for diehards of the Left. Obviously, it didn't and doesn't.

To find myriad examples of Marxism's dismal outcomes being obfuscated by moral narcissism, look no further than Bernie Sanders's 2016 presidential campaign. The self-described democratic socialist Vermont senator touts the economic success and social justice of Scandinavian countries to adoring crowds even as those same nations abandon socialism for capitalism for their own survival or, in the case of Sweden, to avoid fiscal collapse.[1] Margaret Thatcher encapsulated the logical inconsistency of Sanders's ideology with her oft-quoted statement: "The problem with socialism is that you eventually run out of other people's money." But the evident accuracy of her statement is easily overridden by the emotional needs of a group, as Sanders's eager audiences have shown. As Sophocles put it nearly twenty-five hundred years ago, "What people believe prevails over the truth."

The current fashionable attraction to multiculturalism and its quasi-fascist forebear cultural relativism is also supported directly by this same morally narcissistic impulse. Indeed, liberalism and progressivism themselves, as presently constituted in our society, would not exist without moral narcissism. They are all about the self as viewed by the self. Without self-approval, liberalism would disintegrate. It holds it together.

That's where the influence of the Least Great Generation comes in. We members of the LGG obviously did not originate moral narcissism, which is undoubtedly as old as our species. Some version of early man thumped his chest and brayed about how he, and only he, had solved once and for all the problem of the saber-toothed tiger and should be rewarded accordingly. History is in part a tale of individuals and groups adhering to maximalist ideas and ideologies, occasionally for the better but far more often with disastrous ends. Communism, measured by those exponential mortality rates as well as by the emotional suffering and poverty of vast populations under its rule, was the worst of them. Immediately post-World War II, despite the revolt against McCarthyism and pleas for the supposedly innocent Rosenbergs, people were gradually beginning to understand the horrors of scientific socialism and Stalinism. Tales of the Gulag and the purge trials, the mass starvation of the Ukrainians, had filtered through, leaving the then young Least Great Generation bereft of its first inspiration, the Soviet Union.

Many chose Maoism instead. I can remember attending performances by the San Francisco Mime Troupe in the early seventies in which the audience was led in a doo-wop style community sing, chanting "Papa Mao M-Mao Mao ... Papa Mao Tse Tung." As we clapped to the beat and sashayed in a conga line, we felt oh-so-modern and oh-so-hip. What did we know? China was so far away and exotic. The slogans of the Great Leap Forward and the Cultural Revolution were unexamined idealistic rallying cries for causes we had only barely heard of. Who didn't want a good harvest? And fighting Lin Biao (whoever he was) and Confucius (he was so old-fashioned) seemed like the intelligent and politically correct (before we had even heard the term) thing to do. Few of us had any idea of what it all meant or what was actually happening in China. And by the time we did, when the horrors of the Cultural Revolution were made manifest to the world and the Tiananmen tanks were on our television screens, most of us had moved on anyway. It didn't matter. Our moral narcissism was focused elsewhere—climate change or the campus rape epidemic, whatever the latest imaginary outrage might have been. Moral narcissism, like the proverbial finger, having writ, moves on. It's not the subject. It's the feeling.

This doesn't mean that old traditions were not reinvented as needed. The Port Huron Statement of the Students for a Democratic Society— written in 1962 by Tom Hayden and arguably the founding document of the Least Great Generation—attempts to restart socialism by painting Stalin as an unfortunate aberration. There were better ways to utopia and we knew how to find them. We wouldn't make the mistake of Stalinist excesses (although years later moral narcissist in extremis Oliver Stone did his best to erase those Stalinist excesses from the record altogether with his television series *Untold History of the United States*).

Others followed in Hayden's footsteps or ran parallel with him, attempting to reconstitute leftism, to give it a new "humanistic" life in the face of its detractors. Writers like Norman O. Brown and Herbert Marcuse, heroes to us at the time, are exemplars of this type of distraction cum rehabilitation, adopting Freud, Gramsci, and other psychological and sociological thinkers to breathe life into moribund nineteenth-century Marxism. The Frankfurt School as well was a united front of moral narcissists dedicated to that end—deliberate obfuscation through art, literature, and obscurantist philosophy aimed at creating "socialism with a human face" or a face that was hidden altogether.

This approach had the desired impact. The Gulag and similar atrocities were largely forgotten and a new generation of leftists was born through the offices of the Least Great Generation. The culture and political theory were mixed together in a confusing stew, sometimes deliberately. Marcuse's most notable concept "repressive tolerance"—the theory that free expression as practiced in Western liberal democratic societies like the United States is actually a form of *oppression*, hence essentially *intolerant*—was a masterpiece of doublespeak, negating almost every possible act of criticism or distinction. This paved the way for the ironically gay French philosopher Michel Foucault's impassioned defense—under the equalizing banner of cultural relativism—of Khomeini's Islamic Revolution in Iran; the "ironically gay" description earned by the well-known repeated hangings of homosexuals from telephone poles under the ayatollah's rule. But still, all cultures were equal. Marcuse's essay on "repressive tolerance" appeared in 1965 and created a sensation in intellectual circles. Not long thereafter (1968) the Beatles were channeling the Beach Boys with "Back in the USSR," playfully establishing an easily swallowed moral equivalence between the United States and the Soviet Union. Everyone got up and danced, that equivalency message seeping into an entire generation and leaving a vacuum easily filled by the feel-good mentality facilitated by moral narcissism. Aren't we hot? Aren't we good? Bebop-alula.

By the time that generation grew up, most of those views had been adopted by the left wing and ultimately the mainstream of the Democratic Party as unspoken givens. William Voegeli in his recent book *The Pity Party* explains how this turned the Democrats into a party of fake, postured compassion, in other words, pity. In a sense, he was being charitable. For many, particularly those in leadership positions, compassion was never the point. Power was. Compassion became a masquerade for selfishness, a way for elites to feel good about themselves while conniving to rule and gain financially. Some of this was conscious on their parts, some unconscious, some undoubtedly a mixture of the two. In the end it didn't matter because an immense power structure, buoyed by a moral narcissism that had trickled down to a large portion of the public, making them especially gullible, was in place. And it was oh-so-profitable to the unquestioned elites who did the trickling. Bill Clinton was already receiving $500,000 for a single speech to oil sheiks in Kuwait.[2] He had previously earned $600,000 for two speeches in Saudi Arabia, no doubt to "progressive" groups, and $200,000 for a speech to a Chinese real estate group. Hillary Clinton received a $14 million advance for her book, surpassing her husband's previous record of $10 million. Neither book came close to earning out those advances or was probably even read much beyond page ten. Perhaps the public recognized they were just a collection of liberal bromides laced with self-justifications. But that didn't matter. The advances did not need to be returned.

These and other financial boondoggles might have been the envy of Boss Tweed, but they provide a certain risk to the elites and to Hillary's presidential ambitions. Well into the second decade of the twenty-first century, American society is at a turning point in that a significant part of the population has rebelled against these ruling elites. An increasing number are becoming repulsed by immensely wealthy public figures like George Soros and Michael Moore telling them what to do and how to live while enjoying lifestyles radically at odds with their prescriptions. And it has reached a point where fewer and fewer believe the masquerade anymore or are cooperating with it. At the same time that the country is trying to work through all the issues mentioned above, a crisis in race relations has risen suddenly to the forefront after seeming to have been improving for decades. This is not by accident. When the public starts to rebel against elites, the focus almost always shifts to a new crisis, providing a deliberate distraction and preserving the ruling class. The role of moral narcissism in manufacturing these crises is crucial.

This book will take each of those issues and demonstrate how they have been infected by moral narcissism and how that worked to the benefit of elites. Later I will try to show how moral narcissism has allowed the Democratic Party to become a hidden party of the rich, thus wounding the middle class and the American dream—and what can be done about it.

I will begin with the issue of climate because I believe it to be paradigmatic. Recently, Barack Obama delivered a speech at UC Irvine (as he did later to the Coast Guard and at West Point) excoriating so-called climate deniers with no reference whatsoever to actual science of any sort, only to what in his morally narcissistic view a citizen is supposed to believe. The coming climate catastrophe was a given, a premise on which all educated and reasonable people must perforce agree. Otherwise, they were barbarians, yahoos out of a Sinclair Lewis novel like *Babbit* or *Dodsworth*. The contradictory details of climate research were beneath mention by Obama, even irrelevant. A "good" person wants to save the earth and is willing to spend billions to do so, even if that means impoverishing the lower classes further, with no discernible evidence that there would be an improvement of any sort to the environment or a true determination as to whether warming is a positive or a negative. The audience, equally infused with moral narcissism and feeling especially good about themselves, gave the president a standing ovation for his pronouncements. As we used to say in the sixties, the personal had become political—or was it vice versa?

That sixties slogan is worth rethinking. More accurate might be that the personal yields the political or, in other cases, that the personal hides us from the political. In the end, for all of us as human beings, the personal is ultimately just that, the personal. We live in our own skins with our own feelings, our joys and pains, reacting to our own friends, family, and coworkers. For most of us, that is our world, at least the most important part of it. The ability to exist comfortably within a social sphere is a significant measure of our sanity. If that ruptures, our peace of mind and that social sphere begin to disintegrate.

That has been the outgrowth of moral narcissism in our culture. It has divided us almost as no other phenomenon. America is a nation emotionally divided because it is ideologically divided and quite rigidly so. Our families are split, many of our lifelong friendships damaged or destroyed. This is particularly true since the events of September 11, 2001, when, for a few months, our country drew together before it inexorably drifted apart to an extent it had not for decades, perhaps since the Civil War itself. Terrified to think anew, people retreated to the traditional views they had had for decades, in many cases since childhood. Now we often live in silence with each other, unable to speak about the most significant things for fear they will cause the situation to get worse, that we will alienate each other further and cause the social fabric to explode.

Almost all of this is because moral narcissism has made us adhere so closely to our ideas, even to identify our entire personalities with them in the most precise manner, when that would not be necessary at all. Bret Stephens, in his *America in Retreat,* speaks of an "overdose of ideals." Perhaps that is what we suffer from. Of course, those ideals come from somewhere. At some point we attached ourselves to them, as I did as a high school student, paging through *The Communist Manifesto.* The question is how to detach our minds from this narcissistic identification to see the world with clarity.

V

Good versus Bad Narcissism: Henrik Ibsen versus Jonathan Gruber

Which works better and will last longer—
A Doll's House *or* Obamacare?

I have painted us all as narcissists, but narcissistic identification is not *entirely* bad. There's narcissim and narcissism. Some narcissists are indeed better than others. "Healthy" or good narcissism exists, as Freud, among many others, has told us. A rational amount of self-love makes a necessary contribution to our lives. It motivates us, sometimes even makes us happy. I wouldn't be writing this book without it—or have done much of anything with my life. Most wouldn't have. More significantly, many of the advances in our science and culture wouldn't exist without a dab of narcissism, often more than a dab. The history of extraordinary achievements in the sciences and the arts can be viewed from one angle as the history of a kind of narcissistic megalomania. Henrik Ibsen is said to have kept a mirror at the end of a stovepipe hat that he would stare down at for hours, admiring himself and his genius while sitting at a cafe table. He wasn't the only one. Well, he may have been the only one with a mirror at the bottom of his hat, but metaphorically he certainly wasn't alone. Tooting your own horn, at least to yourself, may be a prerequisite for success.

An operative difference exists, however, between this healthy, or normally neurotic, narcissism and the moral narcissism under analysis here. One way to look at it is the difference between Henrik Ibsen and

MIT economist Jonathan Gruber, who putatively was one of the architects of the Affordable Care Act, Barack Obama's healthcare reform that has been so heavily criticized. It is perhaps unfair, even absurd, to compare Gruber—a seemingly intelligent though essentially routine academic—with a genius of world literature who helped revolutionize playwriting and the theatre, but it does highlight the difference between healthy, albeit extreme, narcissism and the moral kind—"I *am* best" (Ibsen) versus "I *know* best" (Gruber).

It is this latter type of narcissism ("I *know* best") that is the more dangerous for the citizenry at large and the culture. The MIT economist is one of the prime public exemplars of moral narcissism in recent times, a paradigm figure much in the way global warming is a paradigm theory or movement. Caught repeatedly on video asserting the American public was too ignorant to know what was for their own good, Gruber became a poster boy for elites manipulating the electorate for their own ends. These ends are at once antidemocratic and self-congratulatory and geared, again consciously or unconsciously, toward power, control and, quite often, economic gain.

It's no accident that few, including then majority leader Nancy Pelosi, knew what was in the Affordable Care Act. It didn't matter. They weren't supposed to. The bill itself was written by a small group of unelected and largely unvetted elites like Gruber and Dr. Ezekiel Emanuel, the brother of Barack Obama's former adviser Chicago mayor Rahm Emanuel. All the elected leadership had to do was cooperate with these elites, receive their wisdom, and profit from the appearance of doing something. What the elites wrote had to be good because the elites said it was good and because elites felt good designing it and the leaders felt good enacting it. It's no more than a high-toned shell game—moral narcissism as legislation. And the more byzantine the bill the better because there was no intention that it be understood and debated. As Nancy Pelosi made clear, "You have to pass the bill in order to find out what's in it." The process is more emotional than intellectual or analytical and, while pretending to the practical, is the antithesis of it. Results are immaterial and may never be known. In fact, it's better if they're not.

Inherent in this too, and not so far below the surface, is a buried insecurity. You pretend to know best, because deep down you fear you do not. You also may fear you are unqualified to make the decision or write the bill in the first place, because what really constitutes a qualification? A PhD? (The famous quote from William F. Buckley applies here: "I am obliged to confess I should sooner live in a society governed by the first two thousand names in the Boston telephone directory than in a society governed by the two thousand faculty members of Harvard University.") All of the usual qualifications that define elites may indeed be merely pretensions, something to be mocked like the pompous *Il Dottore* (the Doctor) stock character in the *Commedia dell'Arte*. Your ideas may be defective and you will be unmasked as a fraud. Nevertheless, you have become so thoroughly identified with these ideas that you cling to them more strongly, while making them as complicated as possible, thus wrapping them in a cloak of invisibility. The preservation of power is all.

This process or pattern—famously dramatized by Italian playwright Luigi Pirandello's *It Is So If You Think So* or *Right You Are (If You Think You Are)*—repeats itself over and over in many aspects of our political and social life. I could be polite and say to our detriment. Or I could be honest and say, particularly now, to our destruction. We are living in a time, it has been pointed out by commentators, of increasing global threat to our civilization, not unlike the 1930s. One of the enduring mysteries of that era is how so many allowed Hitler to carry out his dreadful work without forceful opposition until it was too late. There are many answers to that mystery, but moral narcissism is one of the keys to unlocking all of them, possibly *the* key. I will deal with that later, but first . . .

VI

The Weather

Grandmother always said, "In polite society, when you don't know people, just talk about something neutral, like the weather." That was then, this is now.

I am launching into this chapter on a particularly miserable day in Los Angeles, where it supposedly never rains; only today it's been raining at a pace of approximately one inch per hour, enough to create a flood or floods. Traffic lights are out and cars are backed up everywhere. Local news hosts are broadcasting ankle-deep in mudslides washing down from the San Gabriels. Rainfall records are being broken. "Climate change" has struck!

Or has it? Is it just a stormy day the likes of which have ebbed and flowed forever? Or is Armageddon just around the corner? Nobody knows, although many say they do. A new film version of "Noah" was released in 2014, after all. Speaking of floods, 2015 was the year of the Lima Climate Change Conference, the sequel to the Copenhagen Climate Change Conference of 2009. I attended the conference in Copenhagen, which took place in a near blizzard, the furthest thing from global warming imaginable. Nonetheless, the topic was discussed incessantly to the exclusion of anything else, as if the oceans welling up and destroying islands was a foregone conclusion. When I was a kid in New York City, there was a jingle that played repeatedly on the radio at the conclusion of the hourly news as a lead-in to the weather report: "Everybody talks about it, nobody does a thing about it—the weath-ther!"

How times have changed. Now it's "The weath-ther. Everybody talks about it all the time. And we have to do something drastic about it, right now, right away. Otherwise, the volcanoes will erupt, the glaciers will melt, the rivers will overflow, and we're all gonna die—the weath-ther!" According to such scientific wizards as John Kerry and, needless to say, Al Gore, weather—excuse me global warming, excuse me climate change, excuse me whatever new euphemism has or is about to appear—is the great cause célèbre of our era, surpassing even income inequality or, need-less to say, such lesser insignificant crises such as the spread of radical Islam throughout the Muslim world and across the globe, not to mention the Iranian nuclear bomb.

Well, not everybody believes it. There are those people—some them-selves scientists, some not—known as "climate deniers." They have been given a name redolent of the Holocaust to impute to them the status of those terrifying sociopaths who think Auschwitz was just a 1940s version of assisted living. These attacks began over a decade ago in an attempt to make the so-called deniers pariahs. They were often successful, although there has only been the most minor, if any, documented global warming—anthropogenic (man-made) or otherwise—in going on two decades now. Nevertheless, as recently as December 2014 a group calling itself the Committee for Skeptical Inquiry[1] released a public letter to the media urging journalists to use the word "deniers" rather than the gentler "skeptics" to describe those—they particularly had Oklahoma senator James Inhofe in mind—who don't believe in the science. The commit-tee members—who include television "Science Guy" Bill Nye and Carl Sagan's widow—evidently thought the word "skeptics" too respectable. In a May 2015 op-ed for the *Washington Post*, Senator Sheldon Whitehouse, Democrat from Rhode Island, went further, calling for the fossil fuel industry and its trade associations to be prosecuted under RICO rack-eteering statutes for engineering supposed secret payments to scientists in the manner of the tobacco industry. None of this ultimately has to do with whether global warming exists or will exist—and if it does, whether it is man-made and, if so, to what extent. Nor does it deal with the ques-tion of whether warming is finally good or bad.

This is all arguable and *has* been argued ad infinitum. The ins and outs of the science are worth studying, but they are not my subjects here. Although my father was a radiologist who worked for the Atomic Energy

Commission at its beginnings, treating the Hiroshima Ladies and inspiring me to want to be a physicist as a boy, I gradually turned from the subject as a teenager—in part because of lack of ability—toward literature. I am not remotely qualified to discuss the finer points of climate science in any depth, nor do I intend to. I am an agnostic on the topic of global warming, man-made or otherwise, though I assume climate changes eventually. It always has. There was an ice age, several, in fact, and, from what I understand, a medieval warm period with people growing wine grapes in Scotland. What interests me is why people's belief systems arose on this topic and why they think what they do; why they are so certain when they have no demonstrable reason to be.

Most of those who have an opinion on the subject have as little science background as I have, often less. This includes a large part of the Congress, the punditocracy, and the many people you meet at cocktail parties who are convinced that climate change is an approaching catastrophe and that it is necessary to spend an overwhelming portion of the national treasuries of the developed world to avoid this particular Armageddon.

Ask those same people about the second law of thermodynamics and they will most likely give you a blank stare and then, with some justification (it's rude after all), feel insulted that you even brought up such an impertinent question. What does their lack of scientific knowledge have to do with the truth? And if you point out such minor inconsistencies as the lack of hurricanes this year or that the polar bear population is actually expanding instead of declining, the chances of an intelligent dialogue or even a respectful reply are slim. Your words will just disappear into the ether as if you had been flown in from Uttar Pradesh and were speaking in some obscure dialect of Urdu—or they will stare at you as if you had a cognitive disorder. And if a reply does come, more often than not they will deflect the discussion to the supposed consensus of scientists on the matter, many aware of the oft-quoted statistic that 97 percent of scientists agree on the imminent danger of warming (as if it were tooth decay), although the imputation of danger was never part of any larger study and the statistic has been debunked numerous times as inaccurate and, in some cases, deliberately skewed. This is, at base, the oft-debunked "argument from authority," but if you don't know enough science, what else can you resort to? That famous logical fallacy was employed in a tweet by none other than President Obama who declared on his personal Twitter account (who knows who actually writes this?) —"Ninety-seven percent of science [sic] agree: #climate change is real, man-made and dangerous." Note again the use of the scare word "dangerous" that, Alex Epstein explains in *Forbes,* never appeared in the original scientific literature.[2] This is because it's hard to be sure whether warming is good or bad and scientists know this. There are arguments for both—and that's to assume that there is any warming at all. The same *Forbes* article recognizes a measly 0.8 degrees Celsius in the last 150 years, a number which is itself under dispute. Indeed in December 2014, the website *WattsUpWithThat* published ninety-seven articles contradicting the 97 percent consensus.[3] And by February 2015, reports were coming from all over the world of an extraordinary amount of fudging of the temperature data that form the UN report in the first place. This was detailed in an article in the *Telegraph* of London, calling it the "biggest science scandal ever."[4]

Just as contradicting facts go unnoticed, facts that confirm one's narrative tend to linger past their sell-by date and often become indelible. Many will insist global warming is "settled science," even though the notion of "settled science" is oxymoronic—Newtonian physics having morphed into Einsteinian physics, which is itself already revised, and so forth. Roughly thirty years ago *Time* and *Newsweek* trumpeted on their covers that a new ice age was imminent. Now warming is imminent but this time the science is settled. Why is that? Have we finally reached the apotheosis of scientific inquiry, making future study superfluous? That's ridiculous on its face. As late as 1994, *Time* was still warning of an impending ice age, as did important US solar physicists in 2013.[5] Russian scientists have emphatically predicted cooling and continue to, but as a country dependent on energy production, their opinions are suspect. What makes the assumption of warming being "settled science" particularly ironic is that climate science itself is a field that did not even exist as such during the years of those *Time* and *Newsweek* covers. Some say it doesn't actually exist now as a justifiable, separate category of study; that it is just a foregathering of aspiring physicists, chemists, and geologists who couldn't make the cut in their more stringent and demanding disciplines. That's an admittedly severe, and possibly unfair evaluation, but the overall point remains. Science is under assault in the name of science. A new version of Arthur Miller's *The Crucible* could be written about global warming/climate change with the deniers in the role of the Salem witches. Ditto Bertolt Brecht's *Galileo* with the deniers in the role of the great Florentine himself, battling the received wisdom of his day, clerical and otherwise, as he insists the earth really does revolve around the sun.

The manipulation of science for political purposes is not new and the moral narcissism of whatever era is always there as a means to exploit science for ideological purposes, sometimes in a manner that truly is dangerous. In one notable and ominous example, in the 1940s Joseph Stalin used ideas that biologist Trofim Lysenko had derived from the French naturalist Jean-Baptiste Lamarck—that acquired changes such as the enlargement of a muscle through exercise would be transmitted to off-spring—to undermine accepted evolutionary theory and the Mendelian theory of genetic inheritance. Lysenko developed his erroneous conclusions in the field of agriculture, but Stalin and his totalitarian Communist minions exploited them to create the impression that human traits were not genetically determined and that a "new man" could be created in the Soviet Union, free of the encumbrances and reactionary values of the bourgeois past. In 1948, all scientific opposition to Lysenko's theories was formally outlawed in the USSR, literally destroying modern genetics in that country for a generation and turning many legitimate scientists into enemies of the state. The commissars "knew best." You'd better be a "new man"—or else.

To say modern day climate manipulation has gone that far is of course radically unfair. Climate deniers may have been made professional pariahs in some instances, but they're not—unless Senator Whitehouse gets his way—in jail or the Gulag. But the Lysenko story should be a cautionary tale. Science should be shielded in a secure zone away from politicians and political leaders and separate from ideological bias from any side. Admittedly this is a tad idealized and complete innocence of motive is a bit much to ask in human affairs, but it should always be the goal to maintain the preservation of science itself. A significant percentage of environmental science these days— the climate science area in particular but a fair percentage of generalized environmentalism as well—has gone in the direction of virtually unquestioned cant. What was once called conservationism, something almost all people applauded and engaged in, disappeared in favor of a fervent and faith-like rigid belief system exemplified by the ritualized celebration of Earth Day as the modern Christmas. Mother earth had become the new Madonna and Child combined. At the same time, the more the environmental movement centered on climate Armageddon, the less attention we devoted to scientifically verifiable and often solvable ecological problems that will always be around us. They were just not glamorous enough.

How this happened psychologically and emotionally—how anthropogenic global warming became the dominant apocalyptic threat of our time, outdistancing even nuclear war, transnational terrorism, and other perils such as attacks on the power grid or computer hacks of military, government, and corporate facilities that could bring the world to a standstill—is at once fascinating and disturbing. Consistent with the premise of this book, moral narcissism was the culprit in making the weather, even now, the bellwether for determining one's political correctness, one's acceptability in polite society. As with so many trends, it was a matter of timing. A gap needed filling.

But before going further, I should note that at this moment a dawning disinterest by the public at large in the climate change narrative. This is not surprising—it is part of a common pattern. Morally narcissistic ideation typically descends from elites to the masses for their consumption, approval, and adoption. It remains that way until the masses, what Bill O'Reilly quaintly calls "the folks," suddenly wake up and shrug it off—or even begin to think it's cuckoo. But the damage is almost always already done. Legislation has been enacted; government regulations put in place; fraudulent business deals made. So it was with global warming. Late in the last century, elites informed the masses that the earth was warming due to man-caused carbon dioxide emissions, something that as yet can only be proven by statistical inference or computer modeling, not so far by experimental reproduction as per the scientific method. A few of these elites were knowledgeable in the science but most were not. Nevertheless, the much larger latter group—perhaps because they sought a kind of validation by association in a technological age (a makeup grade for college science embarrassment, you might say)—insisted that warming was imminent and potentially catastrophic. It was, after all, consistent with an already prevalent world view—that man was a despoiler. It was the next semilogical step.

Mass media—an ever-willing and in many ways dominant force among the elites because of its permanence—was crucial in this endeavor. A critical mass started to occur as the warming theory approached its apotheosis with the publication of Al Gore's book *An Inconvenient Truth*. This became the documentary for which Gore's producer was awarded an Oscar. (Gore himself was a D student in geology at Harvard, speaking of makeup grades.) When the promised cataclysms never occurred, the rapid warming in the form of Michael Mann's highly publicized "hockey stick" graph not replicated in reality, the elites informed the masses they were confusing weather with climate. Taking a page from Orwell's Ministry of Truth, "global warming" was removed from the lexicon and the new phrase "climate change" promulgated. It was a catchall for everything. Cooling meant climate change, just as warming had meant climate change. Frequent hurricanes, cold snaps, heat waves, and random tornadoes were climate change. And when it was pointed out that there were actually fewer hurricanes rather than the predicted increase, that was climate change too. How this new phraseology differed from the ever-variable weather that the public had seen in front of them all their lives was explained theoretically in various ways, but not in a way that could be easily comprehensible to the public or even to many of the politicians and pundits who were themselves trying to explain it. Theories such as the deep ocean water mitigating warming were proffered and then mysteriously withdrawn or bickered about. Others complained of excessive acidification of the oceans while still others worried about marine ecosystems. In January 2015, more scientists in the Oxford Journal *BioScience* were insisting this was all "group think."

Before that, and more importantly, there had been the familiar email problems. In 2009, years of private communications from scientists at East Anglia University—the hub of climate research in the United Kingdom—had been leaked with indications that data had been fudged to "hide the decline" in warming. (This happened again as recently as 2015, in this case by America's own National Oceanic and Atmospheric Administration.)[6] The motivations for this fudging were all too obvious—professional reputations and cold hard cash were at play. Many rose to defend the scientists involved but the damage was done. So the politicians' opinions were open to mockery, but those opinions, motivated as they were by moral narcissism and by donations from exceptionally

wealthy backers like hedge fund manager Tom Steyer, themselves similarly motivated, rarely varied or even were revised an iota to account for
the embarrassment.

Views based on moral narcissism are most often written in stone.
Changing them can create an unbearable wound to the self, personality
disintegration. Even when Patrick Moore—the cofounder of environmental giant Greenpeace—admitted there was "no actual proof" of man-
made global warming, it made little lasting impression in the high-level
global zeitgeist.[7] The elites—Western leaders—were unmoved by the
apostasy of one of their own. They couldn't allow it. They just pretended
he never existed. Similarly, when so-called "father of global warming"
and mentor of Al Gore former UC San Diego professor Roger Revelle
allowed near the end of his life that his original opinions on warming
might have been "drastic," Gore accused the multiple award-winning
scientist of being dotty. Then, upon his death, Revelle's daughter stepped
in quickly to assure the world that her father had privately told her at the
end of his life that he had never changed his mind. Global warming was a
serious matter. Dissenting opinions could not be countenanced. By early
2014, one Rochester Institute of Technology professor even called for the
political prosecution of "denialists."[8]

After all, that void had been filled. There was no going back. At the
end of the last century the ever-expanding environmental movement
was stalling. Smog had significantly diminished as a major blight on
American cities, leaving them without the most palpable evidence of
looming environmental disaster. The skies even over Los Angeles were
mostly clear. Substitute causes like endangered species and the disappearance of the Amazonian rain forest, while evocative, lacked the immediacy,
not to say proximity, to muster serious adherence and garner significant
donations for an expanding community of interlocking businesses and
NGOs. The movement needed a new cause. This decline in interest
roughly coincided with the disputed, though ultimately failed, 2000
presidential campaign of Al Gore. The former vice-president had been
deprived of a lifetime ambition he thought he deserved and had won. For
a while he acted like a wounded and rather disappointed animal, but then
he found his mojo again. For some years a self-styled environmentalist,
he seized on the opportunity to put forward the momentary imminence
of global climate catastrophe. Almost certainly he did not exaggerate

this deliberately, at least consciously, but if he had merely mentioned the problem as potentially one among many, as yet not fully scientifically determined, nothing much would have happened in the short run, if at all, particularly for him. Obviously, it did. Soon enough he was the most famous environmentalist on the planet, a shared Nobel Prizewinner and a nascent billionaire through green investments and carbon exchanges, the selling of so-called "carbon offsets" between businesses. That most of these investments failed and that the exchanges disappeared after being scrutinized for fraud was beside the point. Gore had already more than filled that void created by those relatively clear skies. These two factors, Gore's desire to remake his mark with a new opportunity and the void in the environmental movement, united to create a climate crisis with moral narcissism as the glue that brought and held them together, that made it possible, and made people *want* to believe. A bourgeoisie, already identifying with the defense of mother earth, was ready to take that step. Controlling the weather was humanity's most important cause.

VII

For The Birds

*Rachel Carson and how "environmentalism" came to
replace Christianity, Judaism, and even Hare Krishna
(well, not so much) as our new religion.*

B ut to understand how this development evolved, to know the process,
we must go back further, over fifty years, to the publication of Rachel
Carson's *Silent Spring* in 1962. This marked the beginning of environmentalism as we know it—the replacement of conservationism with a form of
nature worship. This coincided too with the questioning and ultimately
the restructuring of traditional religion. I remember the time well because
I was one of Carson's readers as a college student, a typical undergraduate
agnostic or even atheist of the period in search of a belief system. We of
the Least Great Generation were at the start of the sixties and just beginning to differentiate ourselves from the previous generation. Soon we
would be working overtime on that separation. *Silent Spring*—an attack
on the use of pesticides as detrimental to the environment, especially to
birds, or what the author called "the silencing of birds"—was the seminal
text in this demarcation. That thousands, perhaps hundreds of thousands,
of Africans ultimately died of malaria due to the DDT ban associated with
the book's publication was to be largely ignored.[1]

A movement had been born. Not long after, Greenpeace was formed—
its existence celebrated by a 1970 Joan Baez concert in Vancouver. Earth
Day was established in the same year, igniting a brushfire. It wasn't long
before there were more ecologically oriented groups than you could

count, filling supermarket parking lots with card tables laden with petitions and knocking on doors for donations like Seventh Day Adventists. Environmentalism was well on its way to replacing organized religion as the premiere faith of the American and global elites and their myriad fellow travelers and acolytes. What a relief not to have to defend the ancient mythologies of Jesus and Moses anymore, all those scientifically troubling miracles. Nature had suddenly become human-centered again, just as it was in the Middle Ages, although then it was man *and* God—now it was just man all by his lonesome. Humanity was now the cause of every problem in the world, maybe even in the cosmos, and it would be up to humanity to solve them. Forget the sun and all those other countless stars, nebulae, galaxies, asteroids, black holes, and the rest of the so-called missing baryons, invisible objects, in an ever-expanding universe. They didn't count for anything or mean anything in the grand scheme of things. They weren't driving gas-guzzling SUVs or leaving the thermostat at seventy-two when it was sixty-nine outside. It was all about us—back to square one before Galileo and Copernicus said all that subversive stuff about the earth revolving around the sun. What could be more narcissistic than that?

Ironically, almost all off this occurred *after* Richard Nixon, of all seemingly unlikely people, signed the National Environmental Policy Act on January 1, 1970. This act did more than any legislation ever had to clean up the air and water in our country—clearly a good thing. Nixon also created the Environmental Protection Agency in 1970, which must have seemed good at the time, but *only* at the time. It was a bureaucracy and like almost all bureaucracies an entity whose own survival became its primary goal, no matter what its members said or thought. Cheered on by that growing claque for whom the environment had become the new religion, the EPA did its best to extend its power under many administrations. It was soon to be out of control, regulating with less and less oversight. In today's world it behaves like a kingdom unto itself, almost no one knowing what it is doing or why until it makes its decrees, upending industries to avert catastrophes real or imaginary in the name of biodiversity or, worse, the latest ecological fad. Like so many idealistic movements, environmentalism was beginning to recapitulate the French Revolution, starting as a positive force and then never putting a brake on itself, continuing on almost entropically until it began to destroy the very things it was intended to save.

I'm not suggesting that Al Gore or anybody else connected with environmentalism is the living embodiment of Robespierre. The only beheadings going on these days are Islamist in nature. We should all be concerned about being good stewards of the planet we live on, at least that should be our intention. But when our moral narcissism runs away with itself, we go blind. The pattern of idealism gone sour, writ so large in the French Revolution, reappears in many—one is tempted to say all—situations on multiple fronts and issues. That is because the thing itself—the idealistic goal—is almost always ultimately subsumed to the needs and projected self-image of the people having those goals. Thus it frequently provides an excuse for outrageous behavior in complete contradistinction to the pronounced intention, like Leonardo DiCaprio circling the globe on a private jet while telling the hoi polloi to restrict their carbon usage, or "working class spokesman" Michael Moore living in nine homes. *Slate* reported several hundred of the delegates to 2015's World Economic Forum arrived in Davos for climate change day in private jets.[2] The examples of wretched excess are endless in a veritable "Lifestyles of the Rich and Environmental." It's as if saying you're Green gives you permission to litter on an exponential scale.

You could say this hypocrisy is finally irrelevant—that it doesn't matter if Al Gore has the biggest houseboat in Tennessee as long as he's on the right side, if his "intentions are good." But excuse me if I'm a little suspicious. What if those intentions really were primarily money and power and the liberal idealism was just a masquerade? Or if it started off innocently enough, with at least the pretense of idealism, and became more sinister? After all, at one point Robespierre was on the right side of things too—or we think he was. Further to the French Revolution analogy, those symbolic (for now, anyway) beheadings were and are used to read people out of the discussion permanently on a subject like global warming/climate change, to smear them in news reports, deprive them of academic appointments and research grants and, most of all, keep them away from the levers of control. That is being done now without the guillotine. You are, in Huey Newton's words, either part of the solution or part of the problem. If you're part of the problem, you are a denier and shouldn't be heard. That this is inherently antiscience is clear, but it is also equally evidently totalitarian in its essence.

VIII

Wonderful Copenhagen

What I discovered to be the true motivations behind the snowbound UN Climate Change Conference in Copenhagen.

What this leads to is a world where actual ideals and even truth are beside the point. People are either *in* or *out* of the game. It's a conspiracy for fun and profit. I was reminded of this while covering the 2009 UN Copenhagen Climate Change Conference at which Obama appeared briefly and gave a speech. Nothing much really occurred there that was substantive other than delegates and press spending a few days in one of Western Europe's most beautiful cities, schmoozing and drinking aquavit. (Climate conferences tend not to happen in Dubuque.) Half the US Congress seemed to be there on a taxpayer-funded junket. When I ran into Rep. Charlie Rangel in the gift shop of the Marriott where most of the delegation was staying and asked the New York congressman whether he believed in anthropogenic global warming, he looked at me as if I were joking. When he realized I might be serious, he waved me away as some kind of crank and returned to the important business of examining the expensive Danish jewelry on display.

More interesting (and telling) was an encounter I had the next day with the delegate from the island of Tuvalu—a tiny place in the Pacific said to be about to disappear under water from the predicted ocean rise due to global warming. We were sitting next to each other waiting for one of these lectures that never seemed to get started, so I commiserated with the poor fellow about the sad fate of his country. He started laughing and tapped me on the arm in a friendly way very unlike Rangel. I suddenly got suspicious and asked hesitantly "You don't believe it's happening?" The man grinned and nodded affirmatively. "Then why are you here?" I continued.

"For the money," he said, as if it were the most evident thing in the world.

You couldn't but like him for his honesty. Half a decade later nothing much has happened to Tuvalu but that hasn't stopped its prime minister, Enele Sopoaga, from warning the world at yet another conference in New York in 2014 that climate change was "like a weapon of mass destruction."[1] Sopoaga, who is seeking cash for the repatriation of his sinking citizens to other countries, further said of his island nation, "We are very, very worried—we are already suffering." How, he doesn't specify, but he did provide a few photos of a few sandbags stacked along the oceanfront. Actual climate data for the island is sparse but records from nearby American Samoa indicate virtually no change for decades.[2]

Tuvalu, of course, is not alone in working the climate change side of the street from a developing world perspective. But the amount of money involved here is the proverbial peanuts compared to the big league game going on in the background at Copenhagen. A new market had recently been formed to trade so-called credits for the use of the supposedly evil carbon, the cap-and-trade strategy. And as with most markets, the numbers of zeros involved boggled the mind and brought out the 3.0 reading glasses—for good reason. According to a December 10, 2009, report in the *Telegraph*,

> Carbon trading fraudsters may have accounted for up to 90pc of all market activity in some Europeans countries, with criminals pocketing an estimated five billion Euros mainly in Britain, France, Spain, Denmark and Holland, according to Europol, the European law enforcement agency. The revelation caused embarrassment for European Union negotiators at the Copenhagen climate change summit yesterday, where they have been pushing for an expansion of their system across the globe to penalize heavy emitters of carbon dioxide. Rob Wainwright, the director of the Interpol serious crime squad, said large-scale organized criminal activity has "endangered the credibility" of the current carbon trading system.[3]

These "embarrassing" carbon exchanges have, not surprisingly, largely disappeared. And if you mention them at a cocktail party to your average climate change true believer—most of whom would be likely to have heard, at most, only vaguely of these exchanges—it is almost certain they will dismiss them with a laugh. After all, bad people can take advantage of all manner of good things. But what if those same people were actually the initiators of those good things in the first place? Here's Maurice Strong—Canadian oil and mining businessman, former undersecretary general of the United Nations, unanimously-elected head of UNEP (United Nations Environment Programme), secretary general of the 1992 Earth Summit, winner of the U Thant Peace Award and the Jawaharlal Nehru Award for International Understanding, and the so-called "godfather of the 1997 Kyoto Protocol": "Climate change is the biggest single challenge humans have ever faced. Unlike other problems, which can be solved regionally or sectorally, climate change affects the very future of life on earth. It is the greatest security problem we have ever faced."

What a man! Have more righteous words ever been spoken? Has a more impressive vitae ever been written? Maybe so, but the reality of this environmental godfather is rather different. Strong has been linked to virtually every scandal coming out of the UN for decades, including the notorious Oil-for-Food debacle—in which unprecedented sums of money were siphoned off from a program that was designed to help the starving in Iraq—to cash being funneled through UN agencies into North Korea. One of the more bizarre of these was a little known UN Strong-directed offshoot in Costa Rica called the University of Peace that gives degrees in "peaceology" as well as foundation grants to the North Koreans. For what is undetermined.[4] Strong is currently living in Beijing with his ties to the UN more or less severed after a controversy concerning his relationship to Tongsun Park—the so-called "Asian Great Gatsby" convicted on federal conspiracy charges over Oil-for-Food—and a mysterious million-dollar check made out to "M. Strong."

But the existence of Strong and other dodgy characters like Northwestern University business professor Richard L. Sandor—father of the Chicago Climate Exchange (whose panicked investors bailed out for $600 million in 2010[5] and who had been named a *Time* Hero of the Environment in 2007) do not themselves mean climate change *isn't* occurring. Indeed, on January 16, 2015, NOAA and NASA jointly announced that 2014 had been the hottest year on record, with several scientists simultaneously concluding that serious man-made global warming was now a certifiable crisis. One of them came to the extreme conclusion that 2014 was the hottest year in five thousand years.[6] Less than an hour later, the gang at *Climate Depot*—a skeptics blog—had launched a counterassault by another group of respected scientists who quickly pointed out that the supposedly monumental warming of 2014 was in the low hundredths of one percent, an immeasurable difference, and that the pause in warming had continued. And so it went—tit for tat—and will go on into the foreseeable future, one would imagine.[7]

James Delingpole in his book *Watermelons: The Green Movement's True Colors* posits the entire environmental movement is like that large melon, green on the outside but red (communist) on the inside. It is a mask adopted to disguise overtly political purposes. There's undoubtedly some truth to that but an argument can also be made that it is instead the ultimate crony capitalism—making up a market that doesn't exist, making a fortune from it, and then closing it down, leaving a gaggle of losers in the lurch. Moral narcissism provides the necessary underpinning either way. People think they're doing either socialist utopian good (money to the poor of Tuvalu) or proving how free markets (via carbon exchanges) are the answers to all the world's problems.

Since most people have nowhere near the scientific expertise to have an educated opinion on global warming/climate change, their opinions on the subject are closer to rooting for a sports team then they are to science. They simply pick a team—in this case, of scientists (or politicians who approve certain scientists)—to believe in, actually root for, and almost always stick with them for the duration, just as most do with their sports teams through the team's ups and downs. Only a few people know the actual names of the scientists on their team the way they do a quarterback in football, but it comes to the same thing. They're with them anyway, largely because the scientists are expressing what the group in question wanted to believe in the first place. Almost all are prey to this. I know I am. I have picked my scientists, admittedly without anywhere close to a full understanding of their work.

One of them is Richard Lindzen, the atmospheric physicist and retired MIT meteorology professor known for his work on the dynamics of the middle atmosphere and ozone chemistry. He was also one of the lead authors of the IPCC Third Assessment Report on climate change. In other words, he comes from the belly of the beast—the IPCC (Intergovernmental Panel on Climate Change) is the UN sponsored body that shares the Nobel Peace Prize with Al Gore. What seduced me about Lindzen was his ability to write well in plain layman's English, making clear that whatever warming may or may not be going on does not merit the terrified alarm bells being rung by politicians. He has also detailed, from the inside of the academy, the interlocking structures of teaching appointments and research funding that have turned climate change into an industry with a vested interest in its own preservation. This didn't win him any popularity contests on campus. Christopher S. Bretherton, an atmospheric research scientist at the University of Washington, told the *New York Times* Lindzen is "feeding upon an audience that wants to hear a certain message, and wants to hear it put forth by people with enough scientific reputation that it can be sustained for a while, even if it's wrong science. I don't think it's intellectually honest at all."[8]

Projection or just an academic pissing contest? I'll see your University of Washington and raise you an MIT. It's easy to understand scientists being passionate about their viewpoints—although, interestingly, many of the most esteemed are more measured. It's their field of endeavor and a few, anyway, have a sense of decorum. But the ferocity of opinion on the part of the rest of us often borders on the comical. At the first Democratic Party debate for the 2016 election, candidate Bernie Sanders, the senator from Vermont and self-acknowledged democratic socialist, in an answer to a question on what was the greatest foreign policy threat to the United States, declared emphatically that it was "climate change." He received a rousing ovation from the audience that seemed to agree. This was in October 2015, when the Middle East was in flames and a revived Russia was making inroads into Syria and Eastern Europe. Sanders, however, was worried about "climate change." He didn't specify whether, in this case, he meant global warming or cooling. Only a few months before (June 2015) the British MET office had warned of a new "ice age" with temperatures possibly the lowest they have been since the seventeenth century,[9] though I'm almost certain that would have been news to Sanders. Not surprisingly, the Vermont senator had almost no background in science, unless you count a BA from the University of Chicago in *political* science and a few months on an Israeli kibbutz in the late sixties. (Perhaps he learned something about agriculture.) Sanders has spent virtually his entire work life in politics.

Sometimes, however, although rarely, opposing viewpoints do seep through to politicians. At one point, John Kerry acknowledged that a handful of people of intelligence might have their reasons for being skeptical about the apocalyptic danger of anthropogenic global warming, but said that the risk of not addressing warming was greater than that of ignoring it—and therefore money should be spent. Of course, the secretary of state was referring to gigantic quantities of money in an already highly stressed global financial system. But even this ambivalent acknowledgement of his adversaries proved to be temporary because Kerry, like Sanders, has since asserted the primacy of climate change as our most important national security concern.

Similarly, and more significantly, Barack Obama cemented his position as Moral Narcissist in Chief by arguing vehemently for climate change as our number one security threat during his State of the Union address in January 2015—this only days after the mass Islamic terror murders in Paris that shook the Western world and brought four million people into the streets in France. "No challenge poses a greater threat to future generations than climate change," said Obama, receiving one of his few standing ovations of the evening. He continued:

> I've heard some folks try to dodge the evidence by saying they're not scientists; that we don't have enough information to act. Well, I'm not a scientist, either. But you know what—I know a lot of really good scientists at NASA, and NOAA, and at our major universities. The best scientists in the world are all telling us that our activities are changing the climate, and if we do not act forcefully, we'll continue to see rising oceans, longer, hotter heat waves, dangerous droughts and floods, and massive disruptions that can trigger greater migration, conflict, and hunger around the globe. The Pentagon says that climate change poses immediate risks to our national security. We should act like it.

Again not surprisingly, Obama also repeated the claim that 2014 was the hottest year on record, although just the day before, that claim had been walked back by one of its key claimants—Gavin Schmidt of the

NASA Goddard Institute for Space Studies—who admitted there was a margin of error in NASA's data, making the likelihood of 2014 being the "warmest year" a far less onerous 38 percent. Moreover, records begin only in 1880, before which year there were many warm periods, some of great length, with temperatures radically in excess of the present day (and during a time there were many fewer carbon polluting humans on the planet, if any). And then there is the question of how temperatures were measured outside the modern era, when most measuring devices were in grassy fields, not on hot tarmacs as they were later.

But never mind. I am breaking my pledge and beginning to argue the science. What was important about Obama's SOTU was that vehement standing ovation he received even from many Republicans. The warmth (excuse the expression) of this response was a manifestation of moral narcissism, not of science, just as were the pronouncements of the president himself. But wait, as they say in late-night television commercials, there's more. And, as in those commercials, the devil is in the details of that hidden more, the unseen payments for postage and handling that often double the cost. In this case, as it is frequently, it is the use of moral narcissism as a motivator for distraction. Obama and also Kerry—not to mention the majority of progressives—seek to use climate change to keep the discussion away from other more important and, to them, uncomfortable subjects, most specifically the danger of radical Islam. Naming radical Islam or Islamism is against their—again, morally narcissistic—entrenched beliefs in political correctness and cultural relativism. (Although the cultural relativism is occasionally tempered for the public with a suddenly remembered obeisance to American Exceptionalism ... of a carefully diminished sort.) So by invoking a general feeling that we all want to save the world above all things—that climate change is truly the greatest of all dangers—the true danger before our eyes, the danger actually killing people in the immediate sense, diminishes in comparison. Questions about Islam are not asked and don't have to be answered. The war is not a war but just isolated crimes committed by random misunderstood extremists from impoverished backgrounds, themselves the unfortunate victims of Western imperialism. A thirteen-hundred-year-old ideology adhered to in various manners by an estimated 1.7 billion people has nothing to do with it.

Moral narcissism changes the subject. It elicits simple answers that the self-regarding want to hear and keeps them from asking, or even of thinking of, questions they should really be asking. That is its method, structurally and emotionally. And that self-regard is something to be manipulated and used by those who understand how to do it, and many do at this point, repeating the same pattern over and over. Enough about me. How do you feel about me? And by the way, if you're unsure of your opinion of me, if you're ambivalent in the slightest, I am absolutely certain the world is warming and it is our fault, humanity's fault, like everything else is, and we better do something about it or we're all going to die in a tidal wave brought on by the melting of the Antarctic ice cap, not to mention the Himalayan glaciers. And don't give me any evidence to the contrary, because that means you're a Republican or maybe a fascist. You agree? Good. Now I can friend you on Facebook.

Well, not quite. Not yet. The dang weather keeps getting in the way, giving the idiots in the public, even some on Facebook, pause. As I was working on this chapter in January of 2015, an almost comic example of this discontinuity occurred. New York City was predicted to have a record-breaking blizzard of the sort never seen in modern times. The city's mayor, Bill de Blasio—the kind of moral narcissist who never found a left-wing cause he didn't believe in and saw fit to have his honeymoon on Cuba (more of him in the subsequent chapter)—urged citizens of his metropolis to batten down the hatches; the equivalent of the Battle of Britain was coming. Roads and the public transportation system were closed as never before in history. Everyone was urged to stay indoors for who knew how long, and to look in on their sick and aged neighbors who would undoubtedly be on death's door. A panicked citizenry cleaned out grocery stores. Well, it turned out to be a routine snowstorm of the type that happens every year or two, sometimes more often. Gary Szatowski, meteorologist for the National Weather Service, tweeted out in embarrassment: "My deepest apologies to many key decision makers and so many of the general public."[10] He promised to examine their computer models. Never dealt with was why we are supposed to believe in climate change, which is also based on computer models, when the weather can't be predicted a day in advance based on similar models. Oh, yes, climate is not weather. But then what is climate other than weather over time? No one has explained.

Elites have to fight hard to convince the benighted hoi polloi of the importance of global warming and, for now at least, it's a losing battle. (Who do you believe—Al Gore or your lying eyes?) Although, as I noted, a scandalous amount of black money has been made, the massive wealth transfer desired by climate change adherents has not happened, and people are still driving around in their retrograde gas-guzzlers, most of which, these days, don't pollute that much anyway. Progress continues in the way it normally does, largely initiated by the profit motive. The future is still in the hands of people like Thomas Edison and Steve Jobs—the ones more likely to bring into being and inspire true advances, despite the best efforts of a swollen bureaucracy. One has the sense that many still adhere to the climate change narrative because to question it would open the door to questioning too many other things. It's the tip-of-the-iceberg phenomenon. Better not to go there or the whole morally narcissistic construct will start to unravel. The most rational approach to climate science I have read comes from *Reason* magazine's science correspondent Ronald Bailey, a climate agnostic: "Whenever you encounter information that confirms what you already believe, be especially skeptical of it." Excellent advice, but few heed it.[11]

The most narcissistic aspect of the climate debate, however, is the odd notion that we humans are more, or at the very least equal to, the sun, moon, and the stars, not to mention the various galaxies, in the effect on our weather. Call this extreme "homocentrism." This viewpoint was made to seem particularly ridiculous in the freezing temperatures of the winter of 2015. At the same period, the center of our solar system, aka the sun, had reached a low point in activity measured in x-ray output, which was flatlining. The sun was also virtually devoid of spots to a degree not seen since 1906. According to *Vencore Weather* for February 17, 2015,

... it is safe to say that weak solar activity for a prolonged period of time can have a negative impact on global temperatures in the troposphere which is the bottom-most layer of Earth's atmosphere— and where we all live. There have been two notable historical periods with decades-long episodes of low solar activity. The first period is known as the "Maunder Minimum," named after the solar astronomer Edward Maunder, and it lasted from around 1645 to 1715. The second one is referred to as the "Dalton Minimum," named for the English

meteorologist John Dalton, and it lasted from about 1790 to 1830. Both
of these historical periods coincided with below-normal global temperatures in an era now referred to by many as the "Little Ice Age."[12]

Brrr ... Are we headed for another ice age? Although New York
City just experienced its coldest temperature in eighty-one years, I
have no idea. But neither does most anybody, if they're honest about it.
Nevertheless, talk about the real climate *denial*, the homocentrist view
of the cosmos inherent in the climate *alarmist's* Weltanschauung, seems
bizarrely primitive, like ancient man staring up in wonder at the sun in
some Stanley Kubrick movie and then thumping his chest in superiority.
Moral narcissism indeed—and in extremis.

When Rajendra Pachauri, the longtime chairman of the UN IPCC
and symbolic Nobel Prizewinner with Al Gore, resigned at the beginning
of 2015 in the wake of sexual harassment allegations (some say he should
have resigned in 2009 in the wake of the "Climategate" scandal), he wrote
in his farewell letter "For me the protection of Planet Earth, the survival of
all species and sustainability of our ecosystems is more than a mission. It
is my religion and my dharma." This confusion of religion and "dharma"
with science is the essence of what is wrong and the reason we all have
to suffer through that endless parade of English majors at cocktail parties
lecturing us on climate Armageddon. It is the Lysenkoism of the trendy.

And yet, other manifestations of moral narcissism in our culture are
far more treacherous in the long run than the vicissitudes of climate and
far more destructive than the mere economic profligacy cum superstition this belief might engender. These manifestations have the capacity
to break our nation apart as never since the Civil War, perhaps more
permanently, both at home and from abroad. "A Republic, if you can keep
it," Benjamin Franklin is reputed to have said when emerging from the
Constitutional Convention of 1787. Those words—often considered more
of an apocryphal tribute to Franklin's wit than an accurate quote—have
suddenly taken on more relevance in today's America, because moral
narcissism has helped create that most reactionary of results ...

IX

Nostalgia for Racism

*How and why moral narcissism helped bring back
racism and the disastrous racial violence across
America at the very time it was starting to diminish.*

"Nostalgia" seemed an odd term to apply to racism in mid-2015 when a twenty-one-year-old white devotee of apartheid regimes in South Africa and Rhodesia had just walked into an historic black church in Charleston, South Carolina, and gunned down nine innocent people, including the pastor of that church, who was also a state senator. When I first heard the dreadful news, I thought I should revise the title of this chapter and perhaps its slant. Like many, I was hugely depressed by the event. And indeed, I knew the terrain of the killings personally, having stayed at the Courtyard Marriott across from that church when covering the presidential election of 2012 for *PJ Media*. It had been the site of Denmark Vesey's ill-fated slave rebellion in 1822 when Vesey and thirty-three others were executed before their revolt could even get started. Hallowed ground.

But on reflection I obviously didn't change my title or what I had already written, emotional as those days in June 2015 were. Evil or criminally insane individuals (depending on your world view) like the homicidal Dylann Storm Roof have existed throughout history and have appeared in every country and among every racial and ethnic group. Until we are genetically engineered, and even possibly after that, they will continue to exist, unfortunately. To consider such a person—Roof was apparently also an abuser of the pharmaceutical Suboxone that has been linked to spontaneous outbursts of violence—as an exemplar of anything except the random tragedy of human life is finally pointless.

Barack Obama, in his typical morally narcissistic style, declared the morning after the event that these mass murders do not occur nearly as frequently in other advanced countries—this only months after the even more extensive massacres in France at the offices of *Charlie Hebdo* and the Hypercacher Jewish supermarket (not to mention the recent mass murder in Norway that left sixty-nine dead.) Perhaps the president had forgotten "*Je Suis Charlie*" because, unlike so many other world leaders, he had decided not to attend the memorial in Paris. Neither did the president mention the steep decline in the murder rate in America in recent decades, only interrupted by an upturn from recent events in Ferguson and Baltimore. Instead, he took the opportunity to propagandize for another of his favorite causes—gun control. He ignored the data, we can assume he was aware of it, that shows a correlation between the growing number of American citizens owning guns and that decline in the murder rate. Candidate Hillary Clinton reacted to the Charleston murders in substantially the same way.

The president and his putative successor both preferred to proselytize in the face of this horrific event, politicizing it, so I am going to do what I originally planned, leave my writings as they were and begin as I did in the halcyon days of 2005. I think we have more to learn from that than from the actions of a psychotic. Yes, nostalgia for racism is involved. It's possibly the most destructive form of moral narcissism extant.

During an interview that year of 2005 with Mike Wallace for CBS television's *60 Minutes*, the Academy Award-winning actor Morgan Freeman said something that today would seem remarkable about how to end racism—"stop talking about it." The conversation evolved this way:

WALLACE: Black History Month, you find …
FREEMAN: Ridiculous.
WALLACE: Why?
FREEMAN: You're going to relegate my history to a month?
WALLACE: Come on.
FREEMAN: What do you do with yours? Which month is White
    History Month? Come on, tell me.

WALLACE: I'm Jewish.

FREEMAN: OK. Which month is Jewish History Month?

WALLACE: There isn't one.

FREEMAN: Why not? Do you want one?

WALLACE: No, no.

FREEMAN: I don't either. I don't want a Black History Month. Black history is American history.

WALLACE: How are we going to get rid of racism until … ?

FREEMAN: Stop talking about it. I'm going to stop calling you a white man. And I'm going to ask you to stop calling me a black man. I know you as Mike Wallace. You know me as Morgan Freeman. You're not going to say, "I know this white guy named Mike Wallace." Hear what I'm saying?

I hear what Morgan was saying. I hear it loud and clear and, as an old sixties civil rights worker, it brings tears to my eyes, because, the way things are going now, that simple wisdom from one of America's finest actors makes 2005 seem ages ago, some distant century or, at least, BBO—Before Barack Obama. Or, more exactly, before Obama, Eric Holder, the New Black Panthers, and the Philadelphia polling place, Henry Louis Gates, and the Cambridge police ("Beer Summit" over nothing), Trayvon Martin and George Zimmerman ("If I had a son he would look like Trayvon"), Michael Brown and the Ferguson police, Eric Garner and the Staten Island police, Bill de Blasio and the NYPD, "Hands Up, Don't Shoot," "Black Lives Matter," Al Sharpton with the president of the United States, Al Sharpton with the mayor of the City of New York, Al Sharpton with the president of Sony Pictures, Al Sharpton everywhere as if the race-baiting ideologue were the arbiter of American social behavior of almost any sort, our contemporary Emily Post. (He was even praised by the mayor of Bridgeport for "fighting the good fight on climate change."[1]) And finally, "What do you want? Dead cops. When do we want them? Now."

As the racial atmosphere continued to overheat, then came the Baltimore riots and those dead, hated cops could now seemingly also be black. Three of the six police indicted for either second-degree murder, manslaughter, or second-degree assault in the death (accidental or deliberate, depending how you looked at it or read the autopsy) of black sometime-drug dealer Freddie Gray were themselves African American. So was the state's attorney Marilyn J. Mosby, who rushed in to indict those police as if they were an adjunct of Murder Incorporated although the worst they could have done, apparently, was failed to secure Gray in a seat belt. Mosby was rewarded for her putative courage with a glamorous spread in *Vogue*—"Meet Marilyn Mosby: The Baltimore Prosecutor in the Eye of the Storm." (The state's attorney is probably unaware that one of the other prominent women recently honored by the fashion magazine is Asma al-Assad, the suddenly hard to find spouse of mass murdering dictator Bashar al-Assad.)

Over fifty years after the Civil Rights Act of 1964, we live in an era where racial charges and countercharges dominate the landscape. Purity of thought—mental cleansing of all possible bias—is demanded of the populace at a level never dreamed or even thought to be attainable. Despite all this, wealth inequality between blacks and whites has continued to rise during the Obama administration. Black households, which had a measly one-eighth the median wealth of white households in 2010, only three years later had a yet lower, some might say astonishingly low, one-thirteenth the median wealth of whites—and this includes, we can assume, such superstars as Lebron James, Beyoncé, Kanye West, Oprah Winfrey (a multibillionaire and listed by *Forbes* as the richest African American), Sean "Diddy" Combs, and Robert Johnson (founder of the Black Entertainment Network). Blacks have their own version of income inequality.[2] It's no surprise that a poll conducted in January 2015 by Monmouth University and Al Jazeera reported 43 percent of Americans thought race relations had worsened under Obama while 40 percent, possibly more cynical about the past, thought it had remained the same. Hardly any of those polled responded that they thought race relations had improved under the first black president.

Something had gone wrong. Even Morgan Freeman had walked back on his previous prescription to "stop talking about it," saying Republicans had a "racist goal" in bringing down Obama.[3] Later he said Obama wasn't even the first black president. He was the first "mixed race" president because of his "white momma." America hadn't had a black president yet. Obviously, he didn't count Bill Clinton, nor was he seemingly interested in Ben Carson, who is of 100 percent parentage. Whatever the case, race relations had indeed deteriorated under Obama. And the relative economic position of African Americans had seriously declined from its already low position, despite decades of well-meaning social programs originally initiated by Lyndon Johnson during his "War on Poverty." The atmosphere between the races had been poisoned as demonstrators marched through the streets of New York chanting for "dead cops" even though many of those same cops were people of color. And all the while, on our college campuses—under the newly minted banner of microaggressions—students found racial offense at matters so inconsequential they would make every citizen a racist forever no matter what he or she did or did not do. You were a racist virtually for breathing. The ghost of Robespierre stalked the land—or was it the Chinese Cultural Revolution? The civil rights movement that had begun with such courageous optimism in the 1950s had been turned on its head. How did this happen?

We could go back to the slave ships, but let's begin with events that occurred within the lifetimes of at least a few of the readers of this book. Racism is, after all, a personal, observable matter to all of us because, when it does involve us personally, we are either a victim or a perpetrator of it or a witness to it or some combination of the three. I first realized I was encountering racism the very year (1954) of the Supreme Court decision *Brown v. the Board of Education* that ended school segregation and is often considered the beginning of the formal civil rights movement. As a ten-year-old then, I was sent down South to visit family friends in Louisiana and found myself in the world of Jim Crow; "colored" water fountains; segregated restrooms, buses, lunch counters, and the rest. As an impressionable northern boy I was appalled, to say the least, also disdainful. I felt morally superior to my hosts and contemptuous of them. I went home to my family in New York to inform them that everything that was said of the bigoted South was true. It had to be changed. It's not a strange leap that I grew up to join the civil rights movement, registering voters in South Carolina slightly more than a decade later. What I remember about that later period was how good it made me feel, what a fine fellow I thought I was for doing the right thing—and it *was* the right thing. There is nothing I am prouder of than my extremely minor participation in the civil rights movement. I am certain that's true of almost everyone who was involved, to whatever degree.

Not that it was all the kumbaya of "We shall overcome" or "Black and white together, we shall not be moved." Not by a long shot. I noticed even back in 1966 the first inklings of a disturbing strain of black nationalism filtering forward from the days of Marcus Garvey. When none other than a then twenty-five-ish Julian Bond (later to be the president of the NAACP) proudly showed me a flyer of the just-founded Black Panther Party of Lowndes County, Alabama, I waved off its in-your-face separatism and potentially violent imagery as a phase. I tried to fight my own innate paternalism or what was later called "white skin privilege." But I had grown up listening to Babs Gonzalez's jazz anthem "We Ain't Got Integration" and dreaming of an interracial society, one in which we would all inevitably be tea-colored. So this separatist impulse made me feel uncomfortable. Still, only five or so years later, as a young screenwriter in Hollywood, against my better judgment I ended up donating to the Panthers. I thought then my motivation was "liberal guilt," but this was only partially true. It was an early manifestation of my own moral narcissism. I was showing the world—my friends, family, work colleagues, and whoever else might be interested—how I was on the cutting edge of the civil rights movement, that I knew best, even if that meant turning a blind eye to "armed struggle," hatred of whites, drug dealing, and often murderous, internecine warfare. In fact, the further out on the edge I went, the more morally narcissistic pride I could feel. I was special.

And I was not alone, far from it. Many others turned that same blind eye then and still do, for similar reasons. This has been terrible for white *and* black people. It set up an atmosphere of mutual dishonesty and bad faith. And when people are treated in bad faith, on some level they know it and react in various, almost always troubling, ways. Black people faced with whites who papered over extreme Panther-like behavior knew those whites were either suppressing true feelings or were what Lenin supposedly called "useful idiots," possibly both. White people lived in suspicion they were despised by blacks who blamed them for centuries of cruelty even though these same whites were not alive, in most cases by decades, at the time. Buried rage increased on both sides, as the position of African Americans in our country grew worse in many ways despite the celebrity status and consequent economic success of those prominent blacks. Great Society programs like affirmative action had not really worked; often they had even exacerbated the problems they were intended to solve. People's natural good feelings—the will to get along and move past the tragic history of slavery and Jim Crow—fought against a continuing racial frustration that would not go away.

This frustration began to bubble up in the early 1990s, with a new or renewed rift growing between the races exemplified and in many ways actually heightened by the trial of retired football star O. J. Simpson. Much has been written of the minutiae of the evidence surrounding the murder of Simpson's ex-wife Nicole Brown and Ron Goldman. But far more interesting in the long run was the racial divide that characterized reactions to his guilt or innocence that often overrode that evidence. Despite Simpson having lived a lifestyle that could be described as upper class white in highly privileged Brentwood, California, black people rallied around him in a manner that transcended traditional indices of culpability and spoke to grievances well beyond whether Simpson had committed a heinous crime. This in turn caused a division in the white community, many of whom had sympathy for the plight of blacks but couldn't understand why that sympathy should extend to a wealthy celebrity who had killed two innocent people. Emotions were riled and the case became almost a national obsession, contributing more than any other event to the development of the media culture we live in now. The trial also contributed greatly to the enhancement of a renewed separatism going into the modern era. If black and white people could see evidence of murder in such a radically different manner, it was unlikely that they could live together. The dreams of integrationists were being cut to the quick, often without them even being aware of it.

People, particularly whites, found it difficult to be honest about this rift, which undoubtedly made it worse—not that blacks were much better. They took satisfaction in a victory over a justice system they perceived to be racist, no matter how unjust that victory might be, how disrespectful of physical evidence, DNA or otherwise. Without knowing it we were entering an era of nostalgia for racism, an era that would bring racism back while pretending to solve it. This was paradoxical, because at the same time we were finally having a chance of reaching a postracial society via the method articulated so succinctly by Morgan Freeman in 2005—end racism by deemphasizing it, by rising above it. Indeed, that truly is the only way to actually end racism, a technique that is very much like the bamboo Chinese toy many of us played with as children, wherein you stick two fingers in a woven bamboo tube and try to pull them apart. If you yank hard with your opposing fingers, the tube squeezes tight and you are stuck. If you simply take it easy and don't try to extract the fingers, the tube falls off and you are out. Racism is gone. In Freeman's words, I will call you Mike and you will call me Morgan. Forget those other useless activities, all those breast-beating panel discussions and tedious academic studies.

Racism in our culture was now appealing only to fringe personalities. It had been against the law for years. Nobody wanted to bring it back. Let it go. Let the wound heal. But we couldn't. We had to scratch the scab until it got worse. Nostalgia for racism got the better of us—a decrepit nostalgia with moral narcissism as its secret instigator, its psychic Mephistopheles.

What do I mean by nostalgia for racism? Well, an entire generation of people, many black but a fair number of whites, yearned for those halcyon days of the civil rights movement when good was good and evil was evil. Bull Connor and his racist ilk were monsters and Martin Luther King and John Lewis were heroes and we all knew what to think and feel. It was nostalgia for a simpler time, nostalgia for an era when everyone bathed in the glory of doing the right thing, a time when good people, black and white, could parade their righteousness for the world to see. But then life got complicated. Nothing was getting resolved. The inner cities remained what they were—inner cities—with little hope for their occupants and the same old solutions for the same old problems. And when someone offered a new idea, it seemed to disappear in a maw of conventional wisdom, never to appear again. How could we get back to that better time? How could we resolve these feelings of discomfort that all of us had—black, white, and yes, brown? By scratching that hardening scab of racism and bringing the devil back to life. After all, none of us are pure. Everybody is a racist on some level. Everybody profiles. Even Jesse Jackson admitted he crossed the street to the opposite sidewalk when he saw some gangbangers heading his way. The bias is there, the bigotry. They say the Klan is gone, but it's really not. You just have to search for it, ask enough questions, and keeping scratching that scab until it appears again, maybe have a few colloquiums and conferences to understand our original sin, how we have never been able to work through our inherent racism. And then soon enough we are back to square one—the 1950s again and the redneck sheriffs are swinging their truncheons. But that's not bad. That's just what we needed. We can start over. "Hands up! Don't shoot!" And by the way, I'm a good guy. I'm on the right side. I know best. I know the sad truth. We're all racists. I have everything I have only because of white skin privilege. I was born with a silver spoon in my mouth, even if I was white trash living in a trailer in Appalachia and the only spoon in the house had melted from freebasing. I will apologize and change that. Mea culpa. Mea culpa. Mea culpa. Am I exonerated now?

These were the self-defeating and impure, conflicted emotions brought out before and after the O. J. trial and they have gotten worse ever since. People naturally fought against them. They wanted, oh how they wanted, to put paid to this racism thing, to put an end to it, so the whole country could bask in the glow of a postracial society in which everyone marched together into a politically correct sunset. So Barack Obama was elected president, a man with only the slightest of records, a Moral Narcissist in Chief to fit a morally narcissistic age. That he delivered that aforementioned speech accepting the 2008 nomination of the Democratic Party on an elaborate columned stage resembling a Greek temple at Denver's Invesco Field before eighty-four thousand fans now seems almost bizarrely apropos. Ditto his most famous mantra "hope and change"—that open, one-size-fits-all expression suitable to be object of any projection. We, the good people, know what it means; you, the bad people, don't. The night of Obama's election, nearly all of America, myself certainly included, had tears in our eyes, our hearts going pit-a-pit given that our long national nightmare was over. We would be free at last, in the words of Dr. King. We had elected an African American president.

How long did it take to realize that something was wrong? Not long if you were paying attention, but few did. Moral narcissism, which was Obama's inspiration, was also his ace in the hole. From the beginning of his administration the public was mesmerized as, in a sense, was he, mesmerized by his own words. Idealistic pronouncements were the same as policy. If you said something, it WAS. No need to follow up. Despite the president having a Democratic House and Senate for the first two years of his administration, Obama did little or nothing to substantively improve the lot of African Americans. Even community-based tax incentives, which would have been attractive to both political parties, were not put in place. It was as if Obama's election were sufficient: "I am, therefore it is." Moreover, most of the traditional liberal solutions to the plight of African Americans had been tried and had failed, multiple times. Normally, this would be an occasion to try something new and different, but Obama—whose own perfection made such outreach unnecessary—was actually highly conventional in his approach, never really trying anything new. In a larger sense, he evinced little interest in the poor in general, only in *saying* or *appearing* to have an interest in them. Obama's operative term for demonstrating this appearance was "fairness," in order to meet his supposed goal of ending "income inequality." But evidence that this was mere rhetoric surfaced as early as his first campaign for president in an exchange with Charlie Gibson of ABC News.[4]

> GIBSON: All right. You have, however, said you would favor an increase in the capital gains tax. As a matter of fact, you said on CNBC, and I quote, "I certainly would not go above what existed under Bill Clinton," which was 28 percent. It's now 15 percent. That's almost a doubling, if you went to 28 percent. But actually, Bill Clinton, in 1997, signed legislation that dropped the capital gains tax to 20 percent.
>
> OBAMA: Right.
>
> GIBSON: And George Bush has taken it down to 15 percent.
>
> OBAMA: Right.
>
> GIBSON: And in each instance, when the rate dropped, revenues from the tax increased; the government took in more money. And in the 1980s, when the tax was increased to 28 percent, the revenues went down. So why raise it at all, especially given the fact that 100 million people in this country own stock and would be affected?
>
> OBAMA: Well, Charlie, what I've said is that I would look at raising the capital gains tax for purposes of fairness. We saw an article today which showed that the top 50 hedge fund managers made $29 billion last year—$29 billion for 50 individuals. And part of what has happened is that those who are able to work the stock market and amass huge fortunes on capital gains are paying a lower tax rate than their secretaries. That's not fair.

Let's leave aside the perplexed expression that flickered across Obama's face during this television interview, as if he had never heard of this concept before, did not appear to recognize the well-known economic theories of Arthur Laffer, or the curve he drew tracing the point at which increasing tax rates actually depletes government coffers. What Obama seems actually to be saying here is that *even if* government revenues increase by lowering the capital gains rate—thus fattening the coffers for what you would assume he would applaud, liberal income redistribution—he still objected to lower gains rates because they weren't "fair." To an objective observer, Obama's "fair" was not "fair" at all. It was the opposite. It demonstrably hurt the people it was supposed to help. But in the world of the moral narcissist it was "fair" because it had the appearance of being "fair." Appearance trumps reality any time. Another way to look at this was and is that something is only "fair" when it punishes your adversaries or people of whom you disapprove or you believe to be undeserving. But moral narcissism is not based on anything rational like the analysis of data or fact. It is a purely emotional reaction.

This leads us back to the race question. From the beginning of the Obama administration the preference was to punish those he perceived to be the enemies of black America, even if they were unconscious enemies or secondhand enemies (anyone who could be profiting from "white skin privilege"), rather than to uplift the African American community, something to which he paid scant attention. New approaches for helping that community help themselves were suggested by libertarian-leaning senator Rand Paul and were essentially ignored. (Actually, they weren't that new. They were, Paul himself admitted, largely borrowed from one-time vice-presidential candidate and football star Jack Kemp. The new book by Morton Kondracke and Fred Barnes—*Jack Kemp: The Bleeding-Heart Conservative Who Changed America*—details the full extent of Kemp's contribution.) The idea that self-reliance and responsibility might have something to contribute to a black renewal was barely addressed, let alone discussed. Fresh legislative initiatives did not occur. No one in Obama's administration seemed to have a single original notion or creative thought about what to do about the problems of black America.

Meanwhile, the situation in the black community was going from bad to dismal. The statistics are clear. The black unemployment rate continued to be double that of whites, but more tellingly, during the Obama administration the crucial labor participation rate that measures the actual percentage of people who even want to be part of the labor force, fell to its lowest number since the Carter presidency. This was especially true for blacks. Only 65.6 percent (not even two-thirds) of adult African American men considered themselves part of a potential workforce. The other one-third plus had simply opted out, creating the backdrop for a potential criminal or even pre-revolutionary class. Compounding that potential, black teenage unemployment was at record levels.[5] By 2013, in a trend that had been gradually increasing for decades, 71 percent of births to African American women were out of wedlock. Not surprisingly, considering the all-around situation in the community, the black-on-black murder rate in the African American community continues to be truly depressing, especially since murders in general are down in the United States. In 2014 the rate for black male victims was 31.67 homicides per 100,000; for white males it was 3.85. The overwhelming number of those murders in the African American community are black-on-black; the police killings of blacks trumpeted by the media on practically every occasion—regrettable though they are—are minuscule by comparison. Indeed, it's likely the police save far more black lives than they hurt. Finally, according to the Pew Research Center, the median net worth, adjusted for inflation, of black households in 2011 was approximately 7 percent lower than it was in 1984, while the net worth of white households was almost 11 percent higher than it had been in the same year.[6]

None of these depressing statistics have been responded to in any way by the Obama administration or, for the most part, its followers. To do so might open a whole series of questions about conventional liberalism, which dominated the culture ideologically over most of the period of decline. Why, when affirmative action was in place, when most schools and businesses had opened their doors to minorities—often giving them preference either through law or goodwill—when prominent African Americans were in positions of power in our country as never before, did such a perplexing downswing occur? *Wall Street Journal* editor Jason Riley has many answers in his excellent and exhaustive *Please Stop Helping Us: How Liberals Make It Harder for Blacks to Succeed.* The essence of Riley's response is in his title. Nevertheless, however sensible Riley's analysis might seem and however in tune with an objective observation of human behavior it may be (Does it help or hurt to give an addicted relative more heroin?), liberals leaving blacks alone is unlikely to happen because of the very moral narcissism under discussion here. To stop would cause an unraveling of the liberal mindset. The entire way they had defined themselves, in this case in regards to race, would be called into question. Had they not been "good"? Had they not done the "right thing"? To think otherwise would be intolerable. Even more intolerable is the possible imputation that *they* would be racist. That's obviously wrong. Liberals were the ones who called *others* racist. That's the way the game is played and has been for decades. (Well, up until the last couple of years on our college campuses where virtually everyone is a racist.)

Obama understood the rituals of this pattern almost instinctively. He had lived it. From the backrooms of Chicago politics to the pews of Reverend Wright, he had seen it all—a perfect storm of moral narcissism and what talk show host Larry Elder calls "victimology." (Elder, a black man himself and called "the Sage of South Central," describes the problem this way: "The American left teaches 'minorities' and women to think of themselves as victims, Republicans as victimizers, and Democrats as rescuers.") These two approaches to life were born to reinforce each other. The moral narcissism soothed and justified the victimology. Blacks were victims, therefore whites were villains, or quasi villains in a kind of purgatory, waiting to be cured or forgiven. Pope Obama was now there. They voted for him, waiting for their expiation.

So the chances of his instituting new policies were nil and always would be. When it came to race, "hope and change" was actually the same old same old. Instead, Eric Holder was installed as attorney general to be a kind of racial point man. He could do the hatchet work as if we were still just at the beginning of the civil rights movement and only baby steps, maybe one or two scissor steps forward, had been taken, Morgan Freeman be damned. Holder instituted a policy of blaming racism for as many things as possible at a point when racism itself was on the decline. Not only was this nostalgia, it was a deliberate exacerbation to preserve and enhance power. This explains his not pursuing the New Black Panther case when militant thugs in black leather and berets appeared to be vetting voters entering a Philadelphia polling place. Racism could only go one way. Blacks were not capable of it. They were automatically exempted or exonerated.

Slowly, the nostalgia built. The next step in the resurrection of racism was the so-called "Beer Summit." If ever there were an event that could have been ignored, this was it. A crusty university professor locked out of his own home lashed out at a clueless cop who arrested the prof on a disorderly conduct charge that was completely dismissed a few days later. No one even got his hair mussed. If Henry Lewis Gates hadn't been black and famous and the university involved not Harvard, the incident wouldn't have made the back pages of a suburban throwaway. But wait. … The Cambridge police officer involved must have been guilty of "racial profiling," right? Well, maybe not. Turns out the officer, Crowley, had taught a course in racial profiling himself at the police academy and had even, while a member of the Brandeis campus police, tried to revive Boston Celtics star Reggie Lewis with mouth-to-mouth resuscitation after the basketball player had a fatal heart attack—a pretty far cry from refusing to drink at a "colored" water fountain. Not only that, other Cambridge police officers, including African Americans, thought Crowley a stand-up guy and not a racist at all. But that would not be sufficient. As media coverage increased, endless murky details of the case came forth—Crowley's past, the past of people who might have known Crowley or known people who knew people who might have known people who had met Crowley—so on and so forth. It was enough to make a talmudist's head spin, though none of it was remotely conclusive or probative. Nevertheless, the president of the United States decided this crucial situation deserved a White House face-to-face with all parties to set things right—hence, the Beer Summit.

Other than generating a ton of news coverage, the summit didn't amount to much. Crowley and Gates apparently didn't particularly like each other, which at this point was hardly surprising. But not even that imaginary talmudist could determine how much racial bias, if any, was at play here. The event did serve an important purpose for the president, however, reminding the public that race was still an issue, that they could not forget it even though he had been elected president. There would be no free pass. For the Moral Narcissist in Chief, abandoning race would have meant abandoning a key, in fact the most important, lever on power. And beyond that, abandoning race as an issue might have meant … well … abandoning race as an issue, which might have meant there was really not that much racism after all. And then what? With the Ku Klux Klan long gone and discrimination outlawed and basically vanished from American society—at least considered an extremely repellent characteristic not welcome anywhere—we might just have to live with each other and forget about skin color. An entire industry and social structure built around the presence of racism would become worthless and have to be dismantled. Blame could no longer be properly assessed.

Racism, therefore, could not be abandoned under any circumstances.

Thankfully, along came the Trayvon Martin case. This one was slightly more promising than the Beer Summit because it was about a lot more than ruffled egos. In Florida, a seventeen-year-old hoodie-clad youth had died at the hands of an overzealous neighborhood watchman who, despite carrying the name George Zimmerman, was inconveniently Hispanic and possibly "of color" himself. Even though it was difficult to tell if Zimmerman, who had clearly sustained wounds in his tussle with Martin, had a history of racism—as with Officer Crowley, there were counterindications—accusations were immediately made. President Obama quickly weighed in on a decidedly local crime (or accident, as the case may be), informing the world that if he had had a son, he would look like Trayvon. No one would dare state the obvious—that that was as absurd as a President Bush saying any recently deceased white youth could have been *his* son. Such a statement by Bush would, of course, have been branded as racism—and beyond that simply silly. But moral narcissism and its handmaiden white liberal guilt would not allow the questioning of the president's risible comment, even though Obama had grown up comfortably middle or even upper middle class and attended the most exclusive private school in Hawaii. Trayvon had far more in common with the whites who lived down the street from him. But real comparison was never the point. The idea was to racialize society. It was never to be ignored that we were tribes, not one people. The melting pot was a distant idea out of some sentimental poem by Emma Lazarus. "Give me your tired, your poor . . ." was replaced by "You never stop, do you, Mister Charlie?" What whites had done to blacks would never be forgotten, no matter how long we or anybody else lived. Obama and his (literal) bad cop Eric Holder would see to it.

To what degree this was a conscious decision on their parts is hard to say, but it didn't have to be. Since childhood, it had been imbued deeply in the fabric of their personalities. You could say you were free of racism and you could even act as if you were, but that was only superficial. America was a racist culture and always would be, despite our best efforts. Like rats in a maze we would be forever chasing the chimera of a postracial society. That this continued division had obvious electoral implications, creating a perpetually aggrieved class as a permanent voting block, although an important corollary, was only part of the story. The real story was innate white racism even, as in this instance in which the perpetrator—if he was indeed a perpetrator and not simply a nut case—was Hispanic. That was just a temporary setback. Zimmerman was quickly deemed a new category that was provided conveniently by the always-complaisant media—the white Hispanic. The man couldn't be brown, after all. He had to be white, as if this semiliterate Florida loser were a direct descendant of Goya or Velazquez. The media, as it usually does, knew best.

But all of this was just a warm-up, a minor orchestral prelude, to the events of summer 2014 in St. Louis, New York, and later Baltimore, which have yet to play out fully, and may not for some years. When Michael Brown, an eighteen-year-old black man, was fatally shot by twenty-eight-year-old Ferguson police officer Darren Wilson and a grand jury exonerated the cop, black America, at least the part of it the media chooses to show, exploded. The subsequent exoneration of a Staten Island police officer in the chokehold death of Eric Garner exacerbated the situation, with demonstrations—not to mention looting and fires—metastasizing across the country. It wasn't with quite the intensity of the Watts riots of 1965, but it was close enough and brought the country back full circle to those days only a year after the enactment of the 1964 Civil Rights Act. Race relations in America had become another version of Groundhog Day, to be repeated over and over.

Sad as this situation is, you can't help but think it's a comfort zone for many. Change is threatening and a nonracist America represented new territory, at least so we were told. The narrative had always been that the United States was a country born of racism and, struggle how we may, it will always be with us. Never mind that on an individual basis people treat each other well. They didn't really mean it. They were just pretending. Never mind that in most business and academic settings, preference was given to people of color in the name of political correctness or just a sense of wanting to do a good deed. That is all hypocritical or insufficient. Deep down we are racist and the events of Ferguson and Staten Island proved it. Eric Holder had known this all along. That is why he staffed the Department of Justice with attorneys for whom civil rights violations were a primary, almost the sole, obsession. (Christian Adams has documented this thoroughly in his *Injustice: Exposing the Racial*

Agenda of the Obama Justice Department.) Visiting Ferguson, Holder seemed vindicated, as if on a victory tour. The world as he saw it had not changed. This was his America.

And not just his. We have arrived at a time when Ivy League colleges like Dartmouth are giving post-Ferguson courses like #blacklivesmatter (hashtag in the course literature)—as if black, or all lives, had not previously mattered. The über-state (elite liberals in control of the federal government and its bureaucracies) is largely seen as beneficent, especially to the extent that Democrats are in power, while the local constabulary, the men and women in the street actually doing the hard and dangerous work of preventing crime and saving lives, are assumed to be bigoted and ruthless. This view persists—and has been applauded and encouraged by those same elites and the media—despite grand juries not having found evidence of police malfeasance in either the Ferguson or Staten Island cases. Against all logic, almost to the point of cognitive dissonance, the cases have been compared to the death of Emmett Till, the fourteen-year-old black boy who, in 1954, was dragged out of his great-uncle's Mississippi home into a barn where he then was murdered, his eyes gouged out, for the alleged crime of flirting with a white woman.

These views continue in the face of facts, even when the facts most directly contradict them. According to the Center for Disease Control and Prevention's fatal injury database, in 2012, only 123 African Americans were shot dead by police in the United States, a country with then some 43 million blacks. The statistics do not give the details of those shootings—we can assume that some could have been avoided—but that amounts to only .000003 percent of African Americans being killed by a cop. By comparison, an estimated one hundred thousand Americans die every year from medical error. Taking blacks at 13 percent of the population, that's thirteen thousand African Americans, more or less. Ergo, an African American is roughly a hundred times more likely to be *accidentally* killed by his doctor than by a cop. (Maybe there should be a new demonstration—"What do we want? Dead docs!")

Of course, the chances of them being killed by their doctor are minuscule and the whole charade is a grotesque distortion of real life. Many of the small, though still unfortunate and regrettable, number of police who kill African Americans clearly did so in self-defense. They had to do it, very often to save the lives of other black people. And yes, blacks as a percentage of their population are more likely to be killed at the hands of the police than whites, but, as we also all know, since there is considerably more crime in black communities, it could not be otherwise until that changes. In fact, a strong argument could be made that the police are the first line of defense for African Americans. And so they have been, as murders in black communities, indeed across all communities in the United States, have declined. We should be thanking them. And yet the narrative continues.

X

Booker T. Washington Really Did Know Best

The great African American educator knew long ago that the Sharptons of the world were the real racists.

Moral narcissism dictates that some things never change. They're not supposed to. If they changed, the moral narcissist would have no way to express himself, nothing to complain about, no way to feel superior. Nowhere is this more prominent than in the area of race. And nowhere does it more obviously hurt the very people it claims to be helping. Anyone who has lived in a big American city for a significant amount of time, as I have in Los Angeles, knows this to be true. The conditions in South Central Los Angeles have barely changed since the days of the Watts riots, although the number of social programs put in place by consistently liberal governments is now almost uncountable. The same faces have stalked the land throughout those years as spokespeople for the black community—locally Representative Maxine Waters, nationally Jesse Jackson and Al Sharpton, to name the most prominent—always recommending the same solutions and demanding the same fealty like medieval lords. Booker T. Washington recognized this pattern over a hundred years ago when he said: "There is a class of colored people who make a business of keeping the troubles, the wrongs and the hardships of the Negro race before the public. Some of these people do not want the Negro to lose his grievances because they do not want to lose their jobs. There is a certain class of race-problem solvers who don't want the patient to get well."

These days Booker Washington is not in favor with elites for what he wrote back then, nor are other prominent black conservatives like Thomas Sowell and Shelby Steele who have written updated versions of the same message, in many instances with an eloquence considerably in excess of their liberal counterparts of any color. But their views advocating personal responsibility for black people have been largely drowned out by such widely reported comments as Mayor de Blasio warning his mixed race son to be wary of the New York City police when the teenager ventured beyond the well-guarded precincts of Gracie Mansion. Sadly, what we have had since the Civil Rights Act is basically fifty years of cynicism and manipulation undermining at nearly every turn what would have been a natural progression to racial equality. At every moment when we appear to have left racism behind, at least to the extent that is possible in human life, somehow it seems to rear its ugly head again. If that seems deliberate, it is. Repetitive cycles of this nature of course breed cynicism and this cynicism has percolated well into the black community itself. We see that cycle of decline in the themes of that great African American achievement, black music, which has descended from the transcendent agony of the blues, through the inspirational anthems of the civil rights movement, on into the love songs of Motown and soul to reach today's rap lyrics, championing drug dealing, misogyny, homophobia, and greed. The musical quality, for the most part, remained high but the subject matter turned toward the self-interested nihilism we see in the entertaining film *Straight Outta Compton*. Who could blame those rappers for their nihilism? (Well, Dr. Dre seems to have done pretty well.) Why be optimistic anymore when everyone knows the game is fixed?

The rise of the Reverend Al Sharpton—a character straight out of classic portrayals of black race hustlers in Ralph Ellison's 1952 *Invisible Man*—is evidence in itself of a fixed game. Anyone paying the slightest attention for the last several decades knows Sharpton is an Elmer Gantry-like opportunist—half race-baiter, half racist himself—and yet he is welcomed at every door from the White House to the board room of Sony Pictures. The unspoken intention of this welcome is not really to improve race relations in the United States. It is to inoculate Sharpton's client against those accusations. It's rather like the Spanish Inquisition with somewhat, for now, less fatal results, though careers are ruined and people made to repent. Thus, Sharpton is able to appeal to the morally narcissistic instincts of politicians like Obama and de Blasio as well as to our self-appointed guardians in the media. Indeed, he provides a certain frisson for all of them, coming as he does from a history of violent confrontation, the exact details of which, including overt anti-Semitism, are conveniently forgotten or ignored. The Sharpton of the Crown Heights riots and the Tawana Brawley case has been defanged to become a now bowdlerized version in the way Huey Newton and Angela Davis had their histories cleansed. All that's important is that he's "been there." He knows what's really happening, how "bad" it is, but he's willing to help us get better if we will only listen—and of course pay the necessary bulto. Sharpton's change from fringe demonstrator and low-grade Mafia collaborator[1] to a member of the respected mainstream is taken at face value. At the same time it is taken at face value that most of white America *has not* changed and is still largely what it was, either closet Klansmen or boardroom bigots, no matter how we pretend otherwise. This is one of the bright shining lies of moral narcissism, as it is one of its basic theorems. If Sharpton did not exist, someone like him would have to have been invented—a little too strident perhaps, but basically honest and true. Morgan Freeman had to be rolled back. Indeed, he had to roll himself back. And as we have noted, he did.

So what hath moral narcissism wrought in the twenty-first century with regard to race? An America clearly more obsessed with it than it has been for years. But is the country in actuality more racist? That's hard to say. Most of us fight against it. Although the charge of racism has been made so frequently and so easily it has often become absurd, we are not entirely anesthetized. It remains the scarlet letter of our time, even when the accusation is completely unproven. A famous instance of this in recent years was the offer of $100,000 by the late Andrew Breitbart to anyone who could provide evidence of racial slurs at a Tea Party demonstration. The racial charge had been made by a group of African American congressmen, including the legendary John Lewis from the congressional Black Caucus, who had been passing through the event and claimed to have been racially vilified. No one ever stepped forward with proof to take Breitbart up on his offer, despite its size. This is not surprising. Nostalgia for racism is so strong that it often makes the devil appear where it doesn't exist. Lewis et al. may have thought they had heard the N-word, even when they didn't. Its ghost was sufficient. Just as with global warming/climate change, the supposed universality of alleged racism has overtones of the Salem witch trials. Proving that you're not a racist is in the realm of the impossible.

What has become clear is that the races are regarding each other more warily than they have for some time. Our political parties are increasingly separated racially, the Republicans, the party of Lincoln, becoming an all-white party. That this risks making the GOP a permanent minority is almost too obvious as demographics change. Also it makes whites withdrawn and sullen while it turns blacks into a bitter shame culture always blaming the other party. This was even the case at the 2015 Grammy Awards where dancers aped the "Hands Up, Don't Shoot" mantra of the Ferguson rebellion as if it were the latest step, a boogaloo for our times.

The final irony, however, is that this racial moral narcissism—specifically that widely held view that slavery is America's original sin and therefore anything that happens to blacks now and into the future, anything they do, is justified by that atrocity—is the very excuse that has led to the "crumbling" of the black family predicted fifty years ago by Daniel Patrick Moynihan when he was an assistant secretary in Lyndon Johnson's Labor Department. Blacks are not responsible for themselves because whites had already ruined their lives. That can be argued, of course, but if you succeed in winning the argument, it will be a self-fulfilling prophecy. It will excuse all sorts of bad behavior from gang warfare to mob violence with the looting and torching of largely black owned businesses. In other words, the moral narcissist insists that #blacklivesmatter, while achieving, even unconsciously desiring, the reverse. Everything is stood on its head. The ones who suffer most from these declarations are African Americans.

Since we live in a society where preserving racism has become more important than conquering it, all of us—white, black, Hispanic, and Asian—are trapped in a monumental catch-22. Any time you downplay racism (which usually improves the situation), you are accused of racism. Every time you *make* an accusation of racism, you exacerbate it further, often out of line with the level of the crime. So we are caught in a racially overheated America for no reason, with only the ability to make it worse. The moral narcissism lurking in shadows, reinforcing this trap, does not allow us to escape, even to relax. If you believe the primal theorem, there is no way out. And if you express even partial skepticism of the primal theorem—that slavery is only *partly* responsible for the fate of African Americans today—you are yet again a racist. Catch-44.

Will there be an end to this? It's hard to see it and it's hard not to be depressed by the situation, although certainly the Republican presidential candidacy of retired neurosurgeon Ben Carson gives hope, no matter how this candidacy turns out. Nevertheless, the racial situation is extremely depressing for those of us who participated in the civil rights movement and depressing for our children and our children's children, who will now have to deal with it yet again. This is particularly true of the younger generation, who are surrounded by a racial witch-hunt of unprecedented proportions, permeating our schools and almost all other public institutions, masquerading under the rubric of political correctness or, more recently, microaggressions. In this world where the moral narcissist is king, many of these young people become cynical, others frightened, still others regress or seethe with hatred. Whatever the result, it bodes no good for the future and is indeed ominous. Those who most loudly claimed they were seeking a postracial America are the ones sabotaging it.

Everything is inverted in the world of moral narcissism. It is also oversimplified, so that the truth is obscured and change is impossible or unlikely. As we will see in the next chapter, just as the moral narcissist views race in the most rigid and simplified manner, he or she looks outward to the world with the equally rigid conviction that most of the significant global problems were solely generated by the West and hardly ever by the people actually causing them. Whatever terrible things are happening are finally our fault. We are responsible for our own demise. In a way, they are right. But not in the way they think they are. Locally and globally, moral narcissists are the ones doing themselves—and us—in.

XI

Selfies from Raqqa

How moral narcissists fight the War on Terror to lose.

Edward Said's *Orientalism* may be the most influential book of our time that few people have read and only slightly more have heard of. Published in 1978, it posited that almost all Western analysis of the Orient—in Said's world largely the Islamic Middle East—was inaccurate, self-referential, and terminally biased by being a product of triumphalist imperialism. Scholars like Princeton's Bernard Lewis had been wasting their time at best, deliberately and perniciously misinforming at worst, in their explanations of Islam for the West. Everything they said was basically a lie designed to further the exploitation of the East by that same West, even if Lewis didn't understand that himself. The scholar was the victim of his own propaganda. Lewis struck back in a 1982 issue of the *New York Review of Books*, pointing out that Said's arguments were as ridiculous as saying classical scholars' works were invalid because they were not native Greeks. He also went into many specifics about Islam, conveniently ignored by Said. Nevertheless Said's approach prevailed, dominating nearly all the Middle East studies departments of American and European universities where so-called postcolonial studies prevail to this day. Hardly coincidental was the simultaneous rise in influence of such postmodern philosophes as Jacques Derrida and Michel Foucault with their deconstruction/cultural relativist world views. The irony that the societies they so "relativistically" considered equals were among the most misogynistic and homophobic on the planet, not to mention fascistic, was somehow beside the point and not worthy of discussion or even attention.

Roughly at the same time (1997), the term Islamophobia was coined. Commonplace as this neologism is today, it came in through the back door via an obscure report by the Runnymede Trust, a left-wing British think tank. Six years before 9/11 someone in that group thought to apply the phobia (irrational fear) suffix to Islam. Whoever did it was something of an evil genius, equating criticism of Islam to a clinical neurosis. It would fit perfectly with the twenty-first-century zeitgeist. We are not superior to other cultures, quote unquote Michel Foucault et al. You had to go on the couch or take a double dose of Prozac if you thought anything as reactionary as that. This proved to be superb preventive medicine. Serious study of Islamic ideology and/or theology was kept carefully at bay after the 747s hit the World Trade Center. To brand all, or even some, Muslims with this action would be and was Islamophobia. For the more intellectually sophisticated, you would be guilty of Orientalism, in Said's words. What did we know, after all? What could we know? We weren't them. So almost no one learned much about Islam, even after our country was attacked in the name of Islam at a level equal to Pearl Harbor. For years after that, Islam was called "the religion of peace," when anyone with two-minute's worth of research on Google could have found out the truth. It had nothing thing to do with peace, quite the contrary. Islam literally meant "submission." The definition and intention of the religion was no more or less than worldwide submission to Allah. For everyone. When the British Islamist imam Anjem Choudary gleefully explained as much multiple times direct from London on American television, it appeared to surprise or even shock a fair percentage of the audience.

How was and is this possible a decade and a half after 9/11? Where did this "willful blindness," as Andrew McCarthy puts it, come from? Lassitude is clearly part of the answer, as is ignorance. In a country where a significant percentage doesn't know the name of the vice-president, how can they be expected to know the details of an alien religion, even if those details could have mortal consequences? Further, to be ignorant is not having to act. And acting is hard work with unforeseen results. But far more important than lassitude and ignorance, crazy as it sounds, we had come to a time that, for most Americans and certainly a vast majority of the media and the academy, the fear of being labeled a bigot was greater than the fear of dying at the hands of those same bigots. The achievement of moral narcissism had been that extreme and powerful. The elites had decreed it and their decree had been, more or less, fully received. Islamophobia was more dangerous than Islam, even in the religion's fundamentalist form.

This, more than anything, accounts for what can only be called the post-9/11 Thermidor, only this time it was not Robespierre's radicalism from which we were retreating, but common sense and reality. It was okay to oppose Islamism or Islamofascism or whatever it was to be called for a while, but at a certain point, after a very few years, this opposition drew too close to the line of prejudice and had to end. These were the disadvantaged of the third world, the victims of imperialism, as Said would have it. If they did us wrong, it was because we did them wrong for a longer time and more deeply.

This closed the door, if it was ever open, to learning what Islam really was and is in any of its various strains. If you were the equivalent of a racist even for raising the question, then why raise it? Why risk the opprobrium, professionally or socially? This perpetuated the ignorance to the degree that later Barack Obama could say, with a straight face, that the Islamic State was not Islamic. Napoleon in Orwell's *Animal Farm* could have done no better. We were living in a form of dictatorship without knowing it. If Communism was the dictatorship of the proletariat, we lived in a dictatorship of elite moral narcissists who decided between right and wrong, what exactly was the truth, before we could even begin to evaluate the facts for ourselves. They were gone in a flash. The differences between Islam and the Judeo-Christian tradition were deliberately obfuscated and blurred. Only those who actively went out to study the differences could learn them—and few did. In the view of our elites, all religions were equal on the surface, while religion itself was treated with disdain, as old-fashioned, so any distinctions between Islam and Western faiths was therefore irrelevant in the first place. Religion was something passé or to be used as a source for chastisement, as when Obama reminded an audience of evangelical Christians at the National Prayer breakfast that bad deeds had been committed by Christians during the Crusades, the intellectual equivalent of informing those same people that the sky is blue. Of course he did it for a reason—to silence those who disagreed with him under the false flag of moral equivalence between religions, and to distract from the true culprit in an era when people were butchered and heads lopped off with regularity in the name of Allah. We're supposed to see this violence as an extreme and temporary aberration, not even part of the religion, and avert our eyes from the original texts from which it all derived. We're supposed to ignore the history of the Muslim Brotherhood (and groups that followed them like Al Qaeda, and later the Islamic State) that revived and relied upon those texts, and then to cooperate with that same Muslim Brotherhood and its allies against the Brotherhood's enemies for mutual political ends. This is moral narcissism at its purest, distilled to its essence, a pas de deux that uses a superficial pseudomorality to exploit people's natural impulses to seem good and openhearted for what, consciously or not, ends up being the most evil and destructive of purposes. And, as many have been quick to point out, much as it is with African Americans, those who suffer most from Islamic extremism are the Muslims themselves. That, of course, is in the process of changing, as larger and larger numbers of Muslim people migrate into Europe.

The self-described liberals and progressives that pretend to themselves and others that what is occurring in the Islamic world is just that kind of temporary aberration are so deeply locked into their world views that they can see neither reality in front of them nor remember history, if they ever read it. Against all evidence, they are determined to adhere to the overall gestalt of blaming the West for the problems of the East. On the surface this is again much like blaming slavery for the 2016 problems of African Americans, but the story is considerably more complex, deeper, and longstanding, beginning in the seventh century with the founding of Islam and continuing through the Battle of Tours (732) and the Siege of Vienna (1529) to name just the obvious signal events. Islam and Christendom have been in violent competition for centuries. Said's strategy was to win that battle from within, boring into the confidence of the dominant West, presaging what Robert Spencer later called "stealth jihad." Said was successful because he was able to leverage the moral narcissism of those who wanted to feel superior to their peers by joining in the attack on Western imperialism. His timing was excellent because the West was near its peak and he was able to exploit liberal guilt and self-laceration. Also, in the period after the Vietnam War, it was "cool" to be anti-American and anti-Western. That didn't change even as Vietnam receded. No one wanted to be seen as imperialist. Indeed, the West seemed so strong that no amount of Islamic-inspired violence could possibly hurt it anyway. So why worry? It was all a game and far away. Even an event as impactful as 9/11 did not really alter the narrative and isolated incidents such as the attack at Ft. Hood or the bombing at the Boston Marathon, even (just barely) the mass murders in San Bernardino, could easily be ascribed to crazed malcontents.

But that wasn't all. At the same time, moral narcissism masked actual fear. It was a way of hiding from the true, and frequently mortal, results of terrorism under a cloud of rhetoric and rationalization. Although ludicrous on its face in the era of ISIS, Islamic terrorism was often equated by liberals to such wildly divergent activities as deranged evangelicals bombing abortion clinics, events that happen infrequently and are therefore dismissible and safe. Few were seriously worried about being assassinated by an anti-abortionist, though they might pretend they were, but Al Qaeda was another matter. Best not to think about the latter while focusing on the former. Liberals can avoid reality while simultaneously punching the moral equivalency card, leaving values unruffled and unchallenged. I am good because I do not oppress the East. I am not a colonialist. I don't even play one on TV.

The rise and election of Barack Obama represented the apotheosis of this Western self-abnegation. Said's ideation had arrived in the White House. It's no accident that one of Obama's good friends in Chicago was Rashid Khalidi, Said's successor at Columbia as director of the university's Middle East Institute. The president, while still an Illinois state senator, attended Khalidi's 2003 bon voyage party to New York for his new appointment. The *Los Angeles Times* was given a tape of this event, which according to their cursory report, was a decidedly pro-Palestinian Israel bash. The extent and content of Obama's participation is unknown. The *Times* will not release the tape, claiming that would be counter to its agreement with its source. This agreement has never been made public, but whatever the case, the tape has remained hidden. This could be insignificant. Most of us have friends with whom we do not consistently agree. So may it be between Obama and Khalidi. But considering what has occurred since, it is more than arguable that the paper should release at least a transcript of this tape. That has not happened. It's hardly surprising. The *Los Angeles Times*, like so much of the media, has operated under the principle that the enemy should not be named. Until quite recently it called terrorists "activists" and "militants" and showed extreme reluctance to use the word Islam in relation to them, as if they had no motivation other than poverty, which was very often not the case.

If we go back into the Bush administration, we see a schizophrenia on the part of Bush 43 and his advisers regarding who or what this enemy was. Like everyone else, they had bathed in the inescapable lukewarm bath of moral narcissism that made all but the most orthodox conservatives prey to political correctness. But immediately after 9/11, on 9/20 to be exact, Bush demonstrated he was able to see events with some clarity during a speech before Congress when he addressed the question of "Who attacked our country?":

> The evidence we have gathered all points to a collection of loosely affiliated terrorist organizations known as al Qaeda. They are some of the murderers indicted for bombing American embassies in Tanzania and Kenya and responsible for bombing the USS Cole. Al Qaeda is to terror what the Mafia is to crime. But its goal is not making money, its goal is remaking the world and imposing its radical beliefs on people everywhere. The terrorists practice a fringe form of Islamic extremism that has been rejected by Muslim scholars and the vast majority of Muslim clerics; a fringe movement that perverts the peaceful teachings of Islam.
>
> The terrorists' directive commands them to kill Christians and Jews, to kill all Americans and make no distinctions among military and civilians, including women and children. This group and its leader, a person named Osama bin Laden, are linked to many other organizations in different countries, including the Egyptian Islamic Jihad, the Islamic Movement of Uzbekistan.[1]

No, Bush did not say we are at war with radical Islam or, heaven forbid, Islam, but he did at first describe Islamic extremists as under orders to kill Christians and Jews—in other words, we were in something of a quasi holy war. Sadly, he walked this back to various degrees over the next six or seven years. He did, however, act forcefully during "the Surge" that overcame Al Qaeda in Iraq—at least temporarily. Nevertheless, he appeared always to look over his shoulder at those who would accuse him of racism, Islamophobia, and virtually any other factor that could indicate bias against the supposedly impoverished of the third world. Some of this was strategically necessary to a certain degree. And some of Bush's behavior was due to old alliances—his family ties to the Saudis and the "realist" foreign policy advisers to whose ideas his father sometimes subscribed—former Secretary of State James Baker, National Security Advisor Brent Scowcroft, and others. But what interests me here was how the atmosphere in our country was building, how moral narcissism and political correctness worked together to make victory over fundamentalist Islam increasingly impossible. The idea of winning a war by smashing the enemy as we had in Dresden and Tokyo at the end of World War II was disappearing from the table, if it was ever really on it or could be. Removing such discussion from foreign policy arguments was one of the most significant outgrowths, if not the most significant, of the rise of moral narcissism and political correctness in the post-Vietnam era. If all cultures were equal, or even nearly equal, then to annihilate, even severely wound one, was inexcusable. This was true although they were trying to annihilate us and had publicly declared as much on multiple occasions. Paradoxically, we were so superior—or thought we were—that we didn't have to worry about anything they did or said. "Death to America" was no more than a Boy Scout slogan for Iranian *basijis*. They supposedly didn't take it seriously, so we didn't. To compound the paradox, the ones suffering most, at least as of this writing, from our military politesse were the very people we claimed to be supporting: that indeterminate and shifting mass of mysterious, moderate Muslims. It was as if we had decided to go easy on the Nazis in order to protect the "good Germans" from being overwhelmed by them, a patently absurd strategy. Whatever the case, George Bush's famous "axis of evil" had faded into oblivion. We lived in a world of "different strokes for different folks."

This prepared the way for Barack Obama. When he made his speech about hope and change, there was, of course, no mention of radical Islam, except the unspoken message of peace and understanding to our Muslim brother and sisters. Shortly thereafter he went to Egypt and gave words to that unspoken pledge in a much-discussed speech at Cairo University. The United States, he said, had misunderstood the Islamic world and been substantially unfair to it. We would make, in Obama's words, "a new beginning" based on "mutual understanding." The speech ultimately meant very little but it sowed the seeds of what was to come, especially in the relatively immediate future, as the United States sided with the Islamist Muslim Brotherhood in the "Arab Spring" that shook the Middle East. The Muslim Brotherhood might have had a dangerous and violent past, not to mention an ultra-expansionist and vehemently anti-American jihadist ideology, but Obama ignored that. He and his secretary of state Hillary Clinton took the position that there were good and bad Islamic fundamentalists and if you supported the "good fundamentalists," all would turn out well.

Needless to say, it didn't. Mohamed Morsi, the man they backed in the ousting of longtime American ally strongman Hosni Mubarak, although the first democratically elected head of state in Egyptian history, was quickly revealed to be a religious despot who made Mubarak look genteel. Within days of his election, Morsi had granted himself unlimited powers, followed by proffering a draft of a new Islamist constitution placing Egypt virtually entirely under Shariah law. This would have morphed the somewhat more liberal state—for an Arab country anyway—into a virtual Sunni clone of the Shiite Islamic Republic of Iran. Demonstrators took to the streets and chaos broke loose. Soon enough the military took control, as it had before, and General Abdel Fattah al-Sisi was in command of Egypt, to the consternation of the United States.

XII

Islam Denialism

*If you think all religions are equal,
you can skip this chapter.*

What had attracted Obama and Clinton to Morsi in the first place? On the surface, you would think the doctrine of the Muslim Brotherhood, with its heavy dollop of misogyny and homophobia, not to mention that anti-Americanism and unwavering advocacy of the monolithic primacy of mosque over state, would be anathema to them. Indeed the Brotherhood's twentieth-century thinking had been largely inspired by the Egyptian writer Sayyid Qutb who, after briefly attending Colorado State College in Greeley in the late 1940s, criticized America for its materialism, but even more for its "animal-like" mixing of the sexes that "went on even in the churches."[1] He also described the American girl as "well acquainted with her body's seductive capacity. She knows it lies in the face, and in expressive eyes, and thirsty lips. She knows seductiveness lies in the round breasts, the full buttocks, and in the shapely thighs, sleek legs—and she shows all this and does not hide it."[2] Qutb was no feminist. This and other similar statements and behaviors, including extremely drastic ones such as Islamist attitudes toward rape in which women had almost no rights—made by the Muslim Brotherhood—does not seem to have bothered Hillary, at least not enough to impede her support of the Islamists. Nor has Obama's Christianity—if we can really call Reverend

81

Wright's church Christian—deterred his support for the group that gave rise to Al Qaeda and ultimately the Islamic State.

So what accounts for this support beyond the more obvious aspects of realpolitik (choosing the winning side, etc.), which proved to be inaccurate in this instance? For the elite American moral narcissist, anti-imperialism would appear to trump all things, even extreme sexual discrimination and homophobia. Anti-imperialism has become a control mechanism that was too hard to resist. This is particularly true for Obama whose Islamic background as a child in Indonesia meshed emotionally with a political bias against the West. Of course, this bias was not simple and as Obama grew older he must have become aware of the dark side of Islam. This darker side had long been evident before he became president and only increased during his presidency. But he did his best to hide this and deny religious culpability, making pronouncements that Al Qaeda was on the run and later that the Islamic State was merely a jayvee team. And neither of these groups, not to mention Boko Haram, Islamic Jihad, and the like, was really Islamic. What they were, he did not say. Perhaps nothing. Or social clubs. But behind the scenes he had quietly tried to bottle this dark impulse through drone attacks and the use of Special Forces. Though these strategies were largely ineffective and the threat continued to grow, he persisted in denying the doctrinal link between Islam and violence. Perhaps he had been playing hooky from the madrassa as a child but he didn't seem to know or to acknowledge the passages from the Koran and the Hadith that advocated world domination and justified jihad. If he acknowledged them at all, he equated them to other religions, reminding that Christian audience at that prayer breakfast of the horrors of the Crusades and the Inquisition, long-ago events of whose excesses that audience was already fully aware and condemnatory.

But historical analysis or comparison wasn't exactly Obama's intention. His goal was much more clearly to distract, to keep the eyes off the religion that was actually causing problems in our times—huge and growing problems. The narrative, his version of the narrative, decreed that Islam itself could not be isolated as the sole culprit. That would undermine the narrative that the West was to blame in all things. The moral narcissism inherent in that view, the ability to separate yourself from the great unwashed and prove your goodness above those who sought petty vengeance on poor victims of imperialism, would come unstuck.

And then what? The center would not hold. Islamic violence had to be described as "random," not doctrinal. We just didn't understand what jihad really meant. It was a striving for spiritual growth.

This was made more evident at the three-day summit on Countering Violent Extremism held in Washington by the president in February 2015. This event took place only days after the murders at the *Charlie Hebdo* offices and the Hypercacher kosher market in Paris, some further mayhem in Belgium and Denmark (where the target was again Jewish, this time at a synagogue), and some extraordinarily savage activities by the Islamic State, including burning a man alive in a cage and simultaneously beheading twenty-one Coptic Christians. And yet the words "Islamic" and "extremism" remained detached from each other. The supposed explanation for this separation—the narrative that was offered through various administration sources—was that to name radical Islam as the perpetrator of the violence was playing into the hands of the Islamists who would then claim that the United States was at war with Islam and use that claim to gain still more adherents. The same, of course, could have been said of naming Nazism or Communism—or any enemy for that matter. It was an extreme form of political correctness that allowed Obama to flip the conference on its head, turning it into a defense of Islam, warning his audience that they had to "address their [Muslims] social, political and economic grievances." It was the old "root causes" argument, a moral narcissist standby that exonerated the perpetrator of a crime while elevating the "goodness" of the speaker, making him morally, even intellectually superior, to the listener. Obama further admonished the older Muslim imams in his audience not to be "boring" with their younger constituents or the young 'uns would run off to join the Islamic State or Al Qaeda. It was coolness, doncha know, that made otherwise normal young men slit people's throats and throw women in rape rooms. If only they found another way, maybe a Muslim rap song about tolerance with a catchy backbeat, everything would work itself out. Dr. Dre would handle it. They could give out his music, together with a set of earphones, to prospective terrorists.

At his conference, Obama did everything in his power not to acknowledge that Islam had ideological problems in its actual texts and history that was causing the violence, problems that were not so easily solved, because, unlike the Bible, the Koran was the verbatim dictation of

Allah to Muhammad. Only weeks before Egyptian president al-Sisi—who could pay with his life for such statements, as Anwar Sadat had paid for his rapprochement with Israel—had courageously spoken out at Cairo's Al-Azhar University on the need for an Islamic reformation. Not a peep out of Obama on such a thing or any comment on what al-Sisi had said. The Egyptian president was never to be mentioned. He is what is referred to in the White House colloquially as a "PNG"—persona non grata. Instead, at the conference, Obama emphasized the dangers of domestic Islamophobia, while not mentioning actual anti-Semitic acts that far outnumbered anti-Muslim acts in the United States. Why?

It sounds corny to say that the tentacles of moral narcissism run deep and express themselves in different ways, but it's true. Obama and his political allies in his administration and the media see racism and bigotry as the original sin and therefore can't see past them into the reality of events. Willful blindness, as I have mentioned, is what former US attorney Andrew McCarthy has memorably called this phenomenon, but it is more than that. It is a kind of *pathological* blindness linked to personality disintegration. So much of one's self is tied up in seeing the world in a certain way that to alter or even question that view constitutes an assault on the self. We see this in the intellectual handstands and cartwheels performed by Obama and his minions at the conference and through the press in an effort to justify at least partially the activities of the Islamic State, to nudge the blame not altogether subtly back in the direction of the imperialist West, personified of course by the United States. This reached the level of the risible when—only two days after Islamic State terrorists had simultaneously decapitated those twenty-one Coptic Christians in Libya—the administration suggested that the problem was that terrorists could not find "jobs." If only we took heed of that old Silhouette's 1950s standard "Get a Job," all would be well and all these malcontents from Toronto to Timbuktu would trudge back from Raqqa and sign up for a work/study program at their nearest community college, hopefully majoring in something useful like computer programming. (Unfortunately, many already had, but not exactly as intended, as the jihadists' presence in social media made all too clear.)

Meanwhile, the Islamic State was offering eternal life and seventy-two virgins to its potential convert—not to mention a bevy of sex slaves in the present day. It's hard to imagine a job at Walmart would be more attractive, even at the highest managerial level. And that's not even touching on the literally orgasmic excitement inherent in believing you are doing God's will—and therefore saving the world—in bringing about the Apocalypse, murdering as many infidels as possible in the name of Allah. Forget *Fifty Shades of Grey*. Forget *Game of Thrones*. It was the computer game of all time, only real. (Ironically, the only job more attractive or exciting would be an elite executive or political position, like Barack Obama's and John Kerry's, enabling you to fly around in government or private jets to terrorism conferences in the Caribbean or make an annual pilgrimage to Davos to complain about the climate or perhaps income inequality. The food would be considerably better and the women more attractive. You didn't even have to import the lingerie, as the Islamic State was allegedly doing. (Ask Dominique Strauss-Kahn.) This ludicrous jobs suggestion by the administration was not an accidental act but one of ideological desperation cum manipulation. They were terrified of the truth, which was creeping up around them, and they had to do something. The jobs trial balloon would have been no more than laughable had not so many accepted such an absurd rationalization or at least given it an impartial listen. After a while, after the brouhaha died down, it could even become conventional wisdom. After all, something close to it always was—that traditional "root causes" explanation. The original 9/11 report had pointed to Islamic theology as the source of the violence of that day, but that was quickly and easily forgotten, swept under the political correctness rug. Recent events, ghastly as they may be, could be too, and the comfortable status quo returned. All would be happy again in this best of all possible worlds, Dr. Pangloss. Preservation of world view at all costs was indeed about the self.

Not inconsequential in this too is the similarity between this approach to terrorism (Islam denial?) and the unquestioning global warming orthodoxy discussed in an earlier chapter. In both instances, a continual effort is made to blame us, the United States and the West, for forces and results that are largely external. This is quite narcissistic in a directly personal way—preserving our role as the centerpiece of the universe—while, in the case of terrorism, it is racist in its essence—ignoring, as it does, that Muslims (Arabs, Iranians, et al.) are capable of having real opinions on theological matters, which, like it or not, they truly believe, have thought through, and are prepared to act upon. The aforementioned Sayyid Qutb and Hassan al-Banna of the Muslim Brotherhood are just two seminal examples of this, as are, of course, Usama Bin Laden and Ayatollah Khomeini. All of these men were obviously well aware of the economic differences between East and West, but not in the slightest preoccupied by them. (Bin Laden was a billionaire anyway.) Their considerations were about values and lifestyle and ultimately were entirely religious in nature. They were anti-Western theocrats that did not, Sunni and Shiite, believe in nation states—only in caliphates. Obama's Islamic denialism is an attempt to avoid confronting this or, more accurately, to prevent us, the American public, from confronting the obvious reality around us. Hence we end up with Obama-approved euphemisms like "man-caused violence" that would border on the laughable if they weren't so dangerous.

How far from the Islamic life of reality is the morally narcissistic bowdlerized version believed in or force fed by Obama. It is wildly distant from the concept of the "strong horse" described by Lee Smith in his book of that name, a theory actually supported by Bin Laden himself— that Arabs, a tribal culture, will follow the strong horse, the strong man leader, in almost every instance. Surely, Obama was aware of this theory and of its numerous real-life examples from Saddam Hussein to Bashar al-Assad and now al-Baghdadi of the Islamic State. But his ignoring or turning away from this theory or anything similar or indeed from any direct link between violence and Islam at all seems to come from a deeper place—shame.

Barack Obama—both of whose parents deserted him serially when he was very young—spent his early childhood during those emotionally difficult years attending Indonesian madrassas. A man so cosseted and soothed by a religion as a particularly vulnerable child would find it extraordinarily difficult to acknowledge that the religion that protected and nurtured him would be capable of mass killing and violent jihad. It would almost make no sense. He remembers kindliness and poetic quotations from the Koran. (No wonder he considers the sound of the muezzin the most beautiful in the world.) And yet it is reality. The violence is everywhere and has been since Muhammad himself slaughtered his enemies to start the religion. This is shameful and Obama himself most probably is ashamed of it—wouldn't we all be—so he hides it from the world and to a great extent, apparently, from himself. And Islamic life is, to a great degree, as many have discussed, a shame culture.

This does not mean I think Obama believes in stoning adulterers to death, cutting off the hands of thieves, or throwing homosexuals off towers (in the manner of the Islamic State), or hanging them from telephone poles (as in Iran). He loathes these things, as most decent people would. But he can't look at or examine their context because to do so would interfere with his intentions. His most important foreign policy goal from before his inauguration has been a rapprochement with Iran, a nation he considers a natural ally of the United States. He was able to stick to this goal even during the massive antiregime protests by the Iranian Greens who called out to him "Obama, Obama, are you with us or are you with them?" meaning, of course, the ayatollahs. Obama said nothing, an extraordinary display of lack of basic empathy. He must have known that many in the leadership of these protests, not to mention the anonymous rank and file, had been and would be tortured in the notorious Evin Prison. Others would be murdered. Yet Obama persisted in his goal. Why?

Some of the answers to this remain mysterious, although clues exist in his relationship to Valerie Jarrett, who was raised in Iran, and in the frequently mentioned desire for some positive legacy for an administration sorely lacking in foreign policy success. But an equally important answer still resides in that aforementioned emotional connection to Islam from his childhood. Whatever the case, he has been unshakeable in his goal to make a deal with the mullahs and their representatives even while they appear to have outwitted him completely in the negotiations, reportedly berating and insulting Secretary of State Kerry at meetings in the process. The most remarkable thing is that anyone in the United States supported this enterprise, yet many did. This is a testament to the extraordinary power of belief systems and the degree to which they make rational observation impossible. When Obama declared ISIS to be a jayvee team, his constellation of beliefs may actually have made him think that way. He probably didn't even take the time to look closely at the details—or didn't want to for fear of what could result. This was a new, or relatively new, name to him, just one of many that are hard to keep track of. Therefore they couldn't amount to much. He couldn't be bothered to examine their provenance in "Al Qaeda in Iraq" because to do so would disturb not only his narrative that "Al Qaeda was on the run," but, more importantly, his ideological equanimity.

XIII

The Moral Narcissist Sleep Room

Oh, les beaux jours *when we were all at the barricades, pulling up the pavement in Paris!*

It is this need for ideological equanimity that pervades the culture of the West in regards to expansionist Islam, as if a massive "Do Not Disturb" sign, stretching from Los Angeles to Vienna, had been erected. Needless to say, there have been rips and tears and spatters of blood on the sign from time to time as spurts of terror violence occurred, but for the most part it has remained intact. There were superficial explanations for this. In the United States at least, life was relatively good, the stock market largely up until recently. Even the unemployment figures, fudged as they may be, were down marginally. The complaints about income inequality were mostly for show. Most people knew it was ever thus. Even in Europe with its comparatively high unemployment and shaky economies, things were basically satisfactory compared to the nearly unremitting violence of the twentieth century. The Battle of Tours and the Siege of Vienna were the most distant of memories, events only to be recalled for college admissions tests. Besides, it was natural for humans to seek equanimity. But the need for this equanimity was far more profound than that and contained within it a not insignificant element of fear. And that fear could be hidden from the eye by the morally narcissistic view that Western imperialism was the sine qua non of the world's woes. Those who called themselves liberals and progressives, even those who considered themselves centrists, had indeed bought Said's *Orientalism* without, as I have noted, having even heard of it in the vast majority of cases. Islam had nothing to do with Islam, but everything to do with what we had done *to* Islam.

So the vast majority of the media and almost the entire political class pretended to be surprised and perplexed when significant numbers of the citizens of the United States and Europe, not all of them from Muslim backgrounds, were decamping from their home countries to join the Islamic State in its murderous jihad. They shouldn't have been. If you had been paying the slightest attention, nothing could have been more inevitable. With a rudderless West that was increasingly abandoning its core principles while at the same time drowning itself in the instant celebrity of social media, what else could have happened? Jihadi John, née Mohammed Emwazi, was just another spontaneous YouTube success, his videos depicting the beheadings of journalists and aid workers perhaps a tad more edgy than the norm. From a society where many young men wanted "to be like Mike" (Jordan), we had become a society where a fair number wanted to be like John—slicing heads off in high-definition.

This was not entirely new, just more grisly. Back in 2004 a Muslim convert using the name "Azzam the American" produced a number of videos for Al Qaeda. He turned out to be one Adam Yahiye Gadahn of Anaheim, California, the grandson of a prominent Jewish urologist who was on the board of the Anti-Defamation League.[1] What then seemed like overwrought teenage rebellion was becoming conventional enough to attract tens of thousands of volunteers to Raqqa—the headquarters of the Islamic State—from nations all over the West. Some had little to live for in their home countries, but many did. Emwazi had attended the University of Westminster and was clearly well-spoken. Others came from similar backgrounds. Despite attempts to paint the attraction as being about poverty, it was about ideology as glamour, about being part of the action. A jobs program, as the State Department has suggested, could not possibly counter that. Only a whole new set of values could. But they were nowhere to be found, because they no longer existed. Moral narcissism had replaced the traditional values of the West, just as modern liberalism had replaced classical liberalism.

In the confrontation with radical Islam, indeed with Islam in general, we can see the vacuity of moral narcissism, the emptiness and virtual nonexistence of the ideas the moral narcissist claims to profess. The ideology of Islam, not substantially changed since the seventh century, is ignored in favor of the most traditional of views, most or even all of which were locked into place by the Least Great Generation referred to in the first chapter. This created a society where people chose up sides without reference to data or a changing environment. As I noted earlier, they were like sports fans, true to their teams almost from birth.

Only these weren't sports teams. They were ideologies as frozen as the coldest glacier. We see this in the congressional Black Caucus's boycott of Netanyahu's speech on Iran to Congress. So locked into the view that the Israeli prime minister was "disrespecting" a black president, they couldn't see the obvious: that Netanyahu could care less about Obama's skin color. He was worried about Iranian nuclear weapons and the survival of the country he led. But held by a form of nostalgia for racism, the caucus members had aligned with Obama in the same manner in which the most passionate Bostonians aligned with the Celtics. The president could do no wrong. A disagreement with him was an attack on them. The details of the Iran deal, whatever they were, were of no consequence. The caucus members could then feel good about themselves. They had defended their cause, even though they had no discernible reason to do so because it had nothing to do with their real cause. But that is where moral narcissism leads us. It is about air. But it is dangerous air.

Nowhere has this been more evident than in those negotiations between the so-called P5 + 1 and Iran (really between the United States and Iran). The contest was completely uneven, but not in a way one would expect—the highly technological West lording it over a third world country struggling to modernize. It was tilted in favor of Iran. Our side was motivated by amorphous values and some kind of weak consensus that Iran should not have the bomb, theirs by their conception of God. (Both had a strong business interest, although ours did not admit it. For the mullahs, this was about money—a lot of it.) The negotiation itself was a culture of atheists and agnostics that had forsaken nationalism against a regime of religious fundamentalists who sought and still seek a global caliphate. The fundamentalists do not to have to review what they wanted, nor do they question their goals, nor were they responsible to an electorate that may have overturned their decisions (not that the P5 + 1 really was either).

At base, the Iranians were doing God's will. Dishonesty was then not dishonesty because it was and is in the service of Allah's wishes. This was true in negotiation and in compliance with an actual agreement. It was reinforced by the Islamic doctrines of *taqiyya*—the permission to say something that isn't true when it is for the benefit of Muslims—and *kitman*—lying by omission for the same purposes. All of this put the Western negotiators at a considerable disadvantage especially, as in the case of the P5 + 1 negotiations, the Western side. Under Obama's direction, it seemed to be seeking a deal at all costs for no discernible reason other than to say it had made a deal. The moral narcissistic underpinnings of this are clear. I am peacemaker—never mind if I am really making peace. In fact, I may actually be making war by making peace, but that's irrelevant. I am—to myself and to my peers, that is to the peers I respect and intend to impress, the ones that count—a peacemaker.

This is undoubtedly what Neville Chamberlain suffered from back in 1938. He famously said so himself, hoping for and assuming he would get great acclaim as he returned to London from Munich, declaring "peace in our times." But history has made Chamberlain into a sad joke, an emblem of appeasement in his kowtowing to Hitler. We should have learned from Chamberlain by now, but few have, even though lessons of this nature are not complicated. In our culture, people prefer to make these lessons more complicated, "nuanced" in the terminology made popular by John Kerry, in order to avoid facing uncomfortable truths. Thus when the Iranians chant "Death to America! Death to Israel!" we assume they mean something else. Yelling "Death" to a country is preposterous to Western ears. It must be symbolic of something we don't understand. (Perhaps Edward Said could tell us, were he still alive). But it's not. It means what it means. That death can come now or later, but the intention remains. We should not be fixated on an East-West dichotomy in all this. Totalitarian behavior in the Orient and the Occident is much the same, only the justifications differ at various times. When Hitler said he needed lebensraum, he took it.

So when House minority leader Nancy Pelosi marched out of Benjamin Netanyahu's speech to the US Congress on Iran on March 3, 2015, calling it "insulting" because she had heard it all before, she was more right than she realized. The truth is simple and must be repeated many times before it pierces the narcissistic haze enveloping many of our elites. Often, like Pelosi in this instance, they cannot stand to hear certain facts and start to act out. Pelosi is particularly uninformed, having insisted at the height of the Gaza War that "Hamas is a humanitarian organization." Never mind that it had been designated as a "foreign terrorist organization" in 1997. She had their humanitarianism on the good authority of the Qataris.[2] Whether Pelosi was aware that Qatar was for a long time and perhaps still is the prime financial supporter of Hamas, enabling the terror organization to amass armaments and build hidden attack tunnels under Israel, is unclear. Probably not, if we are to judge by her overall knowledge base. This is the woman who said we had to pass Obamacare in order to see what was in it, a strong indication that she wasn't aware of the details at that time.

This often-deliberate ignorance is common to a certain level of our elites—call them the hatchet men or women for whom a lack of information is useful—but at elevated levels the reverse is true. The mega-elites who consider themselves a guardian class on a plane far above the masses have almost too much confidential information. Much of this unvetted material affects our relationship to the Islamic world, and may even determine it, as we can see from the private emails of Hillary Clinton while secretary of state that were first exposed to the public in early March 2015. A 2013 email to Clinton from Sidney Blumenthal—someone who had not held a government job since his White House post ended in 2001—under the subject line "Comprehensive Intel Report on Libya," contains the warning "THE FOLLOWING INFORMATION COMES FROM EXTREMELY SENSITIVE SOURCES AND SHOULD BE HANDLED WITH CARE." Considering the ungovernable terrorist haven that Libya has become, one can only wonder who those sources might have been that merited such capitalization. But it's easier to imagine the inflated feelings of self-importance Blumenthal had being in confidential communication, able to influence policy on such matters with the secretary of state and putative first female president in her secret email account. Also we can imagine Clinton's pleasure in receiving such "confidential information," placing her even further above her peers.

In another of the memos—"For: Hillary, From: Sid"—Blumenthal refers to "Sources with access to the highest levels of the Muslim Brotherhood in Egypt . . . " This comes from the time when the Obama administration was "all-in" for the Muslim Brotherhood, those famous progenitors of Al Qaeda and therefore ISIS. As will be recalled, Egypt's Muslim Brotherhood president Mohamed Morsi was Obama, and therefore Hillary's, "main man" in the Middle East, if you discount Turkey's Erdoğan, a true believer in a similar cause. It was the contention of our leadership that the Muslim Brotherhood could be turned into, or actually already was in segments, a positive force. It could even be a force for good and not the instrument of a fundamentalist takeover of the Middle East.

Why would they think that? One explanation that stems from Hillary Clinton's relationship to her aide Huma Abedin—whose mother, Dr. Saleha Mahmood Abedin, was a founding member of the Muslim Sisterhood—seems simplistic or, at best, partial. Even the more recently revealed Clinton Foundation donations from such states as Algeria and Saudi Arabia tell only a superficial story of normal corruption. The deeper explanation here takes us back to that Least Great Generation and the values of 1968. Hillary, born in 1947, was an early boomer, very much on the end cusp of the LGG with values totally in synch with them. But the conventional sixties leftist who wrote her Wellesley thesis on radical community organizer Saul Alinsky has morphed into the multi-millionairess from Chappaqua who gives lectures for several hundred thousand dollars a shot while making demands on the tilt of her lectern and the brand of mineral water waiting for her in the green room. Does that leftism then still even exist? Yes, in the sense that it now provides a perfect cover for her present activities. Hers is a morally narcissistic liberal-leftism of convenience, to be trucked out when necessary and shelved when inconvenient. The old beliefs are used to deflect attention from her current lifestyle—give a dollop here, take a dollop there, as long as the natives aren't restless. It's not very many degrees away from the female droit du seigneur of an Eva Peron or a Cristina Fernandez de Kirchner of Argentina. This was completely apparent in the opening coffee klatch of Hillary's aging Wellesley classmates in Edward Klein's *Blood Feud: The Clintons vs. the Obamas*. No idealism here, but plenty of realpolitik cum wardrobe comparisons. Although the book is much maligned, it rings true. The lifestyle had long since trumped the ideals.

Therefore groups like the Muslim Brotherhood—for a brief moment seemingly progressive underdogs, although only to someone who was not only willfully blind, but deaf as well—might provide some of that cover. The interplay here between true beliefs and ambition is key, the latter canceling out the former or at least obfuscating the situation sufficiently so that the beliefs are only unobtrusive ghosts of themselves. Avowed feminists can then support organizations that countenance misogyny at the level of clitoridectomies because these groups supposedly represent the oppressed of the third world. But leaders lost in this confusion are exactly the wrong people to counter those expansionist tendencies of Islam that date back to the seventh century and have only intermittently abated. No wonder Hillary Clinton wanted to hide her emails with Sidney Blumenthal and others from public view. And no wonder the likes of Adam Gadahn and Mohammed Emwazi fled to the other side. Their countries had no leaders that stood for anything, nothing to really recommend or attract. At the same time, as Obama and Clinton chose the Muslim Brotherhood in Egypt, Egypt on its own went the other way, ejecting Morsi and eventually electing the decidedly more modern al-Sisi in its presidency. He is the very man who wants to reform Islam, something Obama and, one can assume, Clinton have given up on or are not even interested in, although it is the only real solution. We thought we knew best, but it turned out the Egyptian people knew best.

Indeed, moral narcissism militates against the reformation of Islam because Islam, as the product of Eastern cultures, is untouchable. The thinking goes: We once exploited them, so everything they say and do is necessarily correct or, if incorrect, none of our business. That comes down to: If they want to kill us, we deserve it—or a country like Sweden, or even Germany, essentially giving itself over to Islamic immigration, its own Enlightenment values be damned. Reading that sentence aloud makes it sound like a civilization gone insanely self-destructive, but it is basically what our culture practices, at least many of its elites. It is a prescription for self-immolation.

Fortunately, however, slowly but surely, this narcissism is increasingly becoming largely the province, almost the sole province, of those elites. The Egyptian people are not the only ones to wake up. A poll taken by (left-leaning) Anderson Robbins Research and (right-leaning) Shaw & Company Research for Fox News at the time of Netanyahu's speech to Congress had 65 percent of the American public backing the use of force to deny Iran nuclear weapons and 84 percent essentially agreeing with Netanyahu, deeming the then current deal a "bad idea." Indeed the deal itself was not a deal at all—it ultimately forbid nothing of significance—it was the "idea of a deal." It was the thought that counted, not the substance. For this reason, among many, Obama did his best to prevent Congress from having the opportunity to review and possibly to block his Iran pact, although it dealt with the most problematic of issues, weapons of mass destruction. It was a deal that a community organizer would make to keep the Mafiosi from selling heroin in his neighborhood, while the Mafiosi smiled and nodded pleasantly, both sides knowing that a week later several truckloads of drugs would be pulling up in the parking lot behind them. The Mafiosi were just giving the organizer an opportunity to look good to his superiors, making it easier for themselves to go about their work. Ultimately that organizer could be his own superior or a superior to many—something the Mafioso, were he a wise one, would have factored in.

In actuality, though of different ages, both Clinton and Obama have similar bourgeois leftist backgrounds with the same developmental pattern—having "sided with the people" early in life, thus anesthetizing themselves from criticism as they rose in wealth and power. They were to be trusted as being one of the good guys. Whether this was deliberate or accidental—probably both—the process is typical. If you are one of the cool ones at the beginning, if you are accepted as what is—in the traditional view—on the side of the people (Hillary in the path of Alinsky, Obama as a community organizer), you will remain one of the cool until the end, no matter what you do, unless you make a truly egregious mistake. And what constitutes egregious is more than a little dependent on how you were perceived at the outset, whether you had that clear acceptance. The more radical your background, up to a point (you might even go as far as Bill Ayers and Bernadine Dohrn and actually practice violence) the more you are anesthetized. I will get further into this pattern ("Nostalgia for Marxism") later, because it is at the heart of the etiology of moral narcissism, but it can lead to terrible, even frightening, public policy, especially where such cosmic issues as expansionist Islam are concerned.

Currently, as is well known, Islam is simultaneously expanding and in mortal combat with itself. Sunni and Shiite battle each other as they have for well over a thousand years while at the same moment the Sunni

Islamic State tries to expand and Shiite Iran tries to expand, often at war with each other. This has been clear for some time to anyone with an Internet who was the slightest bit interested, but it seems either not to have been clear to the president of the United States and to his successive secretaries of state, or to have been deliberately obfuscated or ignored. Confusion has reigned since the beginning of the Obama administration on how to react, a confusion that admittedly began in the Bush administration, and has become considerably worse. Now we are at the point where the president of the United States appears to have taken the Shiite side in the Shiite-Sunni conflict, possibly to secure his deal with Iran or possibly for other reasons that would be even more bizarre. This process has gone on for some time, including the complete turnaround on the murderous totalitarian Assad regime in Syria, with the President's foreign policy only being lightly scrutinized by his adversaries and the complaisant press until far into his second term. Few had wanted to dare criticize the first black president on any serious level until recently for fear of being accused of racism, the most grievous of modern sins, at least in the public sense. More than that, it was the fear of being read out of the club, of what the ancient Greeks used to call *ostrakismos*—a word with far more resonance than our modern English derivative, ostracism. That resonance came from the fact that the original ostrakismos literally meant being expelled from the city-state of Athens for ten years. In the case of our modern ostrakismos, the expulsion contains career and personal implications that are equally as brutal in their own way, at least to us. So we shut up and play along with the moral narcissist game, believing the commands from above and chanting them out—call and response like an obedient choir at a religious service.

That has led to a situation where the Western world is in a more precarious situation than most want to realize. We feel so impregnable, so modern. But so probably did ancient Rome. This has been exacerbated by moral narcissism justifying political expediency, reinforcing each other while blinding us, and possibly the beholders themselves, to the reality of what is happening. This was never clearer than in a March 6, 2015, *Wall Street Journal* article "How America Was Misled on al Qaeda's Demise" by Stephen F. Hayes and Thomas Joscelyn. Hayes and Joscelyn explored the White House claim that the unprecedented haul of secret files obtained from Bin Laden's hard drive when the Al Qaeda leader was killed showed that Bin Laden was an increasingly irrelevant old man who spent his time surfing porn on the Internet. The contents also supposedly reinforced the Obama campaign narrative that "Al Qaeda was on the run,"—a spent force of declining consequence. We were victorious.

None of this proved to be true when—a full year later—the Defense Intelligence Agency was finally able, "after a pitched battle," as Hayes and Joscelyn wrote, to examine even some of the material from the confiscated drives. The narrative that the White House had been putting out was a bright shining lie, as they used to say about Vietnam. The reverse was true; Bin Laden was very much in control. And as for Al Qaeda, according to testimony by Lt. Gen. Mike Flynn, director of the DIA, "By that time, they probably had grown by about—I'd say close to doubling by that time. And we knew that."

And we knew that? Well, not all of us did. Most of the American public that bothered to listen had been told something entirely different, something that came from above, from sources that were impeccable because "they knew best." They better have because Hayes and Joscelyn report that as of now "the public has only seen two dozen of the 1.5 million documents captured in Abbottabad" (Bin Laden's redoubt). Nevertheless, as the world well knows, Obama was reelected by a wide margin. This came after many untruths, including, most notoriously, the monumental lie that the deaths of four Americans in Benghazi, Libya, including our ambassador to that country, were caused by an ineptly made video about Muhammad that nobody saw. As was later made evident by the government's own documents, the true cause was a planned terror attack from Ansar al-Islam, an Al Qaeda affiliate—something that was known almost immediately. Almost as immediately after those Benghazi attacks, a cover-up was clearly engineered at the highest levels of our government to protect the president, the then secretary of state, and various other figures with hidden plans we may never fully understand. These lies went back and forth between the people who told them, being massaged and perfected. Who knows—soon enough they may have believed them themselves or, at least, believed them sufficiently to convince themselves that National Security Adviser Susan Rice was telling some version of the truth when she prevaricated nonstop on practically every Sunday show the weekend after the killings. What did reality matter if you were we on the good, "moral" side of things. As Hillary Clinton famously exclaimed to a congressional committee, "What difference does it make?" This may have been the ultimate statement of moral narcissism.

But what we have learned from the few Bin Laden documents available at this time is even worse than that. Senior Pakistani officials, including many we have worked with, have been more or less permanently in cahoots with Al Qaeda and the Taliban. Yet more concerning, it seems clear that there has been a steady and productive partnership between Al Qaeda and Iran. They were quite willing to ignore the Shiite-Sunni rift when it came to enabling terror, if it was to their mutual advantage—and it often was. This lends credence to Benjamin Netanyahu's statement in his speech to Congress in March 2015 that "the enemy of my enemy is my enemy" as it calls to question the "we can ultimately trust Iran" rationale inherent in Obama's negotiations. Coincidentally, when Cristiane Amanpour called Netanyahu's speech "Strangelovian" or "dystopian," she was more than likely very aware of this entente cordiale between Iran and Al Qaeda. It's her job and her background is Iranian. Nevertheless, the CNN correspondent was expressing the conventional view of many in her class that although relationships of this nature might exist, or have existed, it is in the good judgment of elites that we must ignore them. To pay attention to such things only encourages them, gives them more importance than they deserve, and becomes "Strangleovian," invoking the image of a twisted Peter Sellers struggling out of his wheelchair ("*Mein Führer*, I can walk!") in reference to the Israeli prime minister.

Of course that is absurd. What is really going on in cases like this is the deliberate enhancement of public confusion. A purposive form of obfuscation is being performed by elites that is intended to blur and make us see a situation that isn't there, that they wish should be, and that would be consistent with their world views and the maintenance of their power. When this obfuscation is a self-involved tooting of one's own horn, as in the notorious case of anchorman Brian Williams, who kept repeating his made-up story of having been under fire in a helicopter in Iraq until he seemed to believe it himself, it is harmless enough. But when the lies and obfuscations are about serious matters, as they were with Amanpour, we are all affected directly even when we barely realize it. They are about all of us and our lives.

Soon enough Al Qaeda, supposedly on the run, had morphed into the extraordinarily horrific Islamic State, attracting their own kind of narcissists who began to cross the globe to send back selfies from Raqqa. Obama, the story went, having come into office on a pledge to bring America's troops home, was trapped in a situation where he had to appease Iran to gain their help in defeating the Islamic State. But that may only be part of the story. He seems to have had an instinct to appease Iran anyway, to equalize, in his mind, the odds between East and West. Given that moral narcissism is the enemy of moral clarity, the pronouncements of the moral narcissist are designed to hide the truth. Warnings of the decline of the West are as old as the proverbial hills, but maybe this time it's really happening. A lethargy of acceptance had set in, spreading from Europe into America. The Least Great Generation had done its work. We will now examine how it did it.

XIV

Nostalgia for Marxism

*"I want a revolution where everyone can
drink cappuccino at the Café Royal."*
*—Daniel Cohn-Bendit of the Nanterre Six,
during the Paris "events" of May 1968.*

No one should underestimate nostalgia in our political and social
lives. The fifteenth-century French poet François Villon's *"Où sont
les neiges d'antan?"*—where are the snows of yesteryear?—is a classic for
a reason, evoking an often overwhelming emotion in us of sweet regret,
of loss for a better time that was supposed to have been. I am guilty of
it here—proclaiming there was a better America during an earlier day.
Maybe there wasn't. Or maybe I exaggerate. Certainly there were eras—
slavery, Jim Crow—that were shameful in the extreme.

Nevertheless, nostalgia wields a power over us that can distort and
change reality radically and is one of moral narcissism's most depend-
able allies. As I have attempted to show in an earlier chapter, nostalgia
for racism has worked in a destructive manner and recreated racism in
our time. Nostalgia for Marxism has a similarly destructive impulse,
with some differences. Unless he or she is a member of the politburo, few
actually *want* to live under Marxism anymore. Its results have been catastrophic—economically, socially, and in plain terms of body count. The
excuse was frequently put forth that this failure was because the system
was tried in societies that were too primitive (Russia instead of indus-
trialized Germany) but as time goes by that claim has lost validity. Even
where Marxist principles are tried in advanced countries with the lightest
of hands, as in today's France, the outcome is drastic unemployment and a

stagnant economy. But none of this has stopped people from proclaiming they believe in Marxism or some variant of that philosophy under a new or related name. It is shorthand for saying you are for the masses, for the common good, that you are a moral person. Largely this is pretense—most of these "Marxists" are from upper-middle-class to extraordinarily wealthy families and would be loath to give up their perquisites for the common good—but their views pervade our culture through the academy, the media, and the arts. It is a nostalgia for a Marxism that never was, a pretend Marxism—a philosophy of "as if," as German philosopher Hans Vaihinger put it. But it doesn't have to be real to affect society on basic levels. In fact, it shouldn't be. That just gets in the way. The illusion is all—the memory of those snows of yesteryear when we were all fighting the good fight.

A perfect example of this nostalgia is Warren Beatty's 1981 film *Reds* that recounts the love affair of American journalists John Reed and Louise Bryant against the background of a romanticized Russian Revolution. Interspersed with the narrative are documentary interviews with survivors of the period, a well-executed strategy to evoke sympathy for the idealistic radicals who supported the Bolsheviks. They were the good people. Only the most minor reference is made to the horrors of Communism that followed—the Gulag, Stalin, the mass starvation of millions, the Great Terror, the alliance with Hitler, and so forth—that were largely ignored by most of these interviewees or rationalized by them when they occurred. Comparing this movie to David Lean's 1965 *Doctor Zhivago*—in which these excesses are shown clearly—illustrates how the Least Great Generation (of which Beatty, born in 1937, can be said to be a "card-carrying" member) distorted or ignored truth in favor a teary-eyed, and indeed nostalgic vision of socialist revolution. Both films are basically romances, but Lean, working from Pasternak's novel as adapted by Robert Bolt, at least makes clear that Soviet Communism was massively destructive. Beatty—a filmmaker whose personal lifestyle more closely resembles a Saudi prince than any sort of a man of the people—chooses to avoid these gruesome realities.

It is not only the rich and famous of Hollywood who sentimentalize Marxist revolution. It's a fair swatch of our media and an even larger percentage of the academy, not to mention many in the public at large. Most do not realize what they are doing. Revolutionary heroes have been eroticized like movie stars. Che Guevara is more ubiquitous on T-shirts and posters than Humphrey Bogart, although Che randomly executed people in cold blood, including many of his closest revolutionary compadres and oldest friends. Warhol did multicolored portraits of Mao—easily the greatest mass murderer of all time—identical to his portraits of Marilyn Monroe. They are reproduced everywhere. A twenty-foot-tall chrome Lenin currently dominates La Brea Avenue in Los Angeles. It has been described as "thought-provoking" in the press—for what reasons are unclear. The examples are myriad and continue to this day, becoming increasingly ironic, almost bizarre. In April 2015, Rutgers University invited Mariela Castro—the daughter of Raul and the niece of Fidel—to be keynote speaker at their conference on LGBT rights. Her father and uncle, along with Che, had notoriously built concentration camps to rid Cuba of homosexuals. This is the same Rutgers where, in 2011, students and faculty so vehemently protested the choice of Condoleezza Rice as commencement speaker that the former secretary of state and national security adviser decided to withdraw.

Nostalgia for Marxism? Well, since Marxism, at least in its Marcusean avatar, defines free speech as "repressive tolerance," you might say so. But a game is being played, on the self and on the other. It begins in the academy, a system that is superficially socialistic but entirely dependent on capitalism. Our esteemed Ivy League and similar private universities rely for their massive endowments on the generosity of alumni successful in the capitalist system. Yet the professoriate exists within a socialistic framework usually criticizing that system roundly. This isn't always the case, obviously. Business schools exist and entrepreneurship appears to be one of the latest crazes on campus—an intelligent one given the difficulty graduates have finding work in the current environment. But the humanities and social sciences are so taken over by left-wing ideology that they have turned many of our finest institutions into virtual indoctrination camps. The irony again is that the students are being indoctrinated into something that isn't there and no one really wants—a socialist economy. No wonder the number of students seeking to study in these areas is declining. It has no relevance to anything other than itself.

The role of nostalgia for Marxism and nostalgia in general in this precipitous decline is key. The average college teacher from his or her early thirties even up through early sixties is basically acting out in the classroom what the earlier generation did in the streets. Demonstration envy, you might call it, in a highly protected academic environment, demonstration without risk, since in many cases departments are so permeated by similar left-wing ideology that to act or talk against it constitutes the real risk, a loss of tenure, of appointments. It's a minor league socialist totalitarianism within the confines of the greater capitalist society held together in an essentially parasitical relationship. The highly paid university presidents are tasked with the all-important fund-raising from that larger society for the benefit of the academy. Whether that business plan can survive is moot, but for now it remains successful, our most famous universities as esteemed as ever.

Academic Marxism can exist under many names, from progressivism to liberalism, but its ideological roots are the same in opposition to the capitalist system. The differences are only matters of degree, which change like the weather. When the criticism goes too far, as in the case of Ward Churchill—the University of Colorado professor of ethnic studies, who accused those working at the World Trade Center during 9/11 of being "little Eichmanns"—the perpetrator is expunged from the academy in order to preserve the institution's reputation. But these cases are rare. When Harvard professor Elizabeth Warren was ridiculed as "Fauxcahontas" because she bragged about being Cherokee based on the most minuscule genealogical link, it was finally ignored, with Warren elected to the Senate and regarded as a serious presidential contender. More typical academic behavior these days is the aforementioned treatment of Condoleezza Rice by Rutgers or the even more appalling withdrawal by Brandeis University of its honorary degree to Ayaan Hirsi Ali, the Somali-born author and victim of genital mutilation who has become a famous critic of the treatment of women in Islam. In the end, a Marxism infected by political correctness trumps nearly everything on campus, even and especially freedom of speech. Herbert Marcuse rules over Thomas Jefferson in the academy.

Indeed, nostalgia for Marxism got a notable boost among intellectuals in recent years from the sensational global success of French economist Thomas Piketty's hefty *Capital in the Twenty-First Century,* which was translated into many languages and sold a million-and-a-half copies. Piketty's contention was that income inequality in capitalist societies would inevitably grow because the return on investment capital would necessarily outpace the economy's actual growth rate (r>g, with r being the return on capital and g being the growth rate). As this formula compounded over time, the importance of inherited wealth would continue to increase, worsening the already far-reaching inequality. We were headed for another Gilded Age of extreme riches and poverty. Never mind that in contemporary times the impoverished had flat-screen televisions and smartphones not dreamed of by billionaires ten years before. The inequality was still glaring. Marx lived.

Piketty's ideas were seized upon by many, including the *New York Times'* resident economics nobelist Paul Krugman who virtually anointed Piketty the second coming of the Messiah, calling him "magnificent" in the May 2104 issue of the *New York Review of Books* and ratifying the Frenchman's warning of the control of so much wealth by "family dynasties." The problem was that at that same time Piketty was on his way to recanting his own ideas. In a May 2015 article for *American Economic Review*, the author wrote "I do not view r>g as the only or even the primary tool for considering changes in income and wealth in the 20th century or for forecasting the path of inequality in the 21st century." In the end, "economic development," meaning innovations like smartphones, are more important.

This is not the kind of admission that normally plays well in the academy or the mainstream media—at least the major part of those institutions, the traditional part that preserves this old-fashioned Marxism in such a nostalgic manner. At the same time, a more modern libertarian viewpoint—exemplified by PayPal founder Peter Thiel in his book *Zero to One: Notes on Startups, or How to Build the Future*—has infiltrated these sectors of our society. These views are at war with each other, sometimes unconsciously, because the traditionalists are not entirely aware of what is happening, clinging to their old beliefs as they update the operating systems on their iPhones. This conflict rose to the surface during Hillary Clinton's email scandal. Mrs. Clinton—as pure an exemplar of the top-down, elitist-Marxist approach to governance as one might find in contemporary America—was subject to public ridicule for her assertion that she could only have one email account on her mobile phone—therefore she opted for a private account instead of the recommended or required (depending on legal analysis) State Department one. This was an excuse the vast majority of seasoned smartphone users—virtually everyone—knew to be absurd. It was so absurd, in fact, that it is surprising that Clinton would have made such a claim. A certain desperation factors into this, but a probable explanation is that she assumed it was so accepted by her many followers that "she knew best" that almost any excuse would do. Hillary was on the correct side of things—therefore anything she did or said would be okay. Still, a public outcry ensued. A discontinuity had occurred between the old and the new. Modern technology had created an unforeseen collision because that technology was inherently anarchic or libertarian. It arrived from "out of nowhere" without government instigation or even approval. Everyone had it, no matter their ideology, and it was physically undeniable. It disproved cant. And what Hillary was producing at her press conference at the United Nations was *unmitigated* cant, relying as she did on her gender to make her unassailable. She was the chosen one to break the glass ceiling. There could be no other.

But instead the scandal revealed Clinton to be a textbook case in what I mean by nostalgia for Marxism. Hers is an evolution from a somewhat more liberal (not strict Leninist) Marxism, through progressivism into what might be called that Marxism for the rich and famous. This is far from what Marx himself had in mind, but quite possibly the prevalent, and certainly most powerful, form in contemporary America. The ideas are no longer there, only the justification for action. Clinton's original Marxist roots were quite conventional for her time, the Vietnam era when nearly every intelligent undergraduate espoused some form of socialism in opposition to that "pitiful, helpless giant," the United States. Hillary went somewhat farther than most, allying with Saul Alinsky, but not as far as others (the Weather Underground, etc.). She was always a "reasonable" radical with her eye on the main chance.

The attraction to Alinsky was revealing in its own way. His *Rules for Radicals* was a guide to under-the-radar Marxism, a Marxism that deliberately would not name itself for fear of being rejected before it could ultimately succeed. Hillary obviously saw the value in that and wrote her thesis on Alinsky. Whether she knew of the organizer's links to the Mafia is unknown, but if she did, she forced herself to look away or pretend the alliance was for a "better good." Even her marriage to Bill Clinton can be seen as a form of masquerade, living with a man who was more of a conventional liberal to hide her radicalism. But even then the radicalism was not real and was often more a stance to the self, something you tell yourself to justify your activities—such as windfall profiting in the futures market or through the Whitewater real estate investments: I do not have a position, nor do I care for purposes of this discussion, the extent to which these controversies were justified scandals. I am concerned with how at odds they are with the Marxist goal of aiding the working class, how hypocritical it is.

This hypocrisy is of course not unique to Hillary Clinton. It is shockingly common. In the extreme cases, we have the likes of Fidel Castro, who became a billionaire off the backs of "the People," but it is virtually everywhere in the upper reaches of Western society and has been for decades, almost centuries. The journalist Eugene Lyons coined the term "penthouse Bolsheviks" when, in the 1930s, he returned from Moscow to find the swells of Manhattan still thought Stalin was the bee's knees. (Lyons knew better and had seen the deliberate mass starvation of the Ukrainians.) But true allegiance toward an ideology starts to fade as material ambition grows and soon enough the ideology isn't really there. It's just a ghost. However, the ghost is very powerful and useful. The individual—in this case Hillary—still thinks she's the same girl as the one at the barricades in 1968, only she's wearing a specially designed Ralph Lauren pantsuit and flying in a private jet. And the necessary ingredient to keep thinking and behaving this way is nostalgia for the Marxism that was. It used to be the economy, but now it's the entitlement, stupid.

XV

Luxurious Leftism

The irresistible rise of the "red bourgeoisie."

In modern times, Marxism has become a philosophy of the rich, not in a publicly avowed sense, but as a touchstone. If you look at the *Forbes* list of billionaires, you will see many who have been influenced by these ideas or, more precisely, wish to give the impression they have been. Egalitarian pronouncements provide cover and Marxism formalizes those pronouncements systemically. It's not entirely by accident that Hillary Clinton's famous 1995 speech on women's rights was delivered in Beijing. As Mao Zedong himself assured us, "Women hold up half the sky." The location of the speech was meant to have ramifications. But today there are only two of those same women on China's twenty-five-member politburo, a downward trend from 1969. One of thirty-one Chinese provincial governors is a woman.[1] This is of course no accident as well, just as it is no accident that socialist economies have the *least* opportunity for the underclass to rise. Everything comes from above, even and especially your class in a declassed society. As Lady Gaga would say, they were born that way. Intentional rigidity *is* the system. It's about control, yet the propaganda, usually successfully, obscures it.

That enabled Lenin to see the world's liberals and progressives (to lump together what is blurred terminology anyway) as the "useful idiots" mentioned earlier. Lenin used what others have called "pathological

altruism" to prop up his totalitarian regime. Similarly, when we see a man
ke global financier George Soros advocating for the United States to be
ore like Europe, to expand our country's welfare state and have more
a planned economy, he also has an unspoken intention—to rigidify
es, to keep things as they are with the same people and organizations
top. That has been the hallmark of Europe for centuries. First came
kings, then came commissars. Of course Soros and others like him would
deny this. They would insist they are aiming for "fairness," but the results
are obviously quite the opposite. Although Zambian author Dambisa
Moyo writes primarily about Africa, some of the clearest explanation of
this contradiction can be found in her works that have shown an inverse
correlation between economic success and the amount of foreign aid and
direct interference received by countries in that continent. The same goes
for people everywhere. It's all a kind of shell game with "good works"
being the deception that allows the gamer to hide the pea. The small
percentage of his billions that Soros pays out every year to progressive
organizations like Media Matters is a left-wing version of Islamic *jizya*,
the tax paid by non-Muslims in Islamic states to be left alone and allowed
to exist without fear under Allah. The difference is that it impacts Soros's
bottom line far less than jizya does or did Christians and Jews in those
Islamic societies. The members of his Olympian rich class thrive as never
before in their Swiss redoubts.

This is not meant to assert or even imply I oppose all foreign aid
or domestic social programs from Social Security to Medicare. It is to
demonstrate that nostalgia for Marxism affects our ability to view those
programs with sufficient dispassion so that we can structure them to
actually do what they are supposed to. They are far too imbued with
moral narcissism. The Affordable Care Act became a virtually unworkable bureaucratic monstrosity in part if not largely because of this.
The legislation was propelled by an intense desire for some form of
national healthcare—to achieve parity with the Europeans and finally
say we had a viable healthcare system, although their systems were well
known to have problems of their own. This approach was rational only
in the most superficial way—it was morally narcissistic in its essence.
The result was not just a frequently mocked website—that could be
solved eventually—but a system so complicated few understood it.
And even if they could—because the legislation was written in such a

hurried, unvetted manner, as if it didn't get done in an instant it would never be done—the details of the plan were so sloppily conceived they needed constant changing and revising. Therefore there was no plan really, only a moving target, the notion of a plan, which if it failed, could be replaced by the even more yearned-for single-payer plan, the holy grail of socialized medicine itself. Because of this overriding need trumping rationality, simpler incremental strategies such as requiring catastrophe insurance for all were abjured in favor of a global approach as if the intent were to fill a neurotic hole in the nation's heart rather than actually to improve people's health. The plan was hardly debated in any discernible manner. It was rather visited upon us from above with all the public discussion of one of Stalin's Five-Year Plans. And, not surprisingly, it has been just that successful.

Invoking Stalin in reference to American legislation is, I admit, on the heavy-handed side. But though his predecessor Lenin may have been misquoted as saying "Socialized medicine is the keystone to the arch of the Socialized State," it is easy to see why this assertion, apocryphal though it may be, has had such relevance and staying power. (We don't know whether Trotsky ever really said, "You may not be interested in war, but war is interested in you," but it keeps being quoted for a reason.) The Affordable Care Act is redolent of the dizzyingly top-down methodology of a Five-Year Plan, with the accompanying Stalinist deliberate inscrutability and complete lack of accountability. And, as with command economies, it is based on something close to an ideological oxymoron, a zero-sum game of sorts. Everyone needs healthcare, yet the healthcare crisis can never actually be solved. The moral narcissist pretends that it can, though there is always more demand than supply, no matter what the system. Indeed, socialized medicine has been shown to create unnecessary demand, people arriving in emergency rooms for the treatment of a common cold if the care is free. The attraction of elites to socialized medicine, that "keystone to the arch" in the quote attributed to Lenin, is the same as the attraction to socialism in general. It gives the elites power. They know best, in this case, over our bodies. Of course, Lenin would never be invoked overtly—or his statement even known about in many cases. Never mind that there's only so much medical care to go around, however one wants to finance it. Never mind that under socialized medicine many of our best and brightest will no longer be attracted to medicine. That already appears to be happening. But I am digressing from my topic, the nostalgic attractions of Marxism.

This nostalgia—well, it could have been more than that—surfaced in a yet more purely Soviet manner when, in mid-March 2015, Barack Obama, in the most casual fashion, seemingly floated the idea of mandatory voting. This constituted a veritable cornucopia of moral narcissism as advanced through the methods of democratic centralism. That such a proposal is unconstitutional—the Constitution guarantees the right *not* to vote, according to Rutgers University School of Law professor Frank Askin, an expert in election law[2]—is the least of it. The whole notion of mandatory voting smacks of totalitarian societies that report 99.4 percent of voters support whoever the local despot may be, with the missing .6 percent slated for an indefinite sojourn in their version of the Gulag, if they're lucky.

But this did not seem to disturb Obama when he made his pitch. His concern was to give voice to minorities that tended not to vote and almost always, not inconsequentially, voted for his Democratic Party when they did. That these same people rarely were cognizant of the issues and therefore could not really vote for their own self-interest or even know what it was did not matter. Obama and his cohorts would handle that for them. They knew best. In other words, just as in Lenin's democratic centralism, elites would decide. There literally is no difference when it comes to governing principles. Meanwhile, the feedback loop between those new mandated voters, the results of their votes and the elites whose policies have been decreed for them, would not and does not exist. It's a complete disconnect. Nowhere is this more evident than in the condition of black America detailed in the "nostalgia for racism" chapter. The policies of the elites have not improved the life of the black street one jot. On the contrary, they have worsened it. As the brilliant black conservative Thomas Sowell famously put it, "Socialism in general has a record of failure so blatant that only an intellectual could ignore or evade it."

Yet moral narcissism preserves it now on to forever in one guise or another. Those of us who held those views when we were young, even those like me who abandoned those viewpoints, still respond emotionally when we see the applicable imagery or hear the old songs like "Which Side Are You On," the 1931 anthem of the Harlan County, Kentucky, mine workers. Tears well up in the mist of memory, as if recalling that first girlfriend in high school whose perfection grows as she fades in the distance. Of course there are some who do change, recapitulating the famous quote attributed to Churchill (what is it about these quotes that no one officially owns them), "If a man is not a liberal at twenty, he has no heart. If he is not a conservative at thirty he has no brain." Most do not. This does not mean that these people want to live under Communism or anything close. They've seen the movies with the KGB coming in the middle of the night, but they choose to ignore them, to see them as something "out there" and unrelated to anything that could ever happen to them. Therefore it's not necessary to make a connection that would interfere with their desire to associate themselves with egalitarian ideals. Nostalgia for Marxism allows them to keep that totalitarian link disconnected or hidden, leaving the real Marxism and its grisly results as a chimera.

These links can be small and seemingly innocuous, as when Michelle Obama proposed that all preschool children be subject to mandatory weighing to make sure the three-year-olds were not on the road to slothful obesity. If so, their parents were presumably feeding their children improperly or not creating enough exercise opportunities for the tots, endlessly plopping them down in front of video monitors to play computer games. The parents deserved chastisement and had to be brought into line by the government. In actuality, this proposal—thankfully resisted and psychologically suspect in the first place (focusing children on their weight at such a young age is more likely a promoter of eating disorders than it is a prescription to avoid them)—was another opportunity for government control, here at an exceptionally early age.

Other links are far more obvious, almost to the point of bludgeoning, as with Obama's attempted installation of so-called net-neutrality over the Internet. Using Marxist anti-big business tropes (nostalgic or not) as basic underpinning, he moved for government regulation of the Internet, treating Internet traffic as a public utility much the way Ma Bell was similarly regulated in the 1930s. This would install the government as the administrative judge in the free flow of information—just as in Iran and Cuba. Such an accusation would appall the bureaucrats and Federal Communications Commission but that's what they have and would become—apparatchiks of the online world. How dangerous is that? If Lord Acton was in the slightest correct about his warnings about power, it is *very* dangerous. Already we have seen the results in a similar sphere. At the beginnings of the Obama administration, the National Endowment for the Arts was immediately used for ideological ends—and in an unthinking manner redolent of nostalgia for Marxism. Without any thought that anyone in his right mind would disagree, Yosi Sergant (in concert with White House deputy director of public engagement Buffy Weeks) urged one hundred fellow artists and media members on a conference call to create art promoting the Obama agenda in healthcare, housing, and other favored initiatives. That someone could do this from a supposedly impartial government agency was caused almost entirely by morally narcissistic assumptions. There was only one way to think and you couldn't or wouldn't be an artist if you didn't think that way. (Tell that to David Mamet, Tom Stoppard, or Clint Eastwood.) This attitude is more than reminiscent of the Soviet approach to the arts. It *was* the Soviet approach to the arts. In fact, the Soviet approach may have been superior to the Obama approach because it was more honest, more open, and transparent. Disinformation was always a key to Soviet strategy, but we always knew what they wanted in the macro sense.

But what does Obama really want out of net-neutrality? Superficially again, he appears to be fighting the good fight. Verizon and Comcast will not be allowed to divide the world between them, while we petty men struggle to squeeze out the random bits and bytes, bullied by the big boys as our sluggish home Internet moves so slowly we will never receive the crucial information that informs any true democracy—the crucial information that has been, of course, approved by our masters. In actuality, net-neutrality means more government control for the obvious reason it is the government that now regulates the Internet. We would laugh this off if we were talking about the likes of Cuba or Iran, but the US government somehow gets a pass. It is supposedly benign. And sometimes it is. But a number of times it isn't, although unlike Cuba and Iran, for instance, much of our government's more nefarious activities are done in the name of positive social action or social justice, of "knowing best." (Sometimes it's directly nefarious, as in the political misuse of the IRS. But even that was initiated under the pretense that conservative groups were exploiting the system.)

Thus, a "neutral" Internet would appear to allow the Left and the Right equal access. Blind like Lady Justice, it would adhere to Obama's famous goal of "fairness." But would this policing of the Internet actually be fair or equal? If previous examples of government involvement like the Public Broadcasting System and the National Endowment for the Arts are any indication, that would clearly depend, as they say, on what your definition of fairness is. Those institutions would seem to be largely purveyors of well-packaged left-wing propaganda. The rationale, at least in terms of NPR and PBS, is that the Right already dominates talk radio, so the Left is entitled to government-sponsored equality, including now apparently the Internet. Of course, this bias would be denied, again under that same rubric of fairness.

But what is fairness really? It is what is known these days as a "dog whistle," a coded term used as a signal to the converted that something more important is afoot. In the instance of fairness, that something is socialism, if in a vague and unspecified form. Fairness has thus become a hidden Marxist term, evoking that nostalgia that is the topic of this chapter. Net-neutrality, which seems so just and reasonable on the surface, is similarly a stalking horse for socialism. Undoubtedly, some regulation of the Verizons and Comcasts of the world is advisable, lest they not run amok. But even a cursory evaluation of history shows governments to be more dangerous than corporations. This is not just true in the horrifying body count associated with the Left, but in the more amorphous quality of life as well. Unless you were a member of the ruling class, life under socialism in the Soviet Union, China, or Cambodia was a grim experience indeed, even if you were lucky enough to remain among the living. This is why nostalgia for Marxism is so important. The real thing has its problems. Better to live in dreams.

This nostalgia exploits our moral narcissism. We feel good about ourselves for believing in a perfect society that does not and cannot exist. That nonexistence doesn't matter as long as one is true to the cause in spirit. As noted early in this book, the Students for a Democratic Society, uncomfortable with Stalinism and other Communist excesses, invented a new form of socialism in order to bypass the discredited past form. They didn't care or want to acknowledge that eventually socialism tends to revert to totalitarianism. That was far away. In the meantime, they were being "fair." This process seems to repeat itself over the generations, a generalized appeal to moral narcissism, to knowing best without knowing what. A large part of how this is achieved is the sometimes purposeful, sometimes inadvertent exploitation of language—the attachment of emotional assumptions to political labels that encourage that nostalgia for better days that could be translated into better days ahead. Liberalism and progressivism are seen, without questioning, as positive terms with a future orientation; conservatism is stodgy, connoting the dismal past of the days of robber barons or the most rigid fundamentalists. Who would want to be associated with that, even though actual programs sponsored by the two sides are often the reverse? Conservatism—not to mention libertarianism—is usually open, entrepreneurial, modern, while progressivism is controlled and old-fashioned, its innovations predetermined by political alliances. (Note, by way of comparison, Obama's backing of the now defunct Solyndra solar cell company, a kind of high-tech crony capitalism under the pretense that an ideal, carbon-free system was being created. It never happened.)

C'est la vie á l'invers—the world upside down—as the French say, but it is a world deliberately upside down. It has been arranged for the convenience, power, and profit of an ongoing ruling class, our version of what Marshall Tito's vice-president, Yugoslavian politician Milovan Đjilas once called "the new class" in his criticism of Communism. We have developed our own "red bourgeoisie." They may not be as exclusively "red" as when Đjilas described them, but they are "red enough," occupying positions that are relatively unquestioned and equally permanent. The political rhetoric we live with has been tailored by and for them, revised as necessary from philosophical texts. The terminology involved is deliberately vague or has naturally evolved that way. What is the difference between liberal, progressive, and leftist? Though there are obvious historical antecedents, in the end—not much. Many people make distinctions, but in actuality they are blurry and ever changing to fit the situation. (One day Hillary Clinton will call herself a "progressive," another day a "liberal," yet another day "independent.") They are distinctions, as the saying goes, without differences, in this case practical differences. The results remain the same. The same leaders stay in place.

Meanwhile what do these terms themselves actually mean? There is nothing particularly liberal or progressive about liberals or progressives. It's closer to the reverse. Their world views are quite old-fashioned and have been with us for ages, longer than conservatism in some senses. It's all in the word. Not much substance exists, but that doesn't matter. What matters is that their audience, the public, behaves and responds in the proper manner to the category. And it almost always does. For some, this unthinking ideological belief has become the new idolatry. I am a liberal, therefore I am. I am a progressive, therefore I am. Again, it's a distinction without a difference.

This brings us to one of the great allures of this nostalgia for Marxism—simplicity. We live in a complicated world, growing more complex as it expands technologically. There has to be a way to sort it out—a good that allows us to function and do what we do, a simple answer for everything. Marx provided that. What could be simpler than "from each according to his ability, to each according to his need"? This well-known maxim of Karl Marx is of course not publicly countenanced by our "red bourgeoisie" or even referred to, but what is Obama's "fairness" if not a revamped version of "to each according to his need"? This fairness mantra has been eagerly adopted by this same bourgeoisie and provides a convenient excuse for not doing anything about the inequality they pretend to abhor. Almost nothing is done to promote income equality, yet it is talked about incessantly. The talk is the point, just as nostalgia for Marxism is preferential to living under true Marxism. Nostalgia in general is a form of not thinking. It is a reminiscence, not a reality. By the year 2016 it had become the apotheosis of the Least Great Generation, as empty as the lyrics of John Lennon's "Imagine."

XVI

Anatomy of the American Nomenklatura

And why it's stronger and more pervasive than even the Soviet original.

Most of us have grown up in or lived around an American nomenklatura but few of us understand how deeply our lives have been affected by it, how deeply imbued with it we are. Even though we lived in a democratic republic, our thinking has been more circumscribed than we realized. The original Soviet nomenklatura (literally "name list") was more obvious, of course. It began at the dawn of the USSR with Lenin's appointments to leadership positions and metastasized under Stalin who made such a fetish of *his* appointments that he was called "Comrade File Cabinet." That nomenklatura was a reward system coupled to the most rigid methods of control. You toed the line and you kept your job, generation unto generation. You didn't? Off to Siberia you went. Ultimately the system exploded to reappear in different clothes in the post-Communist world of the oligarchs, a nomenklatura of its own.

Our nomenklatura is more subtle but in many ways more powerful and more durable. The Soviet nomenklatura was cemented by terror. Our nomenklatura is cemented by moral narcissism. Ours, based on self-referential ideals, therefore has the ability to last longer and is not as easily subject to reversal. Play along with the right point of view, say the right things, and you will go on for generation to generation, more surely than the Soviet apparatchiks and without anywhere near the physical danger. No overt coercion is necessary, just the possibility of job loss or ostracism. It isn't a dictatorship of the proletariat; it is a dictatorship of bourgeoisie under the mantle of political correctness, the proletariat (aka "flyover people") be damned.

An example of this dictatorship of the morally narcissistic bourgeoisie emerged around April 1, 2015, in the immediate backlash to the enacting of the Religious Freedom Restoration Act by the state of Indiana. This law, similar to an existing federal one and to those already in place in many states, gave orthodox religious believers the right to petition the judicial system for relief when they felt they were being forced into providing a service that was contrary to the edicts of their faith, for example, having to be a wedding photographer at a gay marriage ceremony. On the face of it, this would seem a recapitulation of James Madison's warnings from the Federalist Papers about the tyranny of the majority, which were woven into the Constitution. But it unleashed an immediate fury, gay rights being the politically correct issue du jour. (As noted in the first chapter, I am a religious agnostic who has long supported same-sex marriage.) Film star and former California governor Arnold Schwarzenegger took to the pages of the *Washington Post* to excoriate his fellow Republicans. "As an American, I'm incredibly concerned about what happened in Indiana this week and the threat of similar laws being passed in other states. As a Republican, I'm furious."[1] He went on from there, as did many others.

The governors of Indiana and Arkansas walked back the legislation. In truth, it was strategically inept on the part of Republicans and a serious misreading of the zeitgeist. But more interesting was the intensity of that backlash over what was truly a minor piece of legislation that would affect only a handful of people nationwide at best. This was a demonstration of the power of moral narcissism, manifesting itself—as it almost always does—as political correctness. You must support gay rights 100 percent even in those minute instances when they run roughshod over the rights of a meaningless and practically invisible minority. Otherwise you will be run out of the nomenklatura. Schwarzenegger was a perfect example of this. His op-ed reeked of panic, personal panic. Yes, Republicans can be part of the nomenklatura if they behave. And, yes, there is even a Republican nomenklatura of sorts. That's the way our system works— twin nomenklaturas working in parallel, a minor one and a major one.

James Madison would not have been amazed, but he probably would have been depressed.

We have all been indoctrinated and this indoctrination began at an early age. For the vast majority it is left-wing indoctrination, culminating in a university system where those views are pervasive. In a 2012 survey conducted by UCLA, 62.7 percent of faculty at our four-year colleges and universities classified themselves as "liberal or Far Left," 25.4 percent as "middle of the road," and only 11.5 percent as "conservative." The *Far* Left outnumbered the conservative.[2]

This is an old story and growing worse. It builds a constituency for politically correct views that form the basis of the American nomenklatura. At first, it would seem paradoxical that the cost of this "left-wing" education is continually increasing out of proportion to inflation (Ivy League schools are now running in excess of $65,000 per annum), but in actuality this is more like a fee or tithe for joining that nomenklatura, for participating in a morally narcissistic class system with its own rules and regulations, which is constantly renewing for its own preservation. You have to keep up or be left behind, read out to the nomenklatura or, in the university sense, not be allowed in on graduation.

The latest rules and regulations concern the concepts of "sustainability" and "microaggressions" that dominate contemporary campuses. Both seem progressive but have a not so hidden totalitarian side that makes them ultimately ironic in their manifestation. Both, under the guise of being modern or postmodern, are actually antimodern. Sustainability is the latest catchphrase for all sorts of environmental uniformity. Everything must be sustainable. We cannot deplete the earth in our construction of buildings and grounds; in our use of energy, our production and consumption of food; in virtually all aspects of our footprint. But as I just mentioned, this is hugely ironic. Much of that irony stems from the monumentally expensive and largely unnecessary physical expansion of our universities that promulgate these views. No longer merely schools, they are virtual country clubs. Most, public *and* private, include such amenities as gymnasiums that would be the envy of the most luxurious spas—replete with climbing walls, steam rooms, and facilities for cardio yoga, Zumba dancing, spin classes, or whatever exercise fad holds sway at the moment. When it comes to campus food, gone are the days of "mystery meat" and stale coffee. Food at today's college is gourmet or a close approximation, with myriad ethnic choices, usually organic, and latte bars at hand in almost every building. Even dormitories are improving, many beginning to resemble four-star, if not five-star, hotels.

Some of this expansion is justified, particularly in scientific areas, but most of it obviously is not. So what is going on? It is driven to a great degree by a keeping-up-with-the-academic-Joneses, Macy's and Gimbels having given way to Harvard and Yale. But the result makes college even more of an indoctrination into the American nomenklatura. Left-wing values are being spouted in the most luxurious of environments that are, on the surface, quite wasteful—while spouting the line of sustainability at every turn. In a world where everything is recycled, life is grand. You can see the message. Play with us, we play with you. Think our way. Join the nomenklatura. The Four Seasons can be sustainable.

At the same time, the "microaggressions" movement solidifies racism on campus, amplifying the nostalgia for racism of the earlier chapter and making it permanent. In the world of "microaggressions" we are all condemned to be racists or sexists forever. Only a few years ago, most people would have found that oft-quoted example of a microaggression—assuming an Asian classmate is good in math when asking for help with a problem—to be a compliment. Now such compliments are verboten. They are hidden aggressions based on invidious racial biases. Such accusations can be extended to virtually everyone, branding everyone a racist for life unless he or she seeks continual, really almost constant, expiation. It's much like an upscale version of the self-criticism sessions practiced during the Chinese Cultural Revolution that made genuine criticism of the society moot. That was mass conformism of nearly unheard of proportions. And now it is being brought here covertly—without donkey heads or dunce caps—through the microaggression system. This new mass conformity is clearly being augmented by what is being preached almost uniformly in the classroom, a nonstop diet of political correctness and multiculturalism. The American university—especially at its now quite extensive highest reaches—is a form of a perfect, even posh, socialist state beyond Marx's wildest imagination. It is very much a utopia outside society itself, its professorate, and increasingly its students, cosseted. But even more privileged are the administrative staffs—what we might call an über-nomenklatura within the nomenklatura—that are growing in number far faster than the faculties. An analysis by a California Polytechnic University professor showed the total administrators in the California State University system growing from 3,800 to 12,183 between 1975 and 2008—a 221 percent increase, dwarfing the increase in the number of faculty for that period. The salaries for the nomenklatura within the nomenklatura were growing at extraordinary rates as well, college and university presidents often drawing seven-figure incomes with perks that would be the envy of many corporate CEOs.

People existing within this system would naturally be supporters of an expanded socialist state for the entire country. It was good to them—why not for others? This has led to a stultified educational system, particularly in the humanities and social sciences. (It has even infected the hard sciences, the so-called STEM subjects, as we have seen from the determinedly biased approach to climate.) With little or no debate, or what debate exists relatively pro forma or for show, what suffers is not just democracy but even more real education and unbiased research in those fields. Social science and humanities faculties these days are largely a collection of morally narcissistic "yes men and women." Students are often forced to comply with their views in order to succeed—or they do so automatically, assuming that it is fruitless to resist. The website *The College Fix* (www.thecollegefix.com) is filled with stories written by the students themselves documenting their situations, which vacillate between the tragic and the absurd. As I write this, the site features such headlines as "PROFESSORS: ACKNOWLEDGING YOUR 'MALE PRIVILEGE' NOT GOOD ENOUGH; FIGHT AGAINST IT" and "STUDENTS WHO BUILT TEEPEE FOR ART CLASS CALLED OFFENSIVE; OUTCRY PROMPTS REMOVAL." The risk to these students on that website and others who criticize the prevailing wisdom is great. The huge sums being spent on their education are meant, consciously or unconsciously, to make them agreeable members of the nomenklatura. To question the narrative, to question the dominant culture in our educational system— a culture that begins in nursery school, continues through elementary, middle, and high school, to be solidified in college and graduate school— is potentially to have wasted that money, with the strong possibility of the individual being required to live a life outside the system. Few would have the courage to resist—and with good reason.

To solve this, a small countereducational system has been established by conservatives. It starts with the homeschooling movement and ends at the college level with Hillsdale College, which was actually established in 1844 but currently features online courses on the Federalist Papers and the films of Frank Capra. Radio personality Dennis Prager also has his own online Prager University with offerings on philosophical questions such as "Do We Have Free Will?" and in the political science realm with "What Is the University Diversity Scam?" These initiatives are certainly laudable and have an impact, but they do not create anything even roughly approximating balance. In some senses, they may even divert our attention from real academic reform, because the "best and brightest" of our high school students, even conservative and libertarian ones, still want to attend Harvard and Yale. They seek to be part of the nomenklatura one way or the other, even if it means compromising themselves and their views. This is normal human ambition, but unfortunately leads to a catch-22. Do you attend an Ivy League (or equivalent) indoctrination camp or do you abjure the upper echelons of the mainstream educational system and forfeit your place in that nomenklatura? What frequently emerges out of this conundrum is a basically timid soul, well educated for the most part in an approved manner, but afraid to speak his mind lest he endanger his position. We see this everywhere in the obeisance paid to certain morally narcissistic liberal causes even when they are being criticized. How often have we seen or heard the equivalent of "I am not a racist, but ..." or "I support gay rights or gay marriage but ..." as a means of self-defense before making a legitimate point that may go against the politically correct conventional wisdom? Frequently in my writing I have been guilty of it myself. Now more than ever we learn that in college, if not before.

Of course there is a counter-nomenklatura of sorts, a network of business and media leaders on the right and center-right, but the tentacles of that network are not nearly as extensive and evolved. That network is by doctrine not socialistic, therefore ad hoc, and unfortunately does not offer the many opportunities of the dominant nomenklatura. Nor is it extensively supported by the other twin pillars that make up the triumvirate of that dominant American nomenklatura with the educational system—the media and entertainment. It is in those two pillars that we find such an excess of moral narcissism that it has the potential to distort, perhaps has already distorted, our democratic republic so that it is virtually unrecognizable. These twin pillars are also highly interconnected to the point of often being indistinguishable, but I shall try to tease them apart from one another for the purposes of our discussion here.

XVII

The Media Is the (Moral Narcissist's) Message

Who is really raping whom?

The first thing to realize is just how indelible is the presence of moral narcissism in the media. It will not change even when exposed. This was brought to the fore recently in the controversy (and reaction to it) surrounding a December 2014 article in *Rolling Stone*, "A Rape on Campus: The Struggle for Justice at UVA." This story, by Sabrina Rubin Erdely, detailed a horrific gang rape at a University of Virginia fraternity as recounted by informant "Jackie" who had several witnesses supposedly corroborating her. However, those witnesses were too "traumatized" to come forward. *Rolling Stone*, despite the widespread bad publicity and disbarment of the prosecutor that followed a false accusation of gang rape by the Duke University lacrosse team, ran the article anyway. Jann Wenner, the publisher and founder of the magazine, approved it. After all, the story fit the narrative. Campus rape, the new cause célèbre for feminists, was a dangerous and growing phenomenon. Upon publication, the University of Virginia and the fraternity members were humiliated. It didn't take long, however, for the article to arouse suspicions and soon enough the *Washington Post* ran a story of its own, alleging—with evidence to prove it—that the entire tale was made up by "Jackie," and her witnesses probably did not exist. Embarrassed, *Rolling Stone* "reached out" to Steve Coll of the Columbia School of Journalism who agreed to do a thorough and open investigation. This resulted in an article that only ratified and extended what had come from the *Washington Post*.

Two interesting phenomena emerged from this case: One, that the original, clearly fictitious, article developed out of its author *deliberately* searching for a case emblematic of the supposed campus rape epidemic. Erdely was the one who initially made inquiries at UVA for a paradigmatic case of sexual assault at the university and then "Jackie" miraculously appeared. The second is that, even after the revelation that the story was fabricated, many in the media still said it was ideologically valid or significant, because it highlighted the increased dangers of that same campus rape epidemic. (This is a similar to the recent Robert Redford film *Truth* that attempted to justify the behavior of Dan Rather—when he was fired by CBS for promulgating obviously forged documents about George W. Bush's National Guard service as being "fake but real.")

These are paradigmatic examples of moral narcissism in our culture. Not only did the *Rolling Stone* article smear the reputation of seven innocent students, accusing them of one of the most heinous crimes known to humanity, it was based on a morally narcissistic myth in the first place. The so-called campus rape epidemic, predicated on an assertion that one in five female students are raped or even sexually assaulted, is simply not true. Even the reliably liberal *Time* magazine said as much.[1] Indeed, young women are far more likely to be assaulted off campus than on. Colleges and universities, well supervised with an emergency phone system almost always within sight, are far safer than normal city streets. What is being promulgated here is a narrative meant to preserve feminism in an era when many of its initial goals appear shopworn. More women are attending college than men, as well as law school and medical school. This portends future change significantly deeper than that ever envisioned by the feminists of the sixties and seventies—a virtual social role reversal. Given this, the initial vision of deprivation and bias against women must be maintained for the preservation of the nomenklatura, especially with Hillary Clinton, one of its most important card-carrying members, contending for the presidency.

Yet more telling is the reaction to the defamatory lies promulgated by the article. Shortly after the Columbia School of Journalism delivered its report, Elizabeth Stoker Bruenig published a response in the *New Republic* entitled "Rolling Stone's Rape Article Failed Because It Used

Rightwing Tactics to Make a Leftist Point."[2] What did Bruenig mean by that? Apparently, Erdely made the mistake of trying to prove a point through a *specific* example, which is (who knew?) a right-wing tactic. According to Breunig, "Pinning an indictment of a system on the story of an individual is essentially a right-wing tactic with a dodgy success rate. It's a way of using an individual as a metonym for systematic analysis . . ." The writer went on to elaborate, using two other well-known events from recent times (nostalgia for racism meets nostalgia for Marxism) where the facts of the case may have proved uncomfortable to her and her colleagues. "The right, on the other hand, tends to understand politics on the individual level, which fits in neatly with a general obsession with the capital-i Individual. Thus, the right tends to pore over the specific details of high-profile cases like those of Trayvon Martin and Michael Brown, concluding that if those particular situations were embattled by complications or mitigating factors, then the phenomena they're meant to represent must not be real either."

Really? This is what Breunig *wants* to believe, what she feels a good person *should* believe. Nevertheless, it's hard to find an example of the Right downgrading the significance of the Ferguson riots because they were instigated by a falsehood. The problems of communities like Ferguson were taken seriously by all sides to the political debate. The difference is the approach to solving them. Breunig's simplistic analysis—coupled with Jann Wenner's incomprehensible refusal to fire anyone responsible for the original article—provides a peek behind the curtain of how the nomenklatura uses media to unite behind their ideas and cement their relationships. But they are rarely so clumsily overt and embarrassing.

The Left would argue, that in terms of the media, our society contains two equally weighted nomenklaturas, one on the right and one on the left. Fox News, after all, is by far the most popular network on cable news and the *Wall Street Journal* the most read daily newspaper. (The *New York Times* outstrips it on Sunday.) Furthermore, the Right has several leading opinion journals (*Weekly Standard, National Review, New Criterion*) and websites (*Daily Caller, PJ Media*). But this is misleading. Opinion journals (the *Nation*, the *New Republic*) and websites (*Huffington Post*) abound on the other side—and Fox News, as popular as it is, has nowhere near the reach of the evening news hours of CBS, NBC, and ABC, which are watched by four times as many people as watch all three cable news networks combined. And the *Wall Street Journal*—unlike the three other most popular papers: the *New York Times, USA Today,* and the *Los Angeles Times*—is bifurcated, its editorial pages leaning right and so-called hard news pages presumptively impartial or centrist. Of course, this is the same "presumption" made by the other newspapers referenced and they are all biased to the left. There's nothing surprising or even bad about that. They are written by humans, a species known to be biased, even and especially when they pretend they are not.

This pretense is the key because left/liberal publications and, notably, the three networks, do not publicly admit to bias. Quite the reverse— they act as if they are evenhanded news organizations letting the pro- verbial chips fall where they may. This is not true, of course. They are entirely biased. The *New York Times* has been tilting left even before the early 1930s when its Moscow correspondent Walter Duranty received the Pulitzer for his cover-up of Stalin's murderous excesses, including the mass starvation of the Ukrainians in the Holodomor. Duranty's portrait remains on the *Times'* wall to this day, because to admit his lies would admit to this extreme bias, to put a chink in the armor, disturbing the paper's loyal audience. That audience—not just lay readers but reporters for many other papers and, importantly, the producers of the network news hours and news shows—looks to the *Times* for the "truth." They look to the *Times* for "All the News That's Fit to Print," that tagline initiated in 1896 and only recently abandoned as unworkable. It is where they get their marching orders, still to this day. The paper trumpets impartiality, an impartiality that is believed by its readers despite the paper's own public editor Daniel Okrent acknowledging in 2004 that "Of course it is liberal." But liberalism equals impartiality. It has been so for the paper's audience since they first opened the Sunday edition as children. They were imbued with the morally narcissistic principles that make our world today. Only the Right can be biased. When Fox News says it is "fair and balanced," it's a lie. The *Times*, after all, has conservative columnists, properly vetted ones anyway. But there is no equality of ideology in the media. Overall, it leans left and has for decades.

The *New York Times* is the Bible of the American nomenklatura, informing them of what they must know and then clarifying for them what to think of it, *Pravda* with special sections for luxury shopping and gourmet cuisine. Although they may be reluctant, even conservatives acknowledge its primacy. When someone dies, even if he or she was the staunchest supporter of the right wing, the obituary must appear in the *Times*. That person, otherwise, lived a life of negligible importance. For a book to succeed, it must be a "New York Times best seller" even if it was published by a conservative press like Regnery and even though the accuracy of NYT book sales measurements has been widely questioned. It remains the Good Housekeeping seal for books, just as it is the seal of approval for so many things in our society—from food to fitness to how to decorate your home—the ultimate arbiter of who is in and who is out of the nomenklatura. In effect, it creates it.

The results of this power are pervasive, ricocheting outward despite numerous symbolic and metaphorical obituaries having been written for the *New York Times* itself. Despite the paper having financial troubles, these obits are premature. It still rules the media, diminished at best by 5 percent simply because it has no replacement. There is no organization on the left ready to fulfill that role, and such a development by a conservative publication or network would be precluded by the nomenklatura. One of the more disturbing effects of this hegemony is that there is very little in-depth investigative journalism coming from the right. The few newspapers that still have the wherewithal to make an attempt to do this kind of labor-intensive reporting with any regularity are the *New York Times*, the *Washington Post*, the *Journal* (again not its right-leaning part) and, once in a while, the *Los Angeles Times*. Investigations are also conducted by the television networks, *60 Minutes*, and others, again almost exclusively from a left liberal perspective, and to some extent by Fox News, especially the estimable Catherine Herridge. The Right, despite compromising some 40 percent of the country, does less than 10 percent of the investigating. These are rough figures, but they are accurate enough. The Internet promised to fill this gap and counter the narrative—and has on occasion—but ultimately the nomenklatura gets its news from the same old trusted (to them) sources. The Truth—the real news cycle—is a perfect circle of mutual reinforcement, with the *New York Times* setting the agenda. Even now, even after embarrassments like the Jayson Blair affair in which a reporter (much like *Rolling Stone's* Erdely) essentially wrote fiction masquerading as fact on the paper's front page, the *New York Times* remains the guiding light of the American nomenklatura.

It may have made mistakes, but they are all forgiven because they were made for a just cause.

In essence, a nomenklatura is a new version of the aristocracy papered over with left-wing or idealistic rhetoric of some sort. The mainstream media in the United States functions largely in that manner. They seek to preserve their perquisites and centrality in the nomenklatura itself, which has endured for decades, often far longer than the politicians they cover. They do this by sometimes subtly, sometimes overtly, injecting bias into almost every story. But it is not felt or seen as bias by the writers because that is prevented by the morally narcissistic overlay. They already "know best." It's reflexive, almost unconscious, an example being the *New York Times'* incipient coverage of the 2016 presidential campaign. On April 14, 2015, after describing potential Republican candidate Scott Walker's visit to European countries to burnish his foreign policy credentials, Patrick Healy wrote for the paper's First Draft section, "Then there is the Democrat, *Hillary Rodham Clinton*, on her road trip to relatability, *ordering a chicken burrito bowl at a Chipotle* outside Toledo, Ohio. Confident that her command of the world stage is well known—hey, Mr. Walker, I visited 112 countries as secretary of state; let me know when you get to Togo—Mrs. Clinton used her video announcement on Sunday to position herself as just one of many Americans (mothers, families, factory workers, gay fiancés) getting ready for big changes." The message is that Walker is a rookie who could never catch up to the experienced Mrs. Clinton, as the *Times* calls her. Healy, not surprisingly, makes no mention of the genuine controversy surrounding her service as secretary of state—the failed Russian "reset," the attack on Gaddafi, yielding a Libyan terror state, the ongoing mystery surrounding the American deaths in Benghazi including Ambassador Stevens, the famous "What difference does it make?" outraged response to questions on the subject at a congressional hearing, and on and on.

One of the strategies that makes the *Times* the *Times* is how they end their articles. While pretending to impartiality, the last one or two paragraphs, often providing a quote from someone supposedly authoritative, give a clue, sometimes more than that, to what they want the reader to think and take away. The article by Healy is no different. After a supposedly evenhanded analysis of the pluses and minuses of Florida senator Marco Rubio's candidacy, Healy concludes his piece:

Mr. Rubio and most of his Republican rivals will be in New Hampshire this weekend for a state party summit meeting, huddling with groups of elected officials and party activists to make their case. So far, no candidate has risen above the rest. "My head tells me that Jeb Bush is the only Republican looking presidential at this point, but my heart vacillates a little," said Barry Wynn, a major Republican donor from South Carolina. "I've heard people say, when they listen to Bush in person, he can come across as presidential. But he and the other Republicans need to become sharper, more sure-footed, if one of them is going to beat Hillary and her I'm-like-you message."[3]

Note how a Republican donor has been chosen to criticize his fellow Republicans and ratify Hillary's "I'm-like-you" message, again without mention of the almost farcical notion that Hillary Clinton, recipient of a $14 million advance for her latest book and a speaking fee of $300 thousand per outing, could be anything approaching "one of us." It is hypocrisy of titanic proportions. One wonders what else Mr. Wynn might have said or how the Republican donor was excerpted, but no matter. The damage has been done and the *New York Times* has ended its foray into electoral politics as it wished—as a superb piece of subtle propaganda that should make the editors of *Pravda* envious. The question is, Why would Healy, an obviously intelligent man, slant it this way? The answer is (not surprisingly!) moral narcissism. Even if Hillary Clinton is a massive hypocrite, she is a hypocrite for the right cause. (This is reminiscent of the famous quote from the emperor Franz Josef—"Ask not whether the man is a patriot; is he a patriot for me?"—that became the title of a John Osborne play.) For Healy that counts for more than any questions that might arise about sincerity and, ultimately, result.

My intention here is not to pick on a particular reporter but to see him as a paradigm—and far from the worst—of a pervasive phenomenon. He has to write the way he does or he will lose his place in the nomenklatura. Like all of us, he needs to survive. He can tell himself the truth is finally elusive. Beyond that, he is just giving his audience what it wants; reassurance that they can feel good about Hillary even though her lifestyle and behavior so extremely contradict her professed values. At the same time, it makes them feel good about their own contradictions. They may not be as rich as Mrs. Clinton, but they are comfortable enough and do not wish to feel guilty about it. That she erased three hundred thousand emails from her private server, although disturbing, can be ignored. After all, the New York Times—in this early instance anyway—is not even mentioning it in their election coverage. It therefore cannot be that significant, just politics as usual. Don't they all do it? (Well, they don't, but who's counting?) They are free now to vote for Hillary as their tribune. She is on the side of the people, after all, and so are they. Call this the Zabar's Nomenklatura, a group that is not just comprised of the Upper West Side of Manhattan where the iconic deli is located. It is all over both coasts of our country and in cities in-between where the New York Times is read or, more importantly, regurgitated in shortened form through multiple outlets. This primacy of attitude over news obviates the believers of the necessity of learning uncomfortable facts. It also dovetails well with the all-too-human resistance to change. Everything old is new again—on and on. You don't have to study the facts because you already know what you believe, what is indisputably "true."

Of course it's not so simple. These same people are being challenged as never before. America is at a turning point, testing whether the American nomenklatura will survive as it has for decades, evolving as it did from the preservation of the values of that Least Great Generation. It may be for a nomenklatura to fall, the society around it must fall, as happened with the Soviet Union in the 1990s. But even that did not entirely destroy the system, which has been resurrected under another name. As has been noted, the American version is yet sturdier than the Soviet. Morally narcissistic ideation instilled in early childhood keeps it together. The ideation is reinforced by early childhood education and even more by the entertainment industry whose devotion to political correctness, especially in children's television programming, is incontrovertible.

This ironclad uniformity is starting to backfire, with not just college students (as shown through the aforementioned The College Fix) but also high school and junior high school students beginning to roll their eyes at the nonstop diversity training to which they are subject. The irony is that these same students already accept and live with diversity on a more basic level than their seniors who are endlessly espousing it to them in diversity classes and similar forums. But, like most people, these students are quickly bored and annoyed with being preached to by their elders, especially when they think their elders are talking through their hats, spouting rote ideology. They retreat to their cellphones, texting each other during required sessions overseen by professional "facilitators" whose backgrounds could scarcely be called academic, but are a new (though only vaguely accredited) occupation of political correctness police. Often these facilitators search for problems that are nonexistent or "scratch scabs," frequently about gender, to create or exacerbate situations, sometimes to the embarrassment of the students. In one case I am familiar with, a Los Angeles high school student was ejected from a gender discussion group sponsored by her upper-crust private school because she was *not* a lesbian.

This kind of behavior is typical of our times. The world is slowly turning upside down, with faculty and administration at all levels of education living in terror of not appearing politically correct while a growing number of their charges think they are toadies or merely foolish. Those same faculty and administrators are desperate to preserve their places in the nomenklatura. They hold on to the views of the Least Great Generation like a life raft, fearful that they will be abandoned if they are not at the forefront of every issue and accused of being reactionaries. (Actually, they are.) Without a strong administration hand, extremist groups dominate campuses—some Islamic and, paradoxically, others on the far edges of gender—while a silent majority of increasingly frustrated students goes about their studies, trying to prepare themselves for employment in an ever-more difficult and complicated world. Many of these students are skeptical of the rebranded socialism promulgated by the Least Great Generation and more interested in free markets and entrepreneurship. They are unimpressed with the endless so-called "trigger warnings" appended to lectures and films by the perpetually offended, and concerned with the censorship inherent in the university banning of such speakers as Condoleezza Rice and Ayaan Hirsi Ali. In actuality, many are beginning to lean strongly in the direction of free market principles, libertarian ideas attracting more undergraduates than ever. This would seem to make our educational institutions potentially ground zero for a revolution of sorts, for the upending of these Least Great Generation values and the beginnings of the serious disruption of the nomenklatura, were it not for one subject—same-sex marriage.

This issue unites the masses of students with the extremist groups as no other. It also almost alone preserves the nomenklatura because the majority of the younger generation of millennials (those born after 1981) has been raised in an era when homosexuality has been accepted. Recent polls find wide backing of gay marriage. A December 2014 CNN poll had 57 percent believing same-sex marriage was "valid with a constitutional right" and an additional 3 percent "valid with no constitutional right." These figures are up from 39 percent and 5 percent in 2008. The trend is clear and has been for some time, especially for millennials; another poll from 2013 showed support for gay marriage among young adults from 18 to 29 at 81 percent.[4]

As this generation grows older, this support will be overwhelming. It constitutes a problem for Republicans seeking the 2016 presidential nomination, especially with their evangelical base that believes equally overwhelmingly in the traditional definition of marriage. Pandering to that base to get the nomination would risk being painted as a homophobic bigot in the general election. The extent of the problem with younger people was made manifest in a small survey of fifty Dartmouth students conducted in April 2015 on the topic of the Hillary Clinton presidential candidacy.[5] While a significant number, indeed the majority, of students interviewed opposed Clinton for her mishandling of foreign policy and for hypocritically pretending to identify with the middle class, those that favored her did so because of social policy. "I think it's ridiculous that we haven't progressed to the point in society where things like gay marriage are still questioned," one student supporter said in favor Clinton, even though the former secretary of state only "evolved" to such a position in 2013.

This accusation of homophobia—justifiable or not—functions as the trump card for the nomenklatura as it is currently constituted. It ratifies what they think about the Right and can easily be generalized and expanded to other accusations, such as racism or greed, even when they don't remotely apply. The moral narcissism factor is used to justify these accusations. They know best: someone who is opposed to gay marriage is a homophobe and most likely a racist. Therefore he or she is also most likely greedy, obsessed with religion, with little interest in the poor but an overweening interest in the Second Amendment. It is basically a recapitulation of Obama's well-known remarks referenced earlier about Middle Americans "clinging to their guns and religion" that were made in 2008 to a San Francisco branch of the nomenklatura. That conservatives of a libertarian ilk, and libertarians themselves, may have positions on same-sex marriage far removed from this stereotype is deliberately ignored. It is not part of the narrative; too threatening to be discussed.

The true underpinnings of the nomenklatura are not ideology, but power and money. The ideology is simply there to serve and preserve them, just as it was in the Soviet Union. It was constructed that way and is decidedly resistant to social mobility while claiming otherwise. This evolved and continues to evolve from the grey area between the conscious and the unconscious. It's unclear which it is or to what degree they reinforce each other, but the results are the same—class stability that is relatively undisturbed save in exceptional cases (entertainment and sports stars, tech entrepreneurs).

No more prime and enduring exemplars of the American nomenklatura exist than Bill and Hillary Clinton. Recent revelations regarding their foundation demonstrate the intentions and methodology of the nomenklatura better than anything thus far. Peter Schweizer's *Clinton Cash: The Untold Story of How and Why Foreign Governments and Businesses Helped Make Bill and Hillary Rich,* published May 2015, details the vast sums of money garnered by the Clintons from extreme reactionary regimes across the world (many misogynistic and homophobic) while the couple publicly espoused liberal and progressive causes, sometimes including same-sex marriage, which they have intermittently supported when it seemed electorally convenient. Much of this occurred when *Mrs.* Clinton, as the *New York Times* quaintly calls her, was the secretary of state. Beyond the obvious monumental hypocrisy, it was also, in at least one instance, more than arguably treasonous.

Those were the dealings in Kazakhstan that led to Russia (and Vladimir Putin) controlling 20 percent of American uranium. The details of these dealings are unlikely to be known fully, given the massive email erasures by Hillary Clinton and the natural inclination not to put influence-peddling on paper. Nevertheless, the legal implications of a US government official taking money from a foreign leader or government are enshrined in the US Constitution, article 1, section 9, known as the Emoluments Clause: "No Title of Nobility shall be granted by the United States: And no Person holding any Office or Profit or Trust under them, shall, with the Consent of Congress, accept of any present, Emolument, Office, of Title, of any kind what, from any King, Prince, of foreign State."

The Heritage Guide to the Constitution puts it succinctly: "The clause sought to shield the republican character of the United States against corrupting foreign influences."[6]

More disturbing emotionally and morally was the principal revelation from the October 23, 2015, Benghazi hearings. Although widely declared a victory for Mrs. Clinton in the mainstream media with the committee Republicans characterized as hectoring old white men bent on partisan destruction, in its lead editorial entitled "Benghazi and Character," the *Wall Street Journal* wrote this: "The select committee led by Republican Trey Gowdy of South Carolina released hitherto undisclosed documents showing that Mrs. Clinton believed from the start that the attack was perpetrated by terrorists. ... This matters because it precedes what became the administration's original story that the Benghazi attack had been motivated by an anti-Muslim Internet video ('the film,' as Mrs. Clinton put it to the Egyptian)."

The undisclosed documents to which the *Journal* was referring were an email from Mrs. Clinton to her daughter hours after the attack saying it was being perpetrated by an Al Qaeda-like group, and subsequent communications to the leadership of Egypt and Libya saying substantially the same thing. As the world knows, for weeks the Obama administration placed the blame on a crude video lampooning Muhammad.

The question remains whether the public has been too brainwashed to care. Whatever the corrupting influences on the Clintons may have been or may be, whatever the level of lying, one of the fundamental dangers of nomenklaturas in general is how they are able to override the possible presence of such prevarication and corruption, making it vanish. An example of the extent of the corruption was the near-accidental revelation that ABC anchor George Stephanopoulos, who had just grilled Schweizer over his book *Clinton Cash*, had himself donated $75,000 to the Clinton Foundation over the last few years and somehow had neglected to report this extraordinary conflict of interest to his employers at the network. Still, ABC did nothing about it, barely giving their anchor a slap on the wrist. If you are a member in good standing of the nomenklatura—and who more than the Clintons and their entourage and press supporters—what you actually do or did pales by comparison to what you say. And even what you say is not of tremendous importance. It is more what you are *assumed* to say and think. You don't have to say it.

In fact, it's better if you don't because the listener/audience can project what he or she wishes. You are, after all, that established member of the nomenklatura. The best is always thought of you. The classic example of this in our time is Obama's famous pledge of "hope and change." It was open-ended and vague on purpose, allowing the individual to use his or her moral-narcissism-based views to fill in the blanks. Everyone had their definition. Whatever you believed to be correct was undoubtedly correct, even if it wasn't. Years later, who can remember what it was anyway?

The Hillary Clinton campaign initially adopted a similar approach, speaking broadly of aid to the suffering middle class without providing specifics. At the same time they did their best to ignore the many accusations against her and the Clinton Foundation or, failing that, to impugn the motives of its accusers. This is standard operating procedure for nomenklaturas throughout the world. The more successful they are, the less likely to face serious opposition. Nomenklaturas constitute a group version of Lord Acton's famous dictum about absolute power corrupting absolutely. The Clintons are as pure an example of this as you could find, essentially leaders of this new class. While thinking they are doing good, or pretending to themselves that they are, they end up doing evil (handing American uranium to Putin), and making outrageous amounts of money. It is at this level that "liberalism" and "progressivism" no longer exist as ideologies but are no more than power structures. This frozen position (reification) evolved out of what to them and others felt like and seemed to be an idealistic youth, that attraction to Saul Alinsky, Herbert Marcuse, and other heroes of the Least Great Generation. Whatever one can say about the "idealism" of those heroes, it has disappeared in the rear view mirror. Everything has been superseded and forgotten in changing times. In his *Rules for Radicals*, Alinsky did not mention navigating the globe in corporate jets as a way of winning the revolution, covert or otherwise. He did not envision a nomenklatura sitting comfortably in David Brooks's Volvos or, even better, saving the world from warming by pulling over to charging stations in a $70,000+ Tesla or a $136,000 BMW i8.

But despite this cushy existence, all is not comfortable for the American nomenklatura. It is under threat as never since the Reagan era or, more likely earlier, since the Reagan era did not finally effectuate a change in the system. Then, the mainstream media, in constant opposition to Reagan, remained almost entirely in place. The entertainment

industry became, if anything, more liberal and supportive of the nomenklatura and its conventional views. And, most of all, educational institutions began to solidify their liberal bias. But now, after the public reaction
to the Clintons' corruption, coupled with years of Obama foreign policy
blunders leading toward disintegration of the world order and a nuclear
armed Middle East, it is not just Internet outliers and Fox News that are
being critical. Mainstream media outlets like the *New York Times* and the
Washington Post are beginning to investigate these situations, something
they rarely if ever did before. Not surprisingly, they are schizophrenic
about it—their editorial pages taking back when their news pages might
give. But it is happening. Whether this can last is another matter. It is
tantamount to a nomenklatura investigating itself to yield a potential
American glasnost.

   The probability is that it won't be sustainable. Too many people live
in fear for their jobs, which is the key to the power of all nomenklaturas.
It's hard to imagine a liberal columnist or reporter in the mainstream
media completely changing sides because it almost never happens,
Charles Krauthammer being the rare exception. Most would not think
to do it under almost any circumstance. The results are too depressing
to contemplate, as they would be for those in the entertainment industry and the educational field, where the professional fear is palpable.
In those fields, however, those in the highest echelons get a pass. The
world-famous director Clint Eastwood can have the politics he wishes,
just as certain academics, once they have tenure, are free of ideological
strictures, not that many exercise that freedom in the current atmosphere.
University administrations seem in full retreat, living in fear of criticism from professors and students as those same administrators operate
under the strictures of Title IX. That portion of United States Education
Amendments of 1972 has morphed into an ax wielded by a veritable army
of federal bureaucrats whose myriad mandates overcomplicate almost
every aspect of our educational systems, drastically inflating costs, laying
down politically correct strictures, and impeding learning.

   In the business community and on Wall Street the picture is less
onerous. Nevertheless many top-level executives mouth morally narcissistic pieties as if applying for some contemporary version of a papal
indulgence. They are "good people" and therefore their stratospherically
high pay and unlimited perks can be justified or at least ignored. Some

of these indulgences go way beyond pronouncements, however, and are purchased with huge corporate sums, as we saw from the revelations surrounding the Clinton Foundation. All contributions, we were told, were for important global charitable causes, yet, according to *The Federalist*, out of the $500 million raised by the foundation between 2009 and 2012, only a paltry $75 million went to grants. The other $425 million were assigned in IRS documents to salaries, travel, and mysterious "other expenses" (a whopping $290 million). Not surprisingly, the Clinton Foundation was never audited, but after exposure of these documents by the *Washington Post* and others, and under the pressure of a presidential campaign, they began to revise a decade's worth of tax filings. Jonah Goldberg has written brilliantly of the ties between liberalism and fascism. Is he correct or is it more accurately a con game devoid of all political theory or principle and totally expedient in its nature? Whatever the case, if you are a good member of the nomenklatura and pay for your indulgences, you make money—a lot of it.

To be clear, these indulgences are not unique to Democrats. Republican Jeffrey Immelt, CEO of GE and recipient of an $18.7 million salary in 2014, had his company donate hundreds of millions to the Clinton Foundation at the time GE was negotiating for a large power plant contract with Algeria. When the controversy broke, Immelt refused to release emails held by GE concerning the negotiation between the company and the State Department, emails whose other end may have disappeared forever with the erasure of Hilary Clinton's server.

The powerful have a lot to give up if they depart from the traditional views of the nomenklatura. No wonder they have a certain level of trepidation. But fear isn't the only motor that keeps them in line. Shame is also a factor. We saw how strong that emotion could be when Academy Award-winning actor/writer/director Ben Affleck fought to keep his family history of slaveholding off the episode of the PBS program *Finding Your Roots* that was devoted to him. His background apparently humiliated the filmmaker, even though the ancestor involved (his great-great-great-grandfather) had died well over a century before Affleck was born. The actor's wishes were revealed in the hacked Sony emails that embarrassed many executives of that company, including CEO Michael Lynton who urged *Finding Your Roots*' host, Harvard professor Henry Lewis Gates (he of the "Beer Summit"), to excise that part of the filmmaker's history even though Gates had his qualms. It would be bad for the show's reputation to be caught tidying up their subject's backgrounds. Ironically, the *Daily Beast* later reported that the program had the story wrong, that Affleck's ancestor did not own slaves and was merely the executor of estates that had.[7] Later still, another report from *Breitbart News Network* did find fourteen slaveholders somewhere in the Affleck family.[8] Whatever the case, it is meaningless. No one is responsible for the deeds of ancestors, especially distant ones. But the intense reaction, indeed over-reaction, on the part of Affleck is an indication of the level of shame attached to these belief systems.

The fear and shame are welded together into views adopted by the nomenklatura that are rarely questioned. And when they are, moral narcissism steps in almost in the manner of Freud's superego to dampen down controversial thoughts that might weaken that same nomenklatura's authority or threaten an individual's place in it. An example of this process occurred in a October 2014 debate on Islam on HBO's *Real Time* between Ben Affleck (again—don't mean to pick on him), neuroscientist Sam Harris, and Bill Maher, the show's host. Harris and Maher had been pointing out that those who espoused the jihadist version of Islam actually constituted a significant portion of the Islamic world, but Affleck was appalled. To him, that was racism. The Islamic world had to be seen as a victim of Western imperialism with jihadists as outliers. "ISIS couldn't fill a AA ballpark in Charleston, West Virginia," the actor said, "and you want to make a career out of ISIS, ISIS, ISIS."[9] It's perhaps unfair to criticize Affleck for that risible remark, as events had yet to unspool, or evidently not enough of them for him. Nevertheless, it was a case of the mind resisting reality. He was unable to countenance the extent of the brutality, even as Harris, who was vastly more knowledgeable, presented facts and statistics. He went on to say "We've killed more Muslims than they've killed us by an awful lot," evidently unaware of the extraordinary numbers of Muslim-on-Muslim murders in recent years, easily dwarfing any Western involvement or anybody else's. But the narrative goes on.

And Affleck was not alone. Many in the audience were sympathetic, applauding first Maher and then him, as if caught between reality and their ingrained belief system. Affleck was finally supported in the debate by a truly head-spinning comment from Nicholas Kristof of the *New York Times*, who was also on the panel. Kristof opined the criticism of Islam has "a tinge of how white racists talk about African Americans and define blacks." Really? Criticism of a jihadist society—where mass beheadings and rape rooms, not to mention the defenestration of homosexuals, was the order of the day—invoked white racists defining blacks? To whom was he referring specifically? No one, because no one exists who fits that profile. It was a totally different subject. Kristof had trumped the room, yet no one reacted, even though his comparison had no basis in truth whatsoever, and in fact was completely phony. Moral narcissistic pronouncements of this nature have become so commonplace in our society no one even notices them.

That is the reason that seemingly inconsequential events like these two examples with Ben Affleck are so important. They demonstrate what is "in the ether," in the air we breathe. This affects all of us. We expect the world to be this way. We expect the vast majority of our college professors to be liberal and our television dramas to lampoon the greed, racism, and sexism of American life. When they are not that way, we are surprised. Our youth are growing up in this atmosphere. Many of them are aware. They roll their eyes at the inanity, predictability, and hypocrisy, but still they are heavily influenced. They know as they grow up they must behave a certain way to be members of the nomenklatura, at whatever level, and they act accordingly in the end. This cycle affirms a nomenklatura more stable, as I said, than the Soviet could ever have been because it is based on the subtle coercion of self-interest. Nobody wakes up to find his father and brother in Lubyanka. Criticism is muted and those that speak loudly are made to seem shrill and marginalized.

Even though it's obvious there have always been ruling classes of one sort or another, our nomenklatura-based society is clearly not what was envisioned or sought by our nation's founders. Madison struggled to overcome the tyranny of the majority in the Federalist Papers, with he and his peers arriving at the republican idea. Yet that tyrannical majority is what has emerged—a tyrannical majority led by a nomenklatura and lost in its own ignorance, a majority of habit and reflex. Dialogue is basically illusory and fresh ideas rare. Most debate occurs around the edges, assuring that little or nothing changes. In that sense, the critique offered by the Tea Party is valid, though rooted excessively in the past and largely unappealing to young people.

XVIII

Nostalgia for Class Consciousness

Nostalgia for Marxism's junior partner.

As with all manifestations of the class system, the nomenklatura depends on an underclass for its existence. The rules of the game defining these classes are complicated, almost like a Kabuki. We are supposed to think certain things, while not allowed to think others, but only express them in a third way. The object is to preserve the status quo while appearing to change it or, more importantly, appearing to *want* to change it. That's the nomenklatura's way of doing things. During the writing of this book, the race situation was once again exploding in American cities, first Ferguson, Missouri, then Baltimore. Satellite demonstrations broke out across the country. Detroit had already shown the way to becoming a dysfunctional city, but Baltimore was rivaling it, having lost one-third of its population from just under 950,000 in 1950 to just over 620,000 today. Almost no one, through all this, was suggesting new solutions, always the same old government programs that had achieved exactly nothing since the Civil Rights Act of 1964. The existence of a nomenklatura militates against new ideas because those ideas threaten the class's power. New ideas mean new people mean new configurations. They are to be avoided. Comments made by Hillary Clinton in the aftermath of the Baltimore riots were identical to comments made by Democratic Party politicians after the 1992 Rodney King riots in Los Angeles, calling for reform to end a "pattern of cops killing innocent black men."[1] But no such pattern exists anymore and the politicians know it. Rodney King was an outlier and the Freddie Gray case in Baltimore was more comparable to the alleged gang rape by the Duke University lacrosse team that proved fallacious than a serious civil rights violation, ironically, in this instance, supposedly by African American police.

But the nomenklatura has no interest in making such distinctions. They are more intent on self-preservation and the accrual of power than solutions to problems. The entrenchment of the nomenklatura indeed militates against new approaches. Former Baltimore mayor and Maryland governor Martin O'Malley immediately said if he were to announce his presidential candidacy, he was going to do it in that city. "We haven't had an agenda for America's cities probably since Jimmy Carter ... We have left cities to fend for themselves. ... But look, the structural problems that we have in our economy, the way we ship jobs and profits abroad, the way we failed to invest in our infrastructure and failed to invest in American cities, we are creating the conditions. Please, Speaker Boehner and his crocodile tears about the $130 million, that is a spit in the bucket compared to what we need to do as a nation to rebuild our country." In other words, O'Malley's prescription for Baltimore was as always—spend more money. It's the nomenklatura way, buttressed, as always, by moral narcissism. He knew best.[2] O'Malley added, "We need to stop ignoring especially people of color and act like they are disposable citizens in this nation." As if we did.

The $130 million he was referring to was the subject of a *Washington Post* article "Why Couldn't $130 Million Transform One of Baltimore's Poorest Places?"[3] The article describes how that large sum failed to resurrect the crumbling neighborhood where Freddie Gray was arrested the day he died. Called Sandtown-Winchester and once home to Thurgood Marshall, Billie Holiday, and Cab Calloway, the state now "spends nearly $17 million just to incarcerate its former residents. Life expectancy is 10 years below the national average." The *Post* quotes Stefanie DeLuca—a Johns Hopkins sociologist who studied the neighborhood—as saying, "It's frustrating. How much money would it take? It certainly seems on an instinctual level that $100 million should have made some difference." Yes, it would. So maybe, just maybe, an alternative approach should be taken.

But to Martin O'Malley the solution is to spend more money, $130 million being "spit in the bucket." Does he really mean this or is he just playing to the crowd, burnishing his bona fides with "people of color" while intending, as per usual, to do little or nothing? Who knows? That is not the point. What he is demonstrating is pure nomenklatura-think. That can be translated as "more of the same," the manner in which our nomenklatura, inherently conservative though superficially liberal—almost always responds. It doesn't matter that this approach has failed or, at best, has been treading water for fifty years; what matters is the preservation of the nomenklatura itself. We can thank O'Malley, no doubt apprehensive that such destructive rioting in the city where he was formerly mayor might interfere with his incipient presidential ambitions, for giving us such a clear demonstration.

So the American nomenklatura, while pretending to liberalism or progressivism, is particularly conservative in style and behavior; ultra-traditional and unchanging in its responses to the world. The Republican (putatively conservative) side of the nomenklatura, if less pervasive, is relatively similar in its hesitancy to come up with something original. Even when they make a new quasi-libertarian suggestion, as with Rand Paul's pushing economic freedom zones (read: tax relief) to encourage entrepreneurship in impoverished Detroit neighborhoods, nothing actually occurs. The pronouncement is the story. This inaction is all the more poignant given that Paul's proposal, the Kentucky senator acknowledged, was simply an adaptation of Jack Kemp's free enterprise zones, first offered at the 1992 Republication National Convention. Little happened then either. Nomenklaturas, whether of the Right or Left, are about stasis. While the private sector, particularly in the technology area, is all about disrupting personal business models, our country's political leadership—the American nomenklatura—replenishes itself in a highly structured manner in order to avoid disruption at all costs.

This approach is occasionally challenged in elections, but usually without much success. Before each cycle, many lament the presence of the same group of professional politicians (Clintons, Bushes), but by the time the cycle is completed nothing very new has occurred. With the advent of Dr. Ben Carson, Donald Trump, and Carly Fiorina, 2016 may be different, but the gaping yaw of the nomenklatura is wide. The same was thought of the advent of Barack Obama. His election had the pretense of the new, but in reality he behaved like a tried and true member of the nomenklatura, selecting Hillary Clinton and John Kerry as his secretaries of state. Other nominations were similarly predictable. Eric Holder, attorney general for nearly Obama's entire presidency, had worked for Bill Clinton. Nearly everyone is recycled. Obama may have moved the ball slightly to the left, but more indelibly he demonstrated how African Americans now had honored places in the nomenklatura—that is, *certain* African Americans, because he also demonstrated just how firmly that community was divided along class lines.

Indeed, he exacerbated that split, creating a branch of the nomenklatura filled with millionaire, even billionaire, blacks from the entertainment industry, sports, and politics (Sharpton, Valerie Jarrett) while the lower classes declined further into the despair manifested by the riots in Baltimore and Ferguson. To a great degree, not even *the illusion* of improvement for this African American underclass was proffered. Everyone would have known it was false. After all, educated or uniquely talented African Americans—never remotely the rioters in the first place—had long since moved to the suburbs of cities like Baltimore, if they remained in the area at all. Many were in Beverly Hills and Malibu. For the underclass, the usual nomenklatura pieties were offered up, similar to those from Martin O'Malley mentioned above. Real change is never the issue, only illusory change. Though seemingly accepted and even applauded, the cries of "No justice, no peace" were not really taken seriously by the nomenklatura because they knew, eventually, after the requisite palliatives, they would go away. Meanwhile, they could be used to flay the opposition, the greedy and intolerant right-wingers who supposedly created the situation.

When we think of the Soviet-style nomenklaturas, we think of extensive power structures dominating a totalitarian state, keeping the impecunious put-upon masses in their place while their leaders enjoy comfortable, sometimes a bit more than merely comfortable, existences. This dichotomy is well described in a recent book *The Double Life of Fidel Castro*, which shows the Cuban dictator living a lifestyle, including yachts and private islands, that would be the envy of George Soros, while his citizens suffer in penury under constant surveillance, the specter of imprisonment looming. The American nomenklatura is, of course, far less brutal and, therefore, as I have argued, far more successful in the long term. But that doesn't stop a large number of them from having a strong attraction to their more rigid peers like Castro. This attraction is nearly romantic, almost eroticized, and fraught with nostalgia for their own lost radical youths, whether they existed or not.

For years the American nomenklatura has sought better treatment for communist Cuba. This goes as far back as Herbert Matthews's fawning interview with Fidel from the Sierra Maestra for which the *New York Times* reporter has been called the heir to the aforementioned Walter Duranty, the *Times* correspondent who, as noted earlier, whitewashed Stalin's mass starvation of the Ukrainians and won the Pulitzer. As Che Guevara himself put it in 1958's *One Year of Combat*, "When the world had given us up for dead, the interview with Matthews put the lie to our disappearance." Fifty-seven years later, Barack Obama has delivered on Matthews's promise, giving the nomenklatura that sought-for rapprochement with Cuba.

It's not a mathematical theorem, but events suggest that the longer nomenklaturas remain entrenched, the more likely they are to turn totalitarian in some form. In supposedly democratic societies, political correctness becomes the enforcing factor, assuring that everyone stays in line. Political correctness, however, is a peculiar term and almost an oxymoron, evolving as it did from cultural relativism, the theory that deems all societies are equal, none above others. But if all societies are equal, how can one particular system or attitude be called "correct"? Confusing, isn't it? Political correctness is a sham unto itself; its intentions were and are entirely totalitarian and coercive. Nomenklaturas enable this goal by providing recognized means through which individuals can have their emotional needs rewarded as those "politically correct" views become socially accepted norms to express their moral narcissism. Thus, in the old Soviet Union, people got to feel good about themselves, feel part of this important group, part of the future and history, by reciting Marxist nostrums about "the ends justifying the means" or "from each according to his ability." Similarly, in today's America a wise member of the nomenklatura blames the conditions of black people on the fruits of "white skin privilege," or "income inequality" on corporate greed. Individual members of either version, Soviet or American, do not necessarily have to believe these things; they just have to say they do. Say it often enough and they will believe it anyway.

Besides encouraging totalitarianism, nomenklaturas, because they rely on the most conventional of conventional thinking, encourage stasis. Most American cities are what they are because they have been controlled by nomenklaturas for decades. Ironically, however, these same nomenklaturas must gradually reinvent themselves to maintain that stasis and control, to preserve the illusion of change and of being edgy, in Hollywood parlance. They evolve at the outer edges, academia, in large part because it is so cloistered from reality, often the center of this evolution. Thus the Democratic Party, which stood for something not so far from classical liberalism during the era of John Kennedy and Hubert Humphrey, over the years turned into a repressive instrument, welcoming, at its fringes, the witch-hunt mentality of those microaggressions now popular on campuses and becoming effectively the enemy, even the eradicators, of free speech.

These witch-hunts have reached extremes that are either risible or frightening or both, depending on how you look at them. An April 2015 op-ed in the *Columbia Spectator*—"Our Identities Matter in Core Classrooms"—written by four undergraduate women, argued that students taking the college's required humanities class should be given advance warning before reading Ovid's *Metamorphoses.* The Roman classic—published in AD 8—contained poetical descriptions of the rape of Persephone that could make contemporary Columbia students, presumably female, feel not "safe," as the op-ed put it. The undergraduate purveyors of these so-called "trigger warnings" may not always go on to become the nomenklatura leaders of the future, but they have injected these new behavioral codes into the zeitgeist where, although ridiculed in the short run by some, they survive to emerge as the received values of the not so distant future.

The values of the Least Great Generation taken to excessive lengths prevail in our schools and, largely, on our television sets. For the most part, they also suffuse our workplaces as well, where human resource departments have become petty tyrannies of political correctness. Despite the country being split down the middle ideologically, those on the right have almost nowhere to turn. Even during national elections, the liberal mainstream media dictate the terms of play with almost exclusively liberal commentators moderating the debates, at least up until 2016. Conservatives can watch Fox News, but they often live half-underground like some modern day version of the *marranos* during the Spanish Inquisition. They only practice their religion, or ideology, privately among the family or at small dinner parties with trusted companions. This is especially true in Blue States where the diktat of the nomenklatura is all-pervasive. In places like New York and Los Angeles organizations have been formed, safety zones, where these people, the new marranos, can breathe freely. The Friends of Abe, a once entirely underground organization of Hollywood conservatives, is one of them. To say this is not a healthy situation is an understatement.

Most dangerous of all is how moral narcissism creates the proverbial slippery slope through which relatively benign nomenklaturas descend into totalitarianism, or already dangerous nomenklaturas become worse. Supposedly ethical pronouncements are made that end up justifying the worst, too often violent, behavior. These declarations can come from as high a position as the leader of the Catholic Church, the Holy See. In May 2015, Pope Francis proclaimed Palestinian Authority president Mahmoud Abbas an "angel of peace." (He also conferred sainthood on two Palestinian nuns.) No mention was made that Abbas had written a Moscow University thesis denying the Holocaust and, more recently, signed numerous alliances with the terrorist organization Hamas that has in its charter a pledge to exterminate all the world's Jews, or that the Palestinian Authority itself sponsored terrorism through its military wing, Fatah, frequently through extreme acts like suicide bombings. More recently Abbas encouraged stabbings of random Israeli citizens. Perhaps to Francis this *wasn't* actual terrorism but the unfortunate response of the wretched of the earth to living in poverty under oppression. Besides denying these people free will, this is moral narcissism of the purest sort, with the *truly* unfortunate result that it gives Vatican cover to all sorts of mayhem, and justifies fascist control of the very people it seeks, somehow, to console. Francis, who supposedly had the ear of God, knew best.

But his words seemed meant largely for the believing Catholic masses in Africa and, most of all, Latin America. Here in the West, we live increasingly in a time of atheism. When it comes to moral narcissism, we make up the pronouncements for ourselves. So did Kim Jong-un, Pol Pot, Stalin and, to break Godwin's Law on the printed page, Adolf Hitler. I am aware I am sounding a little extreme here, but often I fear our country is being prepared on a semiconscious level for such a transition. As generations sit in front of televisions and video games, their abilities to discriminate deadened and their affect flattened while their sensibilities are coddled by "trigger warnings," the dystopian future envisioned by Orwell and Huxley is not only a certainty, it is an understatement.

XIX

Bang! Bang! You're Not Dead!

*How I learned to love the Second Amendment
by outliving my mother.*

My mother hated guns. I mean she *really* hated them and thought they were the root of all evil. After all, a kid with guns would likely grow up to kill people, accidentally if not on purpose. She did everything possible to keep them—meaning cap guns—out of my hands when I was little boy. Several times I was able to overcome this prohibition. Pictures exist of me running around in a cowboy suit at the age of three or four, so one of my parents must have relented at some point, but the message remained deeply imbued in my subconscious well into my adult years— "guns bad."

This is a common form of moral narcissism among middle-class families, even back then in the late 1940s and 1950s. It is particularly ironic that this was exceptionally common, even pervasive, among Jewish families like mine, since the time frame was so close to Hitler's mass murder of the Jews, the vast majority of who were unarmed, marched into gas chambers, or shot en masse and pushed into open pits. I was reminded of this bleak irony by the brouhaha over comments by presidential candidate Dr. Ben Carson, when he said, early fall 2015, that the Jews might have fared better against the Nazis had Hitler not previously expropriated all weapons not in the hands of the likes of his own storm troopers and brownshirts. What Carson said would seem obvious, but the claque of attacking moral narcissists was willing to overlook the Warsaw Ghetto uprising, the Jewish partisans who had to steal from German and Polish weapons caches in order to survive, not to mention the entire state of Israel whose founding evolved out of ad hoc armed groups like the Palmach and the Irgun. "Never again!" was not the watchword of pacifists.

The attack on Carson was a classic case of moral narcissism run amok, exacerbated by the inability of liberals to countenance a black conservative, especially one who is a pioneering pediatric neurosurgeon of great accomplishment. How could *he*, of all people, think such things? So moral narcissism clicks in as a neurotic response mechanism, not allowing the liberals and progressives to hear something as elementary as our Second Amendment exists for a reason—to protect the populace from a totalitarian government. I would imagine they scoff at the idea that that could ever happen here. So did the leaders of Germany's Weimar Republic as detailed in a 2013 article by Stephen P. Halbrook in *National Review Online*—"How the Nazis Used Gun Control":

> The Weimar Republic's well-intentioned gun registry became a tool for evil. The perennial gun-control debate in America did not begin here. The same arguments for and against were made in the 1920s in the chaos of Germany's Weimar Republic, which opted for gun regis-tration. ... The interior minister warned that the records must not fall into the hands of any extremist group. In 1933, the ultimate extremist group, led by Adolf Hitler, seized power and used the records to iden-tify, disarm, and attack political opponents and Jews. Constitutional rights were suspended, and mass searches for and seizures of guns and dissident publications ensued. Police revoked gun licenses of Social Democrats and others who were not "politically reliable."[1]

My own embrace of the Second Amendment came slowly because of the aforementioned childhood indoctrination. It is perhaps the area where I came most reluctantly to a conservative/libertarian position. This was complicated for me by my own squeamishness. The little boy who enjoyed his cap gun was less excited when he had a real gun in his hand. In the late sixties, when I went hunting for the first time with the groundskeeper at the house I was renting in southern Spain (very Hemingway), I became sick to my stomach after shooting a rabbit (again very Hemingway—I felt like Francis Macomber about to have my own "short, happy life").

It was years before I started fully to accept guns. I owe that partly to Rick Perry. Invited by the then Texas governor to go pistol shooting with him on a blogger/press junket at an Austin firing range, I hurried over to take lessons at a Los Angeles range in order not to embarrass myself. I ended up a pretty good shot, hitting the target more often than I missed it while shooting with the governor. Proud of myself I came home from Austin and started to think seriously about the Second Amendment for the first time. Before I had been overwhelmed by what I could call my own morally narcissistic ideation, unable to pay attention to or even to read the material that showed gun violence was greater in the areas with the most severe gun control laws, like Chicago. I ignored the issue to focus on a host of others I found more comfortable. But I was thinking even then about how moral narcissism created a cloud in the brain. It was almost physical, as it made us unable to see. That cloud was lifting. That was seven years ago or so. In December 2015, my mother long dead (it would have driven her crazy), I was a featured speaker at a conference at a ranch near Dallas—on the Second Amendment.

XX

Narcissus in the Time of Atheism

Our society has a gaping hole.

Moral narcissism is obviously not a new phenomenon. Aristophanes's comedies are filled with lampoons of pompous know-it-alls, moral narcissists of ancient Athens, among them Socrates himself, lording it over the masses of the day. But things are different now. The humor is shallow and gratuitously nasty, bloodless. Jon Stewart is no Aristophanes. And there's a reason for that (besides the talent level). There's nothing above, no final judge on human folly, no standard for him to hold onto. He's making it up as he goes along. For large portions of our society, God or even the Gods are no longer in the house. He and they have been replaced by the received wisdom of the nomenklatura.

It's not only the polls that tell us that, although they do. According to a 2014 Pew poll, a record 22.8 percent of Americans now classify themselves as atheists or "nothing in particular." Interest in and allegiance to religion in our culture is diminishing—and rapidly. In May 2015, Melissa Harris-Perry went so far as to discuss, on her MSNBC show, whether religion is "over." Yes, that network is the house organ of the more extreme Left and not exactly a ratings champ, but the attitude is everywhere. Religion, we don't need it. We have good values anyway. We know what's right.

But do we? It's not a simple issue. Good values according to whom? I listen to commentators of the Left and Right and become confused. How exactly do we know what's right? Dennis Prager tells us, in a 2015 book, the Ten Commandments are still the best moral code. But do we need religion to obey them? Or are the commandments simply outmoded? (The Least Great Generation watchwords "Never trust anyone over thirty" do not track well, to put it mildly, with "Honor thy father and thy mother.") Can we not "know best" for ourselves? Even though, as an agnostic, or quasi-agnostic, or recovering agnostic possibly, as this chapter might indicate, I observe religion as an outsider, sometimes an envious outsider, I strongly suspect Prager is right. The Ten Commandments remain the best code. But the absence of God in our culture has made them subject to revision, even disregard. And where there is a vacuum, as we know, nature abhors it. In the case of God, this absence has been filled by people's moral narcissistic ideation. The individual knows best, he or she thinks. Of course, that's not true. The nomenklatura knows best. He or she has been unwittingly influenced by the zeitgeist. They are doing what they are told and telling it back. These days, however, the entire society is floundering. Where do we turn?

The founders of our country relied on "natural law or "God's law" in the writing of the Declaration of Independence, establishing the premise that in America every man could live the life "to which the laws of Nature and Nature's God entitle them." But what is that exactly? Thomas Jefferson elucidated. "Man has been subjected by his Creator to the moral law, of which his feelings, or conscience as it is sometimes called, are the evidence with which his Creator has furnished him. ... The moral duties which exist between individual and individual in a state of nature, accompany them into a state of society, their Maker not having released them from those duties on their forming themselves into a nation."

Considerable debate exists whether Jefferson was a theist or a deist or both at different times. (I can identify with that.) Whatever the case, he based his beliefs on a biblical moral law that means little to the increasingly atheistic America of 2016. One aspect of this is the society has lost self-belief. That the conventional wisdom—at this point you could call it a morally narcissistic mantra, "nation building"—does not work, exemplifies this. We failed at it in Iraq. It made matters worse in the Middle East. We should never do it again. This is absolute cant, of course. Some of the greatest triumphs of our country's history involved nation building, notably turning Hitler's Germany and Hirohito's Japan into vibrant democracies. We should not omit South Korea either, one of the great economic success stories of the last decades, producing ever-more high-tech products for a global market. Had we not fought the Korean War, South Korea today would resemble their neighbors to the north, the most frightening totalitarian nation on the planet where the citizens eat boiled bark to survive. And then, of course, there's the American Civil War itself when more than 600,000 of our citizens died to form a more perfect union, free of slavery. Talk about nation building!

Our culture is in a trap. As religiosity diminishes, there are no received values on which to formulate decisions, no "natural" law. Values must come from the nomenklatura, which makes things up as it goes along, their views a mélange of worn-out sixties leftism and political expediency mixed, as we have seen from revelations surrounding the Clintons and others, with a significant dollop of good old-fashioned greed and self-interest. This is a problem throughout the West as it is faced with the ever-spreading rise of radical Islam or, more accurately, traditional Islam, a culture far more convinced of the veracity of its views. Islam does not have to kowtow to political correctness or cultural relativism. It knows it is the truth, all others merely placeholders until their faith and ideology sweeps the world. That can take thousands of years. They don't care because Allah is on their side. Until they are disabused of that notion, they will continue. The West, however, no longer believes in the Enlightenment, let alone the Judeo-Christian tradition. Godless, it stands for nothing against an adversary that stands for everything, including eternal life, which most Westerners regard as superstition. They have a reason to fight. We don't. As time goes on, that may be a reason to start believing again.

XXI

The Mother's Milk of Moral Narcissism

Alternative title "The Soros and the Pity"
(with apologies to Marcel Ophüls).

I know it's Marxist, or perhaps just materialist, of me, but I see money as the biggest factor behind moral narcissism, both as motivator and reinforcer. Just as—in the now venerable cliché—money is the mother's milk of politics, it is the mother's milk of moral narcissism. Cash, often large quantities of it, is what puts morally narcissistic views in place and keeps them there. Ironically then, moral narcissism is a product of the market, although clearly not its most distinguished or useful one. Conventional ideas mixed with political correctness, itself usually an amalgam of conventional ideas, become commercial structures, guidelines for getting rich or staying rich. Sometimes this expresses itself in salary, sometimes in perks. But whatever the case, stray from the line or even question it at your peril. Loyally toe the moral narcissist line and your life will be assured. You will have what the Israelis call *proteksia*.

We have seen a paradigm in how this works over the long term through the relationship of Sidney Blumenthal and Hillary Clinton. Blumenthal, an opinion journalist initially, came to work for the Clintons during Bill's administration. He was a reliable supporter and confidant, particularly of Hillary, on myriad levels. In the words of a *Wall Street Journal* editorial, "Sidney Blumenthal has served in many roles for Bill and Hillary Clinton, from political Svengali to opposition hit man."

Blumenthal was convinced that the Clintons were on the right side of things—they knew best—so he followed their party line wherever it led and was remunerated for it, both monetarily and via the elusive clout. When Bill came under fire for his Oval Office affair with Monica Lewinsky, Blumenthal rushed into the fray and leaked, against all logic and evidence, that Lewinksy was a "stalker" who had been "rebuffed" by the president. He also disparaged another Clinton accuser, Kathleen Willey.

Years later, when Hillary became secretary of state, the Obama administration—believing the devout Clintonista to be a possibly dangerous loose cannon or too loyal to the Clintons—prevented him from obtaining a position at the State Department, but Blumenthal was rewarded with considerably more lucrative posts at the Clinton Foundation and the progressive media watchdog Media Matters. Thus, when the situation in Libya was heating up, Blumenthal's connection to the Clintons was as steadfast as ever, his ties to Hillary as strong, if not stronger. It is clear from emails exchanged between the two of them that they agreed that the dictator Gaddafi had to go. It was the right thing to do. They would be "good people" for being influential in ending Gaddafi's iron rule. It was a given. The world would applaud. And so the dictator was overthrown. And not to be forgotten, money would be made in the new Libya. Blumenthal injected himself into the mix as a broker between the administration, the frail fledgling Libyan government-to-be, and international business interests anxious to exploit the situation.

The key point here is that neither he nor Hilary Clinton saw anything untoward in this obvious conflict of interest. They had been instrumental in the birth of a new "free" Libya and were entitled to the spoils. The hoi polloi should be grateful. To the victor goes the moral-narcissism-based spoils, more deservedly so because they created a democracy in godforsaken North Africa—or told themselves they were doing so. There's something almost Roman about it and Libya was, after all, once part of the Roman Empire, with some of the world's most exquisite ruins to show for it. Never mind that the death of Gaddafi swiftly led not to democracy but to a failed state symbolized first by the four American deaths at Benghazi at the hands of Ansar al-Islam terrorists (and the subsequent lies about the attacks). This was followed in short order in chaotic Libya by the dominating and murderous presence of ISIS, slicing the heads off Christians by the dozens after parading them along the beach. How could Blumenthal and Clinton have anticipated that? They were only trying to do "good." They knew best how the world should be regulated. So what if it went a little off the rails? In the end it wasn't their problem, not really their doing. They are not to blame and, finally, in the words of Mrs. Clinton herself, "What difference does it make?" Had not the Romanian hacker Guccifer released Blumenthal's email account, no one would have noticed.

Blumenthal represents a microcosm of how greed and ambition are justified by moral narcissism, indeed how it bleeds back and forth between them until all are almost indistinguishable. The embattled consigliere represents the relatively small-time version of this pattern, well-connected though he might be or have been. The life of George Soros is the macrocosmic version. Indeed, Soros is moral narcissism writ large on a global scale and powered by access to immense funds. He first became internationally known for shorting British currency to the tune of 10 billion pounds, nearly breaking the Bank of England in what is now called the Black Wednesday of 1992. These days, however, Soros—among the thirty richest people in the world, according to *Forbes*—is far better known as a leading, if not *the* leading, supporter of leftist causes, having his finger in almost every progressive pie, including pointing an arrow back to Blumenthal and Media Matters, among many, many others. He knows what's best for the entire planet and moves on a large number of fronts through his Open Source Foundation to achieve it, though never at the expense of his own substantial bottom line, which continues to grow.

The story of Soros is instructional because it shows the kind of splitting off inherent in moral narcissism; how personal behavior and political behavior do not track together. The personal is not the political, as the cliché would have it. Indeed it is the reverse. The political is used to disguise the personal, to create a fog around it. This could have started in a deliberate or an unconscious manner, but ultimately the conscious and the unconscious fuse. And materialism trumps all; money rules over values with such a surprising ease the values become almost silly. That movie star and putative "eco warrior" Leonardo DiCaprio could fly back and forth between Los Angeles and New York on a private jet six times in six weeks is an example of this.[1] Would it have been that much of an inconvenience for the wealthy DiCaprio to fly first class on one of the many commercial planes that ply that same route on an hourly basis? Obviously not. He just preferred to ride in style on his own time. But does the obvious hypocrisy restrain the movie star from publicly espousing his ultragreen values? Also, obviously not. The message, not the behavior, is all.

Soros is a much more complicated matter and it is not just about the incalculable number of private jets he might have owned or commanded while bankrolling dozens of organizations warning the world of climate Armageddon or financing various foundations aimed at creating a more equal world, even as the policies of those foundations make the world less fair. These are only the tips of the Soros icebergs, melting or not. He has given billions to left-wing causes, including some extreme ones like ACORN, La Raza, the Tides Foundation, and the once valuable, now reactionary Southern Poverty Law Center. He funded MoveOn. org, whose website regularly compared George W. Bush to Adolf Hitler and ran the New York Times ad calling General David Petraeus "General Betray Us," just as the successful Petraeus-directed surge in Iraq was being launched. It's difficult to find any area of the American Left that Soros has not funded to some extent. There is too much to be rehashed here, and this is not a biography of the financier, but simply a brief attempt to explore moral narcissism and its influence on society. Suffice it to say that just as Gilbert & Sullivan's Major-General Stanley was the "very model of a modern major general," George Soros is the very model of a modern moral narcissist. He has done it all. He has achieved the heights of finance while convincing, or endeavoring to convince, the world that he is its most renowned and respected guardian, often saving it from the evils of US hegemony while living large, gigantically in fact, in Manhattan penthouses and chalets in Switzerland.

Where did this huge split come from? Soros fancies himself some kind of god. He has said as much himself, "I carried some rather potent messianic fantasies with me from childhood, which I felt I had to control, otherwise I might end up in the loony bin." The loony bin? That's rather an extreme statement from a casual interview. Is Soros hiding something, perhaps from his youth? What of his early years? Do they tell us much of his later behavior? Though it may not be a Rosebud in and of itself, his childhood holds a significant key. He discussed it at length in an interview with Steve Kroft of *60 Minutes* on December 20, 1998:

KROFT: (Voiceover) To understand the complexities and contradictions in his personality, you have to go back to the very beginning: to Budapest, where George Soros was born 68 years ago to parents who were wealthy, well-educated and Jewish. When the Nazis occupied Budapest in 1944, George Soros's father was a successful lawyer. He lived on an island in the Danube and liked to commute to work in a rowboat. But knowing there were problems ahead for the Jews, he decided to split his family up. He bought them forged papers and he bribed a government official to take 14-year-old George Soros in and swear that he was his Christian godson. But survival carried a heavy price tag. While hundreds of thousands of Hungarian Jews were being shipped off to the death camps, George Soros accompanied his phony godfather on his appointed rounds, confiscating property from the Jews. (Vintage footage of Jews walking in line; man dragging little boy in line)

KROFT: (Voiceover) These are pictures from 1944 of what happened to George Soros' friends and neighbors. (Vintage footage of women and men with bags over their shoulders walking; crowd by a train)

KROFT: (Voiceover) You're a Hungarian Jew ...

MR. SOROS: (Voiceover) Mm-hmm.

KROFT: (Voiceover) ... who escaped the Holocaust ... (Vintage footage of women walking by train)

MR. SOROS: (Voiceover) Mm-hmm. (Vintage footage of people getting on train)

KROFT: (Voiceover) ... by—by posing as a Christian.

MR. SOROS: (Voiceover) Right. (Vintage footage of women helping each other get on train; train door closing with people in boxcar)

KROFT: (Voiceover) And you watched lots of people get shipped off to the death camps.

MR. SOROS: Right. I was 14 years old. And I would say that that's when my character was made.

KROFT: In what way?

MR. SOROS: That one should think ahead. One should understand and—and anticipate events and when—when one is threatened. It was a tremendous threat of evil. I mean, it was a—a very personal experience of evil.

KROFT: My understanding is that you went out with this protector of yours who swore that you were his adopted godson.

MR. SOROS: Yes. Yes.

KROFT: Went out, in fact, and helped in the confiscation of property from the Jews.

MR. SOROS: Yes. That's right. Yes.

KROFT: I mean, that's—that sounds like an experience that would send lots of people to the psychiatric couch for many, many years. Was it difficult?

MR. SOROS: Not—not at all. Not at all. Maybe as a child you don't—you don't see the connection. But it was—it created no—no problem at all.

KROFT: No feeling of guilt?

MR. SOROS: No.

KROFT: For example that, "I'm Jewish and here I am, watching these people go. I could just as easily be there. I should be there." None of that?

MR. SOROS: Well, of course I c—I could be on the other side or I could be the one from whom the thing is being taken away. But there was no sense that I shouldn't be there, because that was—well, actually, in a funny way, it's just like in markets—that if I weren't there—of course, I wasn't doing it, but somebody else would—would—would be taking it away anyhow. And it was the—whether I was there or not, I was only a spectator, the property was being taken away. So the—I had no role in taking away that property. So I had no sense of guilt.

No sense of guilt? Methinks the magnate doth protest too much. George Soros is a man in hiding, just as he was as a youth during the Holocaust, only now he uses "righteous" causes as his disguise, rather than Christianity. I suspect he is hiding that guilt he feels from himself, because it would be very difficult to endure for many years. Perhaps it would even drive you to the loony bin. But if he isn't hiding it from himself, that is even more disturbing. Likening his behavior during the Nazi atrocities to normal business activity (" … well, actually, in a funny way, it's just like markets … "—because if ". . . I wasn't doing it, but somebody else would … ") is highly revealing and finally indefensible. It takes a lifetime of moral narcissism to justify those few phrases. Soros encapsulates himself in them, a man able to function as the most rapacious of capitalists while exhibiting a worldwide beneficent and charitable persona. After all, the supposedly normal business activity of shorting the pound in a manner that threatened the livelihood of the majority of British citizens is just as he said it was. If he didn't do it, someone else would. And some other people undoubtedly did similar things at different points. Nevertheless, the analogy between confiscating the goods of Holocaust victims and the behavior of markets is not just a bit strained. It is fully delusional—evidence of a mind working overtime, leaving no neuron untouched, in a desperate attempt to avoid culpability in what many call history's greatest evil.

It must be said, however, that Soros has done some good in the world, especially in Eastern Europe where he was to some degree influential in those countries throwing off the yoke of Soviet Communism. Still, once that was accomplished, he directed his attention to help reinstitute many of the same socialist programs across the West, including in the very countries he had helped to free. The result of this switch was and is to instill people with the same dependent spirit, the same victimology, to which they were so easily prey while in the Soviet orbit. The state—or the Soros Foundation—will provide. Essentially, through those foundations, Soros espouses socialism-lite. The irony is obvious, providing camouflage as it sets a pattern for the robber baron of the twentieth and twenty-first century. A nexus is established through which elites, that nomenklatura, rule as they always do through the dispensation of cash and perks, but now that dispensation is under the cover of good works, or at least what sound like good works. Look under the hood and you almost invariably find something more complicated, a different set of circumstances, with money dictating the game as it flows back and forth between NGOs and profit-making enterprises in sometimes unfathomable ways.

Green enterprises—of unquestioned righteousness, at least until recently—provide a particularly convivial ambiance for these

protective webs of affluence that are often no more than crony capitalism. Sometimes, they misfire badly and go belly-up publicly, as in the
previously mentioned Solyndra—the California-based solar company
that went bankrupt after receiving $535 million in federal loan guarantees
from the Obama administration—but more often a subtler game is played
that only rarely comes to the surface. Such a case involved the network
surrounding billionaire hedge fund manager and environmentalist Tom
Steyer that resulted in the February 2015 resignation of Oregon governor
John Kitzhaber. The *Wall Street Journal* headlined the story "Green Love
Is Blind" in its editorial of February 13, 2015, to explain the influence-
peddling by Kitzhaber's fiancée and live-in political adviser Cylvia Hayes
who was being paid $118,000 (evidently unreported to the IRS) by the
Clean Economy Development Center, an NGO lobbying in that field,
plus another $40,000 from an organization connected to Steyer. The
Washington Free Beacon had evidence of greater malfeasance, detailing
a web of what could be dozens of environmental profiteers whose connection to Steyer, Hayes, and Kitzhaber are being investigated and who
are being paid by a miasma of NGOs, corporations, and unions from
Tigercomm to NextGen Climate Action to the SEIU to Steyer's super
PAC. This miasma is all linked together financially in a manner reminiscent of the Mafia. (As it goes with these things, nearly everybody is on
everybody else's board.) Fortunately, however, they are not selling drugs
or prostitutes, only clean air (for the moment), evanescent as that may be
in this case. Steyer, one the biggest Democratic Party donors and said to
have a tremendous influence on Obama's environmental policies, denies
all wrongdoing and perhaps that's true. But as of this writing, the case
is ongoing, with Hayes—who evidently leveraged her relationship with
the now ex-governor to lobby for multiple environmental groups across
several states—delaying the investigation into the deepening scandal by
attempting to block an Oregon State order to turn over her emails. (There
must be something in those email waters these days.)[2]

It's only accidental, of course, that stories like this Oregon tale come
out. The country is filled with similar webs of all sorts, with the commonly accepted liberal dogma tying people together economically with
such strong bindings that nothing gets questioned. To this dominant
nomenklatura, the government must be deeply involved in the development of new energy—not only because they believe in big government

but even more because they make money that way. Government is their money sieve and distribution arm. No wonder people rarely change. The truth is of no use to them.

There is another irony here, of course. If someone in the private sector came up with a cheap and effective source of clean energy, he or she would be richer and more powerful than Henry Ford or Bill Gates in their wildest imaginations. But then, that takes work and originality, an idea. It also takes a willingness to risk. Doing it the government way, even if the payoff is a bit lower, just takes obedience.

Mitt Romney made an oft-criticized statement during the 2012 election when he was recorded privately telling a group of contributors that 47 percent of the country would never vote for him because they were on some version of the federal dole. Romney actually underestimated. The amount of people on some interlocking version of the federal dole far exceeds that, and many of those people are paid vastly in excess of that 47 percent, so far in excess that a significant number of them inhabit the reviled 1 percent. They are part of the game and have triumphed at it. The chances that they will ever change their views are negligible. They are paid off far too well. A new political term should be invented to encompass this system that is not quite socialism and not quite state capitalism but embodies aspects of both: the lower classes living under socialism with the ruling elite enjoying the benefits of state capitalism. In this sense, the United States is more like China and Russia than it would appear on the surface. It's all a matter of degree. European nations live under some version of this system as well. Income inequality is one of the catchphrases of our time, but as should be evident from the foregoing, it is built, frozen really, into the structure that we live under. The so-called charity of people like Soros works to preserve the system even as it pretends otherwise. Moral narcissism acts as the postage stamp that validates the enterprise. It seals the deal.

As I was writing these chapters, another book was published to considerable acclaim—*The Silencing* by liberal Fox News contributor Kirsten Powers. It is Ms. Powers's well-documented contention that liberals and progressives unfairly silence their opposition, making people into targets if, as she says, they "deviate on liberal sacred cow issues." These sacred cows are everywhere and, as we have seen, well entrenched. Many, now including Ms. Powers, someone respected within the liberal church, have pointed this out. That such a person is writing about this phenomenon, albeit for the conservative Regnery publishing house, is an optimistic sign. What Powers describes is the outgrowth of and justified almost exclusively by moral narcissism, although she does not address the issue from that angle.

But a curious problem remains. Powers attacks, and others have lampooned, the more outlying aspects of this silencing—trigger warnings, microaggressions, and so on—but these outliers, absurd and subject to ridicule as they are, ironically become stalking horses for the more common and increasingly acceptable methods of tarnishing people (i.e., calling them racists or homophobes when they quite clearly are not). In other words, the most extreme forms (again trigger warnings and microaggressions) are taken back or decried so that the standard calumnies—constantly calling people racists or homophobes without evidence—can continue with interruption and usually without questioning.

This is equivalent to using the Hegelian dialectic to advance moral narcissism. Trigger warnings are dismissed so that yet more absurd examples can be brought forward. Forget the cloistered environs of academe. The zeitgeist has already moved beyond it. A poll taken on May 29, 2015, by Rasmussen found 35 percent of likely voters, including 53 percent of Democrats, think illegal immigrants should be allowed to vote. Besides running roughshod over the entire concept of citizenship—what does it mean if not the right to vote?—this result seems especially disturbing since the poll was taken less than a month after FBI director, James Comey, announced the presence of ISIS in all fifty states. Comey called it a "chaotic spider web" with Muslim men, many not citizens, being radicalized across America. Apparently those 53 percent of Democrats who supported the idea of illegal aliens voting either were not aware that might include ISIS members or simply didn't care. (Better to have them voting than beheading people, right? Well, maybe.) Yet more likely, the thought of being a good person and allowing everyone to vote eclipsed considerations such as whether we were enfranchising terrorists who want to destroy Western Civilization. And best of all, the vast majority of them, ISIS or not, will vote Democratic. Moral narcissism triumphs over everything.

XXII

Unwinding—The Merry Month of May 2015

Moral narcissism reaches its height in that 2015 month ... until the next one.

Unwinding something as basic to the human psyche as moral narcissism is extremely difficult. "Extremely" may even be too mild an adverb. The catch-22s are exponential. You might even call them catch-22 squared, or catch-484. That's a lot of catches. Demonstrable facts are of little help in this either. More often than not they can be construed to be an irritation, or worse—used fallaciously to disprove themselves. That is the situation of our country now.

Some years ago, the nation's largest city, New York, was rife with crime, often of the violent sort. The streets were strewn with garbage, graffiti defaced buildings and subways, dope dealers were on every (well, too many) corners. People were giving up on New York, the pride of the United States. Then new mayor Rudolph Giuliani decided to improve the execrable situation. He and police chief William Bratton took what is known as the "broken windows" approach, having zero-tolerance for even the slightest malfeasance (broken windows). They also instituted "stop and frisk" policies to make sure potentially violent characters were not concealing weapons or drugs.

It worked. Crime went down. The murder rate went down. New York City was livable again, remarkably quickly. Yet soon enough current Mayor de Blasio—a man deeply imbued with moral narcissism—was elected and began to undo what Giuliani had done. Much as occurred in the international sphere during the years after 9/11, when a once unified nation began to question its commitment to the War on Terror and withdrew troops, the retreat was almost a preordained demonstration of human psychology. The results have been similar as well. In the international sphere, jihadists like ISIS and Boko Haram and the Islamic extremist regime of Iran dominate the Middle East and Africa as never before in recent history, at the same historical moment that violent crime has returned to the streets of New York and many other cities across America. A virtual crime wave of gun violence broke out in the spring of 2015 in the streets of a large number of American cities. This unhappy development was in great part the consequence of what is known as the "Ferguson affect"—police declining to intervene for fear that they will be accused of racism or a crime themselves. And it wasn't just Baltimore, New York City, and Ferguson, Missouri—the sites of alleged police violence—but in every part of the country. Murders reportedly rose 32 percent in Atlanta in May 2015 and shooting and violent felonies were up 25 percent in Los Angeles. The Chicago homicide rate, already notoriously bad, was up 17 percent for the period. Worst of all, blighted Baltimore saw gun violence go up 60 percent with an extraordinary thirty-two shootings reported over Memorial Day weekend.

It's not accidental that this drastic domestic situation was appearing simultaneously with the Middle East's descent into chaos. It is the inevitable outgrowth of leadership by moral narcissism. In both cases, that is what has defined Barack Obama's behavior. He projects his own feelings and beliefs onto the world, making its reality invisible to him and causing or contributing to catastrophe. In the international sphere, several morally narcissistic belief systems or apothegms are at work at once:

1. That Western imperialism is the primary cause of the poverty and totalitarianism of the Middle East.

2. That Islam is the moral equal of the Judeo-Christian tradition and that groups like ISIS are not the true Islam (despite adhering verbatim to the quintessential texts of that religion). The corollary to the second point is that *all* religions are basically the same and to be tolerated temporarily as an inconvenient holdover from a more primitive time.

3. That the state of Israel is a synthetic injection of Western values and lifestyles into the Middle East. It is an unfortunate accident of history that the Jewish state is there. A binational state would have been preferable.

4. Iranian millennialism is a temporary, superficial aberration, not an actual religious conviction. The mullahs' desire for a global Shiite caliphate will fade away as they take their normal place in the family of nations.

These beliefs are not always stated explicitly or even acknowledged, but they govern foreign policy. The domestic situation is a bit simpler, coming down to a simple truism: everything bad that happens in black America is the white man's fault because of slavery. The corollary is that Hispanic Americans (especially if they are of Mexican or Central American background and not tarnished with that convenient neologism "white Hispanics") are similarly the victims of our imperialistic culture and have the right to do as they wish, including crossing our borders at will, a kind of "brown skin privilege." This leads naturally to the belief that police are always, or usually, wrong in the way they treat minorities. Never mind that this concept is racist because it has buried not so deeply a contempt for black (and brown) people as not capable of controlling themselves or raising themselves up. In that way too it is similar to the administration's attitudes toward the Middle East that holds Arabs, notably Palestinians, in hidden disdain as also not being capable of responsibility for their own actions. Consciously or unconsciously, this is what Barack Obama projects outward with his policies.

This leads back to the question of unwinding. Is unwinding even possible while Barack Obama is the Moral Narcissist in Chief, the one who inspires others and sets the tone? Unwinding is highly unlikely, almost impossible. We are deeply in Obama's world and not about to escape until his term is over. And even after that, his Weltanschauung may continue to govern. The approved morally narcissistic beliefs continue to shift with the times and in our case the president guides the shift, smiling on it from above, inspiring it really, like a *roi soleil* beaming down approvingly in an era of instant communication. His beneficence transcends the classes. The self-defeating victim status that had been generated among the poor has been replicated and mirrored among that most privileged of classes, the college students at the elite universities. (After all, they are the ones who have been anointed eventually to take over our society and preserve the vision coming from above.) The pervasive victim culture of our campuses in which so many seem to live in constant fear of offense, becoming delicate wilting flowers that not even Christopher Lasch could have imagined, is largely attributable to this atmosphere established by Obama at the beginning of his administration. These children of Obama are the people who will have to defend Western Civilization as the adherents of the monolithic belief systems of Islamic radicalism grow in strength. It's hard to conceive of them being able to mount any kind of defense or even wanting to. They have been deliberately defanged. Many of our college campuses seem even now outposts of the Muslim Brotherhood at one remove and sometimes closer than that, hiding only under the flimsiest cover of political correctness. We are at an odd point when the children of what is known in Hollywood as "flyover country" are forced to watch over the feckless (that word is too weak) youth of the coastal middle classes. This narcissistic self-involvement is no longer restricted to the coasts, however, as the world of trigger warnings has metastasized across the country.

Meanwhile, another odd dialectic is transpiring on our campuses with standard-issue liberal professors living in fear of their extraordinarily sensitive students. One such professor wrote under a pseudonym for liberal news site *Vox* (vox.com) in June 2015: "I have intentionally adjusted my teaching materials as the political winds have shifted. (I also make sure all my remotely offensive or challenging opinions, such as this article, are expressed either anonymously or pseudonymously.) Most of my colleagues who still have jobs have done the same. We've seen bad things happen to too many good teachers—adjuncts getting axed because their evaluations dipped below a 3.0, grad students being removed from classes after a single student complaint, and so on."

What we have are essentially two tracks of moral narcissism, the older one seemingly more responsible although it truly has begotten the newer one. The younger generation, which normally craves individuation of its own, had ideological debate closed off to them. Only some variant of leftism could be true. Conservatism, even centrism, was mocked in the academy. So in order to rebel, the new generation went to the über-personal. Life was sensitivity training with an undergraduate eponymously known as "mattress girl" endlessly lugging one around Columbia University to protest a rape that did not happen and an epidemic of that crime that did not exist.

In the Merry Month of May 2015, all three threads—Islamic expansionism across the Middle East and beyond (with both ISIS and Iran on the brink of nuclear weapons of various levels), massive black discontent in our cities coupled with nonstop accusations of police racism and campus paleo-narcissism run amok—were at their height, their strains intermingling and building to a crescendo like themes at the conclusion of a symphony. Unwinding this miasma looked like a distant fantasy, especially with the Hillary Clinton candidacy looming. A split country would remain so, with moral narcissism dictating Mrs. Clinton's view of herself and excusing her behavior, her supporters able to overlook her pervasive dishonesty as long as her professed attitudes fit the narrative they all believed in. America stood on the brink of being a country that would elect a president who was a known liar even *before* she took office. This was a recipe for social disintegration, if not a national nervous breakdown. Who would be dancing on inauguration day and why?

It also was a prescription for a society unable to adapt in the face of its own demise. The Republicans, seemingly well positioned to respond to a tired and fruitless liberal narrative, were weakened themselves by a base that adhered to a socially conservative culture that was vanishing. This was particularly true in the area of same-sex marriage. A Pew poll from June 2015 revealed that 57 percent of the country approved of gay marriage, exactly the percentage that opposed it in 2001. The statistics, not surprisingly, were even more skewed for the younger generations, with millennials favoring gay marriage at 73 percent. As these younger people moved into adulthood, the coming national consensus seemed even more pronounced. This social issues tilt also accounted for the leftward shift in the body politic as evidenced by the results of a Gallup poll of May 26, 2015, which drew national attention. This poll detailed changes from 2001 to 2015. Interestingly, attitudes toward such things as approving the death penalty (63 percent approved of it in 2001; 60 percent in 2015) and "married men and women having an affair" (7 percent in 2001; 8 percent in 2015) barely changed. Even the national perspective on abortion appeared basically the same (45 percent in 2015, up from 42 percent in 2001, were pro-choice). But the acceptance of gay and lesbian relations skyrocketed from 40 percent in 2001 to 63 percent in 2015, a change of 23 percent in only fourteen years. (Also shifting is the acceptance of having a baby out of marriage, up 16 percent in that time span. This presents challenges of another sort, especially in the black community where single parent households are the norm with, as we know, unfortunate results.)

Nevertheless, gay rights clearly had become *the* civil rights issue of our time—and successfully so. From the same Pew poll, taken before the Supreme Court decision, 72 percent saw gay marriage as inevitable. This change was not motivated exclusively by liberals and progressives, but also by the libertarians who were often ahead of their more left-wing peers on this issue. This latter group has created a split within the Republican Party with its strong evangelical base. Overall only 34 percent of the party supported same-sex marriage in the Pew poll. (The libertarian branch—vague, in any case—was not tracked separately.) This division seriously threatens Republican success in the 2016 election, again particularly with younger voters. In the battle for primary voters every candidate has upheld the traditional view of marriage, but in recognition of the handwriting on the wall, have allowed, in most instances, that they would abide by the decision of the Supreme Court on the matter.

These candidates thus sought to deflect the issue, but it will not be that simple. Moral narcissism will be in full force and deployed in the general election to paint the Republican candidates, whoever they prove to be, as sexists and homophobes and, of course, racists. These accusations will be untrue, but again moral narcissism will make them *seem* true to a public that has for years, even decades, been inculcated with certain beliefs. The election of 2016 will see the influence of moral narcissism almost as never before, highlighting its ability to block positive change in America and even to negate basic democratic decision-making. Matters of gender and race are so fraught with emotional baggage that they have the capacity to obliterate the rational mind and often do. Only the most determined opposition can overcome them. The contradictions that emerge from this, particularly in the areas of gay rights and women's rights, are revealing of the superficial, one could say "knee-jerk" depth of morally narcissistic beliefs, but also of their intensity.

American feminists pay little or no attention to the brutal treatment of women in the Islamic world (clitoridectomies, honor killings, etc.—just to mention the more vicious aspects of pervasive misogyny), even to the point of reviling more militant critics of Islam like Ayaan Hirsi Ali, denying her awards or opportunities to speak at universities while concentrating on domestic issues like income inequality. The level of irony is sky-high, especially since more women are attending college than men at this point, with the income inequality issue poised to flip.

Also, Hillary Clinton, of all people, didn't bother to pay women equally in her own office, an oversight that she probably came to regret, not out of principle but because it became a campaign issue. In the area of gay rights, American advocates seem far more concerned about the attitude of many Republicans that oppose same-sex marriage on traditional religious grounds than they do about gays being thrown off towers or hanged from telephone poles as they are in the Islamic State and Iran. This can in part be justified as a social issues version of Tip O'Neill's "All politics is local," but the moral narcissism-induced myopia is at least as strong. It is a fear of going "off message" and risking examination of other issues. Ideological uniformity and conformity are characteristic of the Left even more than they are of the Right, although it appears in both.

This uniformity and conformity have become so extreme they can veer to the pathological, taking moral narcissism to unforeseen levels. Blacks have been for some time the designated victims of our society, both by themselves and by the Left. This has led to considerable social identification with blacks on the part of white youth and what we used to call the avant garde. This was recognized as far back as 1957 when Norman Mailer published "The White Negro" in *Dissent* magazine and continued through the rap era as whites of myriad stripes and nationalities started to imitate black people, adopting victimhood themselves, and occasionally making themselves rich in the process. But not until the bizarre case of Rachel Dolezal—the white woman who passed for black and eventually became the chapter head of a branch of the NAACP—did any of them pretend they actually *were* African American in reality. This was indeed moral narcissism crossing the line into pathology. Racial confusion seemed poised to be a new entry in the Diagnostic and Statistical Manual of the American Psychiatric Association, if only that catalogue of mental illness were not itself so morally narcissistic, swaying as it does, or perhaps must, with the winds of social fashion.

But the Dolezal case and its aftermath was a veritable sideshow compared to the most significant example of moral narcissism for 2015 in the global sense as we approached the midpoint of that year. That came from Pope Francis. The pope is a man who can always say "he knew best" better than anyone, because he can speak ex cathedra. He can be infallible. The June 2016 letter by the pope—"*Laudato Sii*" or "Praised Be"—urging rich nations to fight "global warming" doesn't quite claim that infallibility but it is, as the *Guardian* wrote in its headline, an "Explosive Intervention by Pope Francis Set to Transform Climate Change Debate." The British paper further called the letter to the world's 1.2 billion Catholics an "unprecedented encyclical." It is. The pope was advocating an immense wealth transfer from rich to poor countries on ethical grounds and to "honor nature," as he called it. Those rich nations were, not surprisingly, the great despoilers. (Never mind that they were also the great employers.) Natural resources were being hogged by the mighty at the expense of the weak. But in the grand tradition of moral narcissism the pope confuses his feelings with actual science in a manner similar to many described in the earlier chapter on the subject. Though a nonscientist, he chooses to ignore even the measured approach of the well-known Dr. Bjorn Lomborg who, while being one of those who admit to the possibility of a certain amount of warming, has made cogent arguments demonstrating how the massive expenditures used to prevent that unknown amount would seriously hurt the poor, whose lives these expenditures were intended to improve.[1] Indeed, the pope has conflated science with socialism, moral narcissism, as always, providing the justification.

Lest we be confused about this redistributionist politicization of science (rendering it inert and actually reactionary), Francis's right-hand man Cardinal Óscar Rodríguez Maradiaga of Honduras, who coordinates the Vatican's inner council of cardinals, made it clear, also to the *Guardian.* "The ideology surrounding environmental issues is too tied to a capitalism that doesn't want to stop ruining the environment because they don't want to give up their profits." This cliché-ridden drivel is moral narcissism given papal justification. Pope John Paul nobly fought Communism. Francis is doing his best to reinstate it.

In these depressing times, it is *truly* depressing to think of the pope as a moral narcissist, lost in self-regard. And he most assuredly isn't entirely that way. His values can and do come from the best of Christianity. But, as with all of us, these values have been distorted by the world in which we live. As I noted, we are at a period where everything is amped up, and we are near some kind of symphonic finale where we are all being tested to see if we can overcome the pervasive moral narcissism and find our way back toward that nation envisioned by our founders. Why shouldn't the pope in faraway Rome be part of that, especially in our world where nothing is far away and information is simultaneous? America remains the mother ship for moral narcissism, essentially dictating the value system under which the West lives, despite all the criticism our country receives. It's no accident we now have a pope who sounds like Barack Obama with a miter, seemingly more concerned with Gaia then he is with the fundamentalist Islam that threatens the very institution he governs. As America will be distorted, so the world will be. The founders left a system open to reform—as it has been on several occasions. But not open to be *de*formed. "A Republic if you can keep it," in Franklin's pithy expression, which I keep recalling. The founders, particularly Madison, foresaw the problem. "Ambition must be made to counteract ambition," he wrote in Federalist 51. It's almost as if he was envisioning a battle of tyrannical moral narcissists, Godzilla versus Megalon in some Japanese horror movie, so out of control that the rest of us look up terrified or, as is so often the case, join the dominant monster (culture) in its quest for control, for our own self-preservation.

For that is very much the situation we have. It has gone so far in our culture that moral narcissism has even become confused at times with what used to be called good manners. It is the habit of our day, but unlike traditional good manners, it could kill us.

XXIII

Change

How do we get out of this? And can we?

How few people really change their views. How rare they are. I suspect it's always been that way. That famous quote I referred to before, the one apparently falsely attributed to Churchill—"If you're not a liberal when you're 20, you have no heart. If you're not a conservative by the time you're 30, you have no brain"—resonant as it may be, not to mention reminiscent of Allen Sherman's 1963 "Harvey and Sheila" (*Traded their used MG/ For a new XKE/ Switched to the GOP/ That's the way things go*) doesn't happen so much in real life. The Charles Krauthammers who in 1984 were writing speeches for Walter Mondale and thirty years later were key contributors to Fox News and being awarded prizes by conservative organizations—in Krauthammer's case, ironically, the Churchill Prize at the Claremont Institute's annual dinner—are indeed rarities, even if their stories are prominently cited. "Man bites dog" is news and those who switch political sides in our culture may be just that uncommon. Ronald Reagan famously said that he did not leave the Democratic Party, the party left him. Well, it did. But most of the members stayed behind.

Moral narcissism is the enemy of change because it is the enemy of clear thinking. Therefore it is the enemy of democracy, because without the possibility of change, that form of government, republican or not, cannot exist—or more precisely, if it exists, it exists in name only, as in the

Democratic Republic of North Korea. In his 1938 essay "What I Believe," E. M. Forster gave "two cheers for democracy." Those cheers were the importance that democratic governments place on the individual and that those same governments allow for criticism. That was sufficient for Forster. A third, the novelist said, was not even needed. Moral narcissism blocks both those things, placing an emphasis on groupthink and rejecting criticism as "incorrect." (The idea that there is such a thing as "political correctness" is almost as absurd as there is such a thing as "settled science.") Until we do away with—well, at least seriously constrain—moral narcissism, we will be stuck with a static society or, worse, plunged in totalitarianism with code phrases projected on screens out of 1984's Ministry of Truth or *Animal Farm.* "Four legs good. Two legs bad," is just a pig's version of political correctness.

Orwell long ago showed the way to one of the most potent methods of doing away with moral narcissism—unrestrained ridicule. These days there are inklings of this ridicule, though hardly as pointed and effective as *Animal Farm.* Two of the better-known comics of our time, Bill Maher (who occasionally wanders off the ultraliberal reservation) and Jerry Seinfeld, have recently mocked political correctness, saying it was bad for comedy. That may seem relatively trivial, but I suggest that it is not. Humor strikes to the essence of a society and where there is fear of humor, as in the murders of the *Charlie Hebdo* cartoonists, there is fear of freedom. The unfortunate thing is that these comics are not willing to make the next step and do what Orwell did (assuming they had the talent) and take on the nomenklatura itself. There is little chance of that, however, in our culture. They are men of the mass market, concerned for their popularity. They will only go so far and no further.

That is the nature of most social criticism in today's America. Meanwhile, the morally narcissistic status quo, even under this minimal threat, reaches new levels, locking in as never before and making itself impermeable to critique, comic or otherwise. One of the more powerful, though subtle, indications of this is the revision being undertaken by the College Board, a private company, of their advanced placement test in US History. This examination, traditionally intended to be evenhanded in its approach to its subject, is moving determinedly to the left. America is no longer an "exceptional" country but just one among many as the sensibility of the test becomes "transnational." Led by NYU historian Thomas

Bender, the intention is to de-emphasize America's distinctiveness among the nations, paying more attention to our country's flaws in the questions being asked than to its moments of greatness. Since this examination is important to college admissions, students will adjust their answers and, in many instances, their thinking, accordingly. Stanley Kurtz, among others, has written about how the College Board's new approach distorts reality[1] but perhaps more importantly it codifies the dominant view, coercing the young into attitudes they did not freely adopt or often even consider. Now they have them, most often for life. Few will ever change. Democratic choice, even free will, has been headed off at the pass as these students become good little moral narcissists, living under the illusion of democracy but with their views preordained. It is almost the inverse of Marcuse's repressive tolerance. In *The Origins of Totalitarianism*, Hannah Arendt describes how the object of a totalitarian government is to gain power not just over finances and the military but over every aspect of a citizen's life, as in Nazi Germany and the USSR. That is what is being done quietly here, through the unquestioned acceptance of world views. With moral narcissism extending its grip into standardized testing, we may be closer to Arendt's vision than we know. The Least Great Generation will have achieved its goals. Change will have become impossible.

Yet some have done it. The playwright David Mamet woke up one day and discovered the world was not what he had assumed it to be. Conservative thinker David Horowitz did the same thing many years before when he abandoned his "red diaper baby" roots. They were not alone. On the other side there have been those who have changed as well, going from Right to Left: David Brock of Media Matters and Ed Schulz of MSNBC. These are rather disparate figures, to say the least, but they do share that they were able to shuck off deeply held assumptions and see the world in new ways. It could be said they adopted morally narcissistic views on their new sides, identifying too closely with a new suit of clothes. But that would be to deny them the free will of democratic decision-making. And even though, in the cases of Brock and Schulz, I do not applaud those decisions, I would not want to deny that they had made them, that they had their reasons, even if they weren't mine, even if I thought they were completely wrong.

But these are only examples in the public eye. More important is the question of why anyone, celebrated or not, is able to publicly, or even privately, alter their views with all forces—family, friends, career, even primal fears of abandonment—militating against it. What makes an individual free or courageous enough to make such a change? What makes him or her able to live without fear? Did they all have moments like Saint Paul on the road to Damascus? I hadn't and I made some change. In fact, I wrote a book about it—first called *Blacklisting Myself* and then, when slightly revised, *Turning Right at Hollywood and Vine*—trying to explain that change. But I couldn't fully. It had something to do with 9/11 but it didn't. It had something to do with the reversal of racism during the O. J. trial, but it didn't. It remained mysterious to me.

At the beginning of this book, I made mention of how this change was still a mystery to me, how moral narcissism too was finally an enigma, despite all its obvious manifestations and self-serving lies, many of which have been detailed in earlier chapters. I knew from the start that such narcissism was the enemy of change—also that they were deeply entwined—but I wasn't sure how this worked or why. Well, I am beginning to understand. It took me many pages and a much longer time, my lifetime really, to get here, but it is time to stick my toe out of the closet. I didn't have a sudden revelation like Saul of Tarsus on that famous road. No vision appeared before me. I didn't go blind for even a split second and I am not about to become a Christian. I'm still Jewish, maybe even more so. But I did open my mind to a different possibility, a deeper way of looking at the world.

XXIV

The Devil in Disguise

Seeing the devil in morally narcissistic clothes.

The last half dozen years or more have featured one depressing event after another for those of us who care about a healthy United States of America, indeed a healthy world, or even a somewhat peaceful world. I won't go over a litany of those events, many of which have been referred to in previous chapters. Many were exceptionally disturbing, including mass beheadings of the innocent and gassings of civilians, and babies lying inert.

But of all the carnage and despair, perhaps the most intimate moment, and most painful to many Americans, was the murder of nine unarmed parishioners at a prayer meeting in the Emanuel African Methodist Episcopal Church in Charleston, South Carolina. The young man who did it was a racist lunatic of some sort. The newscaster Geraldo Rivera compared him to Charles Manson. That wasn't quite apt, but it wasn't that far-off either. Even so, Manson had followers. This man did not.

I averted my eyes from the news coverage of the event. We had so many awful black-white crises in recent times, whole cities, or parts of them anyway, in flames. This was a bridge too far; a throwback to the days of the Ku Klux Klan. Had we gone that far backward? And no doubt the usual suspects would exploit the situation, reaching for their morally narcissistic bag of tricks, blaming this psychotic act on lack of gun control or any other social ill they could find, hopefully one with political/ballot box ramifications. And they did.

I averted my eyes further. Though a devoted news junkie, this was one media extravaganza I would not allow myself to be glued to. It seemed doomed to take us back decades. I was already plotting my out. Maybe fifty years of political engagement left and right had been a mistake. I should take up nature poetry and decamp to the woods. There was no hope.

Through all this miserable self-regard, my own brand of moral narcissism in a sense, I did not notice my wife tugging at my sleeve. "Did you see that boy?" she was saying. "He's amazing." I nodded my head. I had seen that boy. But I hadn't paid much attention. She was referring to a young black man on the television. Because I didn't want to listen, I had only caught bits and pieces of his statement, hardly anything. Apparently, his mother had been one of the people murdered in the church. Poor guy. I expected him to be angry. In this instance, he more than deserved to be.

But he wasn't. I sat down to watch him on the next endless loop of cable news. His name was Chris Singleton and he was nineteen years old, standing on a baseball field with teammates about to play a game only twenty-four hours after his mother had been shot in a hate crime. He spoke to the camera in a methodical yet heartfelt manner. There was no blame in Chris when he spoke. Instead he said, "We forgive the shooter," and delivered the simplest of words that sent chills down my back: "Love is always stronger than hate. So, if we just love the way my Mom would, then the hate won't be anywhere close to where the love is."

In the person of Chris Singleton good had pushed aside evil, even forgiven it. Not so for others. Surrounding this magnificent young man, the grown-ups played out their charades, exploiting the situation. Barack Obama called for more gun control. Hilary Clinton demanded yet more discussions about race, our national nightmare/scab needing more endless scratching. She said race remained a "deep fault line" in our culture, implying that she was the one to heal it and that we should vote for her.

But was this about race or something deeper? Of course, at first glance it would seem that it was race. Dylann Roof was a classic Southern racist child out of a KKK documentary with his apartheid flags and calls for Jews to turn blue for twenty-four hours so they could be identified. Still, oddly, he had had black friends, at least some of whom had never heard him make racist statements. You could say he was just an extreme clinical psychotic, some variant of homicidal maniac that should have been shuttered away in a hospital for the criminally insane to avoid his doing violence, that this was ultimately a medical issue. But in reality that didn't begin to encompass or explain what had happened, the unspeakable brutality of the act. Roof had sat there quietly with these churchgoers for an hour as they prayed, all the while knowing he was about to kill as many of them as possible. Was this racism or insanity or something even worse?

Puzzling this out, I thought back to 2009 when I had been in Geneva to cover the Durban Review Conference—a United Nations-sponsored festival of anti-Semitism masquerading as a human rights conclave. There I came face-to-face with Mahmoud Ahmadinejad, the then infamous president of Iran who had often called for the annihilation of Israel and denied the Holocaust, among other dastardly accusations, and was to give a keynote speech to the conference. Unbeknownst to me, Ahmadinejad was staying in my hotel and, while I was standing in the relatively small lobby talking, he entered with his security phalanx. He passed within five feet of me, paused, and smiled directly at me, waving as if he were on a reviewing stand and I were an admirer. I immediately felt overcome with nausea, staring at someone I hated as much as anyone in the world, a modern Hitler.

My head started to swim. I had never felt anything quite like it. What was I looking at? Most of my life I would have regarded this as a clinical question. I was looking at someone criminally insane, who should be hospitalized, but this was something more, something not explained by science. I felt as if I were inside a movie like *The Exorcist*, the willing suspension of disbelief having taken over. I was staring at pure evil, the devil in disguise.

Looking at a photo of Dylann Roof I felt much the same thing. It wasn't as extreme as Ahmadinejad, of course, who had within him the capacity and political stature to instigate genocide. Root was a small-time character of the most common sort. But the atmosphere and mood were the same. Again, it was the devil in disguise.

Now I don't really believe in the devil. More precisely I don't *literally* believe in him. But I have come to believe in something metaphorical that is inside humanity, a representation of evil and a, I guess concrete in some way, manifestation of our obvious ability to commit horrendous acts—all of us. Is this the devil? Who knows? But whatever it is, it is beyond, as far as I know, the ability of science to explain and it is truly terrifying, just as Ahmadinejad and Root were, just as all the evildoers, big and small, of history have been. If Adolf Hitler were merely the product of bad parenting or some DNA problem, then there would be multiple millions of Hitlers and, in all probability, the human race would be extinct.

Moral narcissism evolved in part to hide this, to obscure the reality of this human evil from our vision, to occlude the devil, metaphorical or real. It is a way of explaining away evil, blaming all ills on social causes and therefore pushing back the necessity of examining the human soul or one's own, of not seeing the possible darkness within, the levels on which we all contain that evil within us. This creates a peril to society of its own sort, as great in its way as the peril discussed throughout earlier parts of this book—that moral narcissism obscures reality and therefore threatens democracy. That not everything is perfectible, that there is evil in the world, and that evil is likely to remain forever; it is knowledge we must all countenance. But moral narcissism prevents many from doing so. It is another version of the devil in disguise, just not the one in the Elvis recording.

That aforementioned Least Great Generation of which I am a member is greatly culpable in this evolution to the nonexistence of evil. John Lennon's "Imagine," a song that once brought tears to my eyes, is a literal anthem to the morality of an atheism sought to achieve this. It is a musical masterpiece of moral narcissism.

Imagine there's no heaven
It's easy if you try . . .

Speaking of imagine, it's not difficult to imagine how Lennon would have explained the actions of Dylann Roof and Ahmadinejad. The former would have been some mélange of institutionalized racism and the Confederate flag and the latter the product of centuries of Western imperialism. The possibility of evil is gone from the equation and the villain returned to its proper place—bourgeois capitalism, especially of the God-fearing sort. At the same time, the responsibility for doing something real about the problem or problems is diminished—the song is all. If you have sung it, if you have agreed with its message, you have done your job. Back to business as usual, which is usually, ironically, bourgeois capitalism, sometimes at its most rapacious and absent the God-fearing. The Beatles are, and were, a money machine.

Unfortunately, however, the answer to evil in the world—the ISIS and the ayatollah and everything else—is not a song. It is the recognition of evil and the will to oppose it. Moral narcissism—the devil's game—must be brushed aside. (Is it just amusing or accidental that John Lennon, way back in 1963, branded "The Devil in Disguise" as one of Elvis's worst songs and said of Presley "I don't like him anymore"? He also said Elvis now sounded like Bing Crosby, which apparently, in the Lennon canon, was not a compliment.[1]

The question that still arises is how to make a legitimate, solid connection between the genuine evil of a Dylann Roof or a Mahmoud Ahmadinejad and what superficially seems like the (often absurd) propaganda of the more extreme manifestations of moral narcissism. In actuality, evidence of this relationship appears almost every day, if we want to confront or even think about it. Moral narcissist ideation is working overtime to create an atmosphere of hatred and distrust while pretending to exactly the opposite. On the exact day I was concluding this chapter, an article was published in the *Daily Beast*—"The University of California's Insane Speech Police"—that is as good an example of this as you could find. Such statements as "America is a melting pot," "Why are you so quiet?" and "I believe the most qualified person should get the job," are now considered racist or sexist by the administration and faculty of what is regarded as our finest public university, according to the article's author, Robby Soave. The direct line of the restriction on speech inherent in these so-called microaggressions—akin to the behavior of the Islamic Republic of Iran that regularly imprisons citizens for their thoughts and ideas—is evident. The connection to Roof may not seem as clear, but

190 I KNOW BEST

the result of the invention of microaggressions—and they are an invention—is to make racial tension forever irresolvable. There will always be
a new microaggression to throw into the mix, and then another. Thus the
pot is constantly stirred, anger continued, and the Dylann Roofs of the
world forever provided with new deranged justifications for their deeds,
into an unknown future.

Moral narcissism is the very petri dish of evil.

XXV

Envoi: Confessions of a Libertarian Neocon

Living an oxymoron.

Everybody has his reasons, as filmmaker Jean Renoir famously said. A more contemporary way of saying that might be everybody has his biases or everybody has his narrative.

If you accept that idea, however, there is no truth. And I don't accept that. What I do accept, though, is that you lay your cards on the table. You make your biases clear. Just as an unbiased newspaper does not exist, so an unbiased person does not exist. Bias is as American as apple pie ... or as human as ... pick any form of sustenance you want.

So my argument against moral narcissism, my contention that it is the villain in our society unto a veritable *fleur du mal*, is tarnished by my own bias, my own vision of the truth, my own moral narcissism, if you will.

That is why I am confessing, if you have not already pieced it together, that I am a libertarian neocon. What!?, you might ask. In a certain sense, such a thing cannot exist. Libertarian neocon is an oxymoron, the former being the most laissez-faire and noninterventionist of people and the latter being the ultimate busybody, seeking to reform the world everywhere always. I resolve the contradiction this way: I am a libertarian (mostly or often) domestically, and an interventionist (mostly or often) internationally.

Libertarianism is an idealistic ideology to which we can give, as Forster put it of democracy, two cheers. It generally ... sort of, kind of ... works. No system does more than that in any case. All ideologies should be limited. Leave people alone and they have a better chance of succeeding, a still better chance of feeling good about themselves and their accomplishments. Attempt to bolster them continually with government interventions, "nanny state" them endlessly, and you destroy their souls and their confidence—usually. It's like a family. If Cousin Phil has a heroin problem and you give him little bits of it, coddling him and hoping to ease him off the drug, chances are he won't get off it. Chances are it will go the other way and addict him further, often for life. Give Phil some tough love, refuse the horse (or whatever it is), and there's at least hope.

It took me many years to realize that this was the promise of America, that this was a magnificent country because it left us substantially alone. As the state started to intrude more into our lives, I realized how self-defeating that was, however well intentioned, however carefully supported, as it almost always was, by moral narcissism. This was or was not what we ought to be doing, what the good person did. That doesn't mean that I think all state interventions are bad. It just means I think less is almost always more.

But for me libertarianism ends abruptly at the water's edge. The evil-doers of the world—the Ayatollah Khameneis, al-Assads, al-Baghdadis, and Putins, and whatever other candidates come to the fore, as they eventually will—could care less about the degree to which our economy is managed or our laws intrusive. Their only interest is controlling or destroying us. Those who wish to roll up the gangplanks and live in some libertarian nirvana, letting the rest of the world stew, strike me as naive beyond words. If you want to have paradise—or even a halfway decent existence—you have to be prepared to defend it.

So that's my moral narcissism—how "I know best." Factor it in, but as you do, be sure to factor in that of others. It's all around us, the most prevalent disease of our times. I have it, you have it, and everyone else has it too.

ACKNOWLEDGMENTS
(Actually a dedication in the back.)

Having been for decades a novelist and screenwriter, my life took an abrupt turn in 2004 when I co-founded the online media company *PJ Media* (then *Pajamas Media*). A neophyte at the opinion writing we would be featuring, I had the honor and pleasure of hiring a group of extraordinary writers who were far more experienced in this area than I was, and I got to learn from them. I am forever in their debt and wish to acknowledge them by dedicating this book to them.

In alphabetical order, they are: J. Christian Adams, Ed Driscoll, Richard Fernandez, David Goldman, Stephen Green, Victor Davis Hanson, Bridget Johnson, Roger Kimball (editor of this book), Andrew Klavan, Michael Ledeen, Andrew McCarthy, Ron Radosh, Glenn Reynolds, Claudia Rosett, Helen Smith, Michael Walsh, and Bill Whittle.

I also would like to acknowledge *PJ Media* managing editor Aaron Hanscom for his support of my work as I segued from CEO/entrepreneur to traveling scribe covering the 2016 presidential campaign in Diary of a Mad Voter.

My wife, Sheryl Longin, is, was, and always will be my first and best critic. I dedicate everything to her.

NOTES

I. WHY THIS?

1. Jeffrey Herf, "Reframing the Enemy after France's 9/11," *The Blogs* (blog), *Times of Israel*, Jan. 17, 2015, http://blogs.timesofisrael.com/reframing-the-enemy-after-frances-911/.

III. *QU'EST-CE QUE C'EST* "MORAL NARCISSISM"?

1. "Democracy! Whisky! Sexy!," *Command Post* weblog (blog), posted by Dean Esmay, *New York Times*, April 3, 2003, http://www.command-post.org/archives/003688.html.

IV. WHO WAS THE KING OF ALL MORAL NARCISSISTS?

1. Ingrid Carlqvist, "Sweden Close to Collapse," Gatestone Institute, Oct. 17, 2015, http://www.gatestoneinstitute.org/6697/sweden-collapse.

2. Salameh Nematt, "Bill's $500,000 Kuwait Lecture," *Daily Beast*, Nov. 17, 2008, http://www.thedailybeast.com/articles/2008/11/17/bills-500000-kuwait-lecture.html.

VI. THE WEATHER

1. Abby Ohlheiser, "Bill Nye: Stop Calling Sen. Inhofe a Climate Change 'Skeptic,'" *Washington Post*, Dec. 12, 2014, http://www.washingtonpost.com/news/post-nation/wp/2014/12/12/bill-nye-stop-calling-sen-inhofe-a-climate-change-skeptic/.

2. Alex Epstein, "'97% Of Climate Scientists Agree' is 100% Wrong," *Forbes*, Jan. 6, 2015, http://www.forbes.com/sites/alexepstein/2015/01/06/97-of-climate-scientists-agree-is-100-wrong/.

3. Anthony Watts, "97 Articles Refuting the '97% Consensus' on Global Warming," *WattsUpWithThat* (blog), Dec. 19, 2014, http://wattsupwiththat.com/2014/12/19/97-articles-refuting-the-97-consensus-on-global-warming/.

4. Christopher Booker, "The Fiddling with Temperature Data Is the Biggest Science Scandal Ever," *Telegraph*, Feb. 7, 2015, http://www.telegraph.co.uk/news/earth/environment/globalwarming/11395516/The-fiddling-with-temperature-data-is-the-biggest-science-scandal-ever.html.

5. "Global Warming or the 'New Ice Age'? Fear of the 'Big Freeze,'" *Global Research*, Jan. 2, 2013, http://www.globalresearch.ca/global-warming-or-the-new-ice-age-fear-of-the-big-freeze/30336.

6. Christopher Booker, "The Scandal of Fiddled Global Warming Data," *Telegraph*, June 21, 2014, http://www.telegraph.co.uk/news/earth/environment/10916086/The-scandal-of-fiddled-global-warming-data.html.

7. Ted Thornhill, "Humans Are Not to Blame for Global Warming, Says Greenpeace Co-founder, as He Insists There Is 'No Scientific Proof' Climate Change Is Manmade," *Daily Mail*, Feb. 27, 2014, http://www.dailymail.co.uk/sciencetech/article-2569215/Humans-not-blame-global-warming-says-Greenpeace-founder-Patrick-Moore.html.

8. Lawrence Torcello, "Is Misinformation about the Climate Criminally Negligent?," *The Conversation*, March 13, 2014, https://theconversation.com/is-misinformation-about-the-climate-criminally-negligent-23111.

VII. FOR THE BIRDS

1. "Malaria Victims: How Environmentalist Ban on DDT Caused 50 Million Deaths," *Discover the Networks*, http://www.discoverthenetworks.org/viewSubCategory.asp?id=1259.

2. Eric Holthaus, "Hundreds of Private Jets Delivered People to Davos. Also, It's Climate Change Day at Davos," *Future Tense* (blog), *Slate,* Jan. 23, 2015, http://www.slate.com/blogs/future_tense/2015/01/23/davos_climate_change_hundreds_of_private_jets_at_the_world_economic_forum.html.

VIII. WONDERFUL COPENHAGEN

1. "Tuvalu Prime Minister Enele Sopoaga Says Climate Change 'Like a Weapon of Mass Destruction,'" ABC News, August 15, 2014, http://www.abc.net.au/news/2014-08-15/an-tuvalu-president-is-climate-change-27like-a-weapon-of-mass-/5672696.

2. NOAA, National Weather Forecast Service Office, Pago Pago, American Samoa, http://www.weather.gov/climate/xmacis.php?wfo=samoa.

3. Rowena Mason, "Copenhagen Climate Summit: Carbon Trading Fraudsters in Europe Pocket €5bn," *Telegraph*, Dec. 10, 2009, http://www.telegraph.co.uk/news/earth/copenhagen-climate-change-confe/6778003/Copenhagen-climate-summit-Carbon-trading-fraudsters-in-Europe-pocket-5bn.html.

4. Claudia Rosett and George Russell, "At the United Nations, the Curious Career of Maurice Strong," Fox News, Feb. 8, 2007, http://www.foxnews.com/story/2007/02/08/at-united-nations-curious-career-maurice-strong/.

5. Greg Pollowitz, "R.I.P.: Al Gore's Chicago Climate Exchange Has Died," *National Review Online*, http://www.nationalreview.com/planet-gore/252703/rip-al-gores-chicago-climate-exchange-has-died-greg-pollowitz.

6. Associated Press, "The Heat is On; NOAA, NASA Say 2014 Warmest Year on Record," *MyWay,* Jan. 16, 2015, http://apnews.myway.com/article/20150116/us-sci--hottest_year-b64ea00652.html.

7. Marc Morano, "Scientists Balk at 'Hottest Year' Claims: Ignores Satellites Showing 18 Year 'Pause'—'We Are Arguing over the Significance of Hundredths of a Degree'—The 'Pause' Continues," *Climate Depot*, Jan. 16, 2015, http://www.climatedepot.com/2015/01/16/scientists-balk-at-hottest-year-claims-we-are-arguing-over-the-significance-of-hundredths-of-a-degree-the-pause-continues/#ixzz3wahD2hTA.

8. Justin Gillis, "Clouds' Effect on Climate Change Is Last Bastion for Dissenters," *New York Times*, April 30, 2012, http://www.nytimes.com/2012/05/01/science/earth/clouds-effect-on-climate-change-is-last-bastion-for-dissenters.html?_r=0.

9. Colin Fernandez, "Wrap Up, a Mini Ice Age May Be Heading Our Way! Met Office Issues Warning That Temperatures Could Plummet as Sun Enters Cooler Phase," *Daily Mail*, June 23, 2015, http://www.dailymail.co.uk/news/article-3136780/You-need-wrap-UK-set-plunge-mini-ice-age-Met-Office-warns-one-five-chance-temperatures-drop-leaves-seen-17th-century.html.

10. Evan McMurray, "Meteorologist Apologizes for Juno Storm Forecast: We Didn't Get It Right," *Mediaite* (blog), Jan. 27, 2015, http://www.mediaite.com/online/meteorologist-apologizes-for-juno-storm-forecast-we-didnt-get-it-right/.

11. Ronald Bailey, "Temperature Record Chicanery: An Overhyped Scandal," *Hit & Run Blog* (blog), *Reason*, Feb. 11, 2015, http://reason.com/blog/2015/02/11/temperature-record-chicanery-an-overhype.

12. Paul Dorian, "The Sun Has Gone Quiet Again during the Weakest Solar Cycle in More than a Century," *Vencore Weather*, Feb. 17, 2015, http://vencoreweather.com/2015/02/17/29475/.

IX. NOSTALGIA FOR RACISM

1. Ian Hanchett, "Mayor Thanks Sharpton for Climate Change Work during Blizzard Report," *Breitbart News Network*, Jan. 26, 2015, http://www.breitbart.com/video/2015/01/26/mayor-thanks-sharpton-for-climate-change-work-during-blizzard-report/.

2. Rakesh Kochhar and Richard Fry, "Wealth Inequality Has Widened Along Racial, Ethnic Lines since End of Great Recession," Pew Research Center, Dec. 12, 2014, http://www.pewresearch.org/fact-tank/2014/12/12/racial-wealth-gaps-great-recession/.

3. Ibid.

4. Gerald Prante, "Obama and Gibson Capital Gains Tax Exchange," *The Tax Policy Blog* (blog), Tax Foundation, April 17, 2008, http://taxfoundation.org/blog/obama-and-gibson-capital-gains-tax-exchange.

5. U.S. Department of Labor, Bureau of Labor Statistics, Economic News Release, *Employment Status of the Civilian Population by Race, Sex, and Age*, table A.2, http://www.bls.gov/news.release/empsit.to2.htm.

6. Drew DeSilver, "Black Incomes Are up, but Wealth Isn't," Pew Research Center, Aug. 30, 2013, http://www.pewresearch.org/fact-tank/2013/08/30/black-incomes-are-up-but-wealth-isnt/.

X. BOOKER T. WASHINGTON REALLY DID KNOW BEST

1. "So, When Does Rev. Al Sharpton's Suspension Begin?," *Smoking Gun*, Feb. 11, 2015, http://www.thesmokinggun.com/documents/investigation/al-sharpton-lies-657391.

XI. SELFIES FROM RAQQA

1. "Transcript of President Bush's Address," CNN, September 21, 2001. http://edition.cnn.com/2001/US/09/20/gen.bush.transcript/.

XII. ISLAM DENIALISM

1. Sayyid Qutb, *Milestones* (Delhi, India: Islamic Book Service, 2006), 139.
2. David Von Drehle, "A Lesson in Hate," *Smithsonian*, Feb. 2006, http://www.smithsonianmag.com/history/a-lesson-in-hate-109822568/?no-ist.

XIII. THE MORAL NARCISSIST SLEEP ROOM

1. Shelby Grad, "American Al Qaeda Member Adam Gadahn Tells of Jewish Roots in Video," *LA Now* (blog), *LA Times*, June 14, 2009, http://latimesblogs.latimes.com/lanow/2009/06/american-al-Qaeda-adam-gadahn-talks-about-jewish-southern-california-roots-in-new-video.html.
2. Susan Jones, "Pelosi: Qataris Have Told Me 'Hamas Is a Humanitarian Organization,'" CNS News, July 28, 2014, http://cnsnews.com/news/article/susan-jones/pelosi-qataris-have-told-me-hamas-humanitarian-organization.

XV. LUXURIOUS LEFTISM

1. Ruth Marcus, "Ruth Marcus: Chinese Women Face a Political Ceiling That's Hard to Shatter," *Washington Post*, May 30, 2014, http://www.washingtonpost.com/opinions/ruth-marcus-chinese-women-face-a-political-ceiling-thats-hard-to-shatter/2014/05/30/cfbee3ac-e818-11e3-a86b-362fd5443d19_story.html.
2. Cristina Corbin, "Constitution Experts on Obama Mandatory Voting Idea: Never Gonna Happen," Fox News, March 20, 2015, http://www.foxnews.com/politics/2015/03/20/mandatory-voting-experts/.

XVI. ANATOMY OF THE AMERICAN NOMENKLATURA

1. Arnold Schwarzenegger, "Schwarzenegger: Indiana's Religious Freedom Law Is Bad for Republicans," *Washington Post*, April 3, 2015, http://www.washington-post.com/posteverything/wp/2015/04/03/schwarzenegger-indianas-religious-freedom-law-is-bad-for-america-and-bad-for-republicans/.
2. Scott Jaschik, "Moving Further to the Left," *Inside Higher Ed*, October 24, 2012, https://www.insidehighered.com/news/2012/10/24/survey-finds-professors-already-liberal-have-moved-further-left.

XVII. THE MEDIA IS THE (MORAL NARCISSIST'S) MESSAGE

1. Christopher Krebs and Christine Lindquist, "Setting the Record Straight on '1 in 5,'" *Time*, December 15, 2014, http://time.com/3633903/campus-rape-1-in-5-sexual-assault-setting-record-straight/.
2. Elizabeth Bruenig, "Rolling Stone's Rape Article Failed Because It Used Rightwing Tactics to Make a Leftist Point," *New Republic*, April 6, 2015, http://www.newrepublic.com/article/121462/rolling-stone-retracts-uva-rape-story-after-cjr-report.
3. Patrick Healy, "In Perception Primary, It's Folksy Hillary Clinton vs. Statesmen-Looking Jeb Bush and Marco Rubio," *New York Times*, April 14, 2015, http://www.nytimes.com/2015/04/15/us/politics/its-just-folks-hillary-clinton-vs-global-leader-republicans-jeb-bush-and-marco-rubio-in-perception-primary.html?_r=0.
4. Jon Cohen, "Gay Marriage Support Hits New High in Post-ABC Poll," *The Fix* (blog), *Washington Post*, March 18, 2013, http://www.washingtonpost

.com/blogs/the-fix/wp/2013/03/18/gay-marriage-support-hits-new-high-in-post-abc-poll/.

5. David Martosko, "Dartmouth College Students Dish on Hillary's White House Hopes, Saying 'There Was Blood on Her Hands' in Benghazi and 'She Wants the Job More than She Would Be Good at It,'" *Daily Mail*, April 20, 2015, http://www.dailymail.co.uk/news/article-3046586/Dartmouth-College-students-dish-Hillary-s-White-House-hopes-saying-blood-hands-Benghazi.html.

6. The Heritage Guide to the Constitution, Emoluments Clause, http://www.heritage.org/constitution/#!/articles/1/essays/68/emoluments-clause.

7. Brandy Zadrozny, "Exclusive: Ben Affleck's Ancestor Did Not Own Slaves, Tax Documents Show," *Daily Beast*, April 28, 2015, http://www.thedailybeast.com/articles/2015/04/28/exclusive-ben-affleck-s-ancestor-did-not-own-slaves-tax-documents-show.html.

8. Michael Patrick Leahy, "Now 14 Known Slaveholding Ancestors of Ben Affleck throughout the South," *Breitbart News Network*, April 29, 2015, http://www.breitbart.com/big-government/2015/04/29/now-14-known-slaveholding-ancestors-of-ben-affleck-throughout-the-south/.

9. "Bill Maher vs. Ben Affleck on Islam: 'Mafia That Will F**king Kill You If You Say the Wrong Thing,'" *Real Clear Politics*, Oct. 3, 2014, http://www.realclearpolAitics.com/video/2014/10/03 bill_maher_vs_ben_affleck_on_islam_mafia_that_will_fucking_kill_you_if_you_say_the_wrong_thing.html.

XVIII. NOSTALGIA FOR CLASS CONSCIOUSNESS

1. S. A. Miller and Dave Boyer, "Hillary Clinton Seizes on Baltimore Riots, Calls for Criminal Justice Reforms," *Washington Times*, April 29, 2015, http://www.washingtontimes.com/news/2015/apr/29/hillary-clinton-seizes-on-baltimore-riots-calls-fo/?page=all.

2. Daniel Halper, "O'Malley to Announce in Baltimore, Make City Central to Campaign," *Weekly Standard*, May 3, 2015, http://www.weeklystandard.com/blogs/omalley-announce-baltimore-make-city-central-campaign_936812.html.

3. Michael S. Rosenwald and Michael A. Fletcher, "Why Couldn't $130 Million Transform One of Baltimore's Poorest Places?," *Washington Post*, May 2, 2015, http://www.washingtonpost.com/local/why-couldnt-130-million-transform-one-of-baltimores-poorest-places/2015/05/02/0467ab06-f034-11e4-a55f-38924fca94f9_story.html?hpid=z1.

XIX. BANG! BANG! YOU'RE NOT DEAD!

1. Stephen P. Halbrook, "How the Nazis Used Gun Control," *National Review Online*, Dec. 2, 2013, http://www.nationalreview.com/article/365103/how-nazis-used-gun-control-stephen-p-halbrook.

XXI. THE MOTHER'S MILK OF MORAL NARCISSISM

1. Mailonline Reporter, "Leonardo DiCaprio the 'Eco Warrior' Flew on a Private Jet from NY to LA SIX Times in SIX Weeks, Sony Hack Documents Reveal," *Daily Mail*, April 17, 2015, http://tinyurl.com/nr6mm28.

2. Erik Telford, "Oregon's Kitzhaber Scandal Goes Much Deeper than His Fiancée," *Watchdog*, March 16, 2015, http://watchdog.org/206109/oregons-kitzhaber-scandal-goes-much-deeper-fiancee/.

XXII. UNWINDING—THE MERRY MONTH OF MAY 2015

1. Gloria Galloway, "Dr. Bjorn Lomborg Argues the Climate Change Fight Isn't Worth the Cost," *Globe and Mail*, June 12, 2015, http://www .theglobeandmail.com/news/politics/the-professor-who-claims-the-global-warming-fight-is-too-expensive/article24950894/.

XXIII. CHANGE

1. Stanley Kurtz, "How the College Board Politicized U.S. History," *National Review Online*, Aug. 25, 2014, http://www.nationalreview.com/corner/386202/how-college-board-politicized-us-history-stanley-kurtz.

XXIV. THE DEVIL IN DISGUISE

1. Jay Spangler, "John Lennon Interview: Juke Box Jury 6/22/1963," *BeatlesInterviews.org*, June 22, 1963, http://www.beatlesinterviews.org/db1963.0622.jukebox.jury.john.lennon.html.

INDEX

Abbas, Mahmoud, 151
ABC network, 58, 129–130, 138
Abedin, Dr. Saleha Mahmood, 94
Abedin, Huma, 94
Abortion, 14, 77, 176
Academy. *See* Universities and colleges
ACORN, 164
Acton, Lord, 113, 139
Adams, J. Christian, 64–65
Affleck, Ben, 141–143
Affordable Care Act: moral narcissism of elites and, 22, 93; nostalgia for Marxism and, 110–112
Ahmadinejad, Mahmoud, 187–188, 189
Al Qaeda, 76–78, 82, 83, 87, 90, 97–100; Muslim Brotherhood and, 76, 93–94
Alinsky, Saul, 11, 94, 96, 106–107, 139
Amanpour, Cristiane, 99
America in Retreat (Stephens), 20
American Economic Review, 105
Anderson Robbins Research, 95–96
Animal Farm (Orwell), 75, 182
Ansar al-Islam, 98, 162
Arendt, Hannah, 183
Aristophanes, 157
Arkansas, 120
Arts and entertainment, 124–125; liberalism and, 139–140; nostalgia for Marxism and, 102–103, 114–115; political correctness and, 150–151
Askin, Frank, 112
Assad, Asma al-, 52
Assad, Bashar al-, 52, 97, 192
Atheism. *See* Religion, US culture and drift away from
Atlanta, GA, crime in 2015, 172

Ayers, Bill, 96
"Azzam the American" (Adam Yahiye Gadahn), 90, 95

Babacool. See Least Great Generation (*babacool*)
"Back in the USSR" (Beatles), 18
Bailey, Ronald, 47
Baker, James, 79
Baltimore, MD: crime in 2015, 172; failure of liberal social programs in, 146–147; unrest in, 50, 51–52, 64, 145–148
Banna, Hassan al-, 86
Barnes, Fred, 59
Battle of Tours (732), 76, 89
Beatles, 18
Beatty, Warren, 102
"Beer Summit," 51, 61–63, 141
Bender, Thomas, 182–183
Benghazi, Libya, 98–99, 132, 138, 162
Bin Laden, Usama, 78, 86; captured hard drive of, 97–99
"Black Lives Matter," 51, 65, 70
Black Panther Party, 51, 54, 61
Black persons, income inequality and, 52–53, 58–60. *See also* Racism
Blacklisting Myself (Simon), 184
Blair, Jason, 131
Blood Feud: The Clintons vs. the Obamas (Klein), 94
Blumenthal, Sidney, 93–94, 95, 161–163
Bond, Julian, 54
Brandeis University, 62, 104
Bratton, William, 171
Breitbart, Andrew, 69

Breitbart News Network, 142
Bretherton, Christopher S., 43
Brock, David, 183
"Broken windows" policing strategy, 171
Brown, Michael, 51, 64, 129
Brown, Norman O., 17
Brown v. the Board of Education, 53
Bruenig, Elizabeth Stoker, 128–129
Buckley, William F., 23
Bush, George W., 78–79, 97, 128, 164

California State University system, 123
Cap-and-trade. See Carbon exchanges
Capital gains tax, Obama and "fairness,"
    58–59
Capital in the Twenty-First Century
    (Piketty), 104–105
Capitalism: environmentalism and
    crony capitalism, 33, 40–42, 116,
    167–169; versus socialism, 15–16;
    state capitalism, 169; university
    endowments and, 103. See also
    Money
Carbon exchanges, crony capitalism
    and, 33, 40–42
Carson, Dr. Ben, 52, 71, 147, 153–154
Carson, Rachel, 35
Castro, Fidel, 103, 107, 148–149
Castro, Mariela, 103
Castro, Raul, 103
CBS network, 20, 128, 129–130
Chamberlain, Neville, 92
Change: examples of, in politics,
    183–184; moral narcissism and failure
    to change opinions, 1–2, 12; moral
    narcissism as enemy of democracy
    and, 181–183, 184
Charleston, SC shootings. See Emanuel
    African Methodist Episcopal Church
    (Charleston, SC)
Charlie Hebdo attack, 1–2, 83, 182
Chicago, IL, crime in 2015, 172
Chicago Climate Exchange, 41
China, 16–17, 109, 115
Choudary, Anjem, 74
Christianity: Islam and moral

equivalency, 75–76, 82; persecution of
    Christians, 83, 84
Churchill, Ward, 104
Churchill, Winston, 113, 181
Class consciousness, nomenklatura's
    self-preservation and, 145–152
Clean Economy Development Center,
    168
Climate change, 25–48; belief
    system and political purpose
    of, 26–29; crony capitalism and
    environmentalism, 33, 40–42, 116,
    163–164, 167–169; "deniers" of, 26,
    29, 32; environmentalism replacing
    conservationism, 29–30, 35–38;
    importance of shielding science
    from politics and ideology, 29–30;
    media and, 31; moral narcissism
    and, 19–20, 46–48; Pope Francis
    and, 177–179; public opinion about,
    30, 47; questionable data about,
    31–32; as "religion," 35–38, 48; seen
    as dominate national security threat,
    26, 30, 41, 43–44, 85; "settled science"
    as oxymoron and, 28–29; success of
    initial environmental movement and
    need for new cause, 32–33; usefulness
    of changing "global warming" to, 26,
    31
Climate Depot (blog), 42
Clinton, Bill, 18, 52, 58, 106, 137, 148,
    161–162
Clinton, Hillary, 116, 145, 148; Alinsky
    and, 11, 94, 96, 106–107, 139; Benghazi
    and, 98–99, 132, 138, 162; Egypt and,
    80, 81, 94, 95; election of 2016 and,
    128, 132–133; email scandal and, 105–
    107, 109, 134; foreign contributions
    and, 137–138; gun control and,
    186; Islam and, 93–94, 95; leftist
    background of, 96; moral narcissism
    and, 11, 18–19; self-enrichment
    and, 161–163; social policy and, 136;
    women's pay and, 177
Clinton Cash: The Untold Story of How
    and Why Foreign Governments and

Businesses Helped Make Bill and Hillary Rich (Schweizer), 137, 138–139
Clinton Foundation, 94, 137–139, 141, 162
Coll, Steve, 127
College Board, political correctness and, 182–183
College Fix website, 123, 134
Colleges. *See* Universities and colleges
Columbia School of Journalism, 127–128
Columbia Spectator, 150
Columbia University, 174
Comey, James, 170
Committee for Skeptical Inquiry, 26
Communism: moral narcissism and, 16–17; "new man" and, 29. *See also* Marxism, nostalgia for
Communist Manifesto, The, 5–6
Conservationism, abandoned for environmentalism, 29–30, 35–38
Constitution of US, Emoluments Clause of, 137–138
Copenhagen Climate Change Conference (2009), 25, 39–41
Coptic Christians, beheading of, 83, 84
Countering Violent Extremism summit (2015), 83
Crime, in 2015, 171–172
Crony capitalism, environmentalism and, 33, 40–42, 116, 163–164, 167–169. *See also* Money
Crowley, James, 61–63
Cuba, 46, 103, 148–149
Cultural relativism, 16, 45; Islam and, 73–74; political correctness and, 149
Culture of Narcissism, The (Lasch), 7

Daily Beast, 142, 189
"Dalton Minimum," of solar activity, 47–48
DDT, results of ban of, 35
De Blasio, Bill, 46, 51, 68, 69, 171–172
Death penalty, public opinion and, 176
Declaration of Independence, 158
Delingpole, James, 42
DeLuca, Stefanie, 146
Democratic Party, 18–19; election of

2016 and, 43; leftist evolution of, 150; Obama and, 57, 112; Reagan and, 181; responses to R. King episode, 145–146
Derrida, Jacques, 73–74
Detroit, MI, 145, 147
DiCaprio, Leonardo, 37, 163–164
Dissent magazine, 177
Djilas, Milovan, 116
Dohrn, Bernadine, 96
Dolezal, Rachel, 177
Domestic policy, results of Obama's, 172–174
Double Life of Fidel Castro, The (Sanchez), 148
Dr. Zhivago (film), 102
Duke University, lacrosse team and false accusation of rape, 127, 146
Duranty, Walter, 130, 149

Earth Day, 30, 35
East Anglia University, 31
Eastwood, Clint, 114, 140
Education. *See* Universities and colleges
Egypt, 79–81, 84, 93–95, 138
Elder, Larry, 61
Election of 2016: Clinton and, 128, 132–133; Democratic Party and, 43; media coverage of, 132–133, 136; public opinion and same-sex marriage, 176; Republican Party and, 71, 132–133
Emanuel, Dr. Ezekiel, 22
Emanuel African Methodist Episcopal Church (Charleston, SC), shooting at, 49–50, 185–190
Emoluments Clause, of US Constitution, 137–138
Emwazi, Mohammed (Jihadi John), 90, 95
England, Soros and shorting of currency of, 163, 167
Entertainment industry. *See* Arts and entertainment
Environmental Protection Agency, creation of, 36
Epstein, Alex, 28
Erdely, Sabrina Rubin, 127–129, 131

Evil, recognizing and opposing of,
    49–50, 185–190
Extramarital affairs, public opinion and,
    176

"Fairness": capital gains tax and, 58–59;
    nostalgia for Marxism and, 109–110,
    114–115, 117; Obama and, 58–59, 117
Fatah, 151
Federalist, 141
Federalist Papers, 120, 124, 143, 179
Feminists, ignoring of treatment of
    Muslim women, 176–177
Ferguson, MO, 50, 51, 64–65, 70, 129,
    145–148, 172
Finding Your Roots (television program),
    141–142
Fiorina, Carly, 147
Flynn, Mike, 98
Forbes, 28, 52, 109, 163
Foreign aid, inverse relationship to
    recipients' economic success, 110
Foreign policy, results of Obama's,
    172–174
Forster, E. M., 182
Foucault, Michel, 18, 73–74
Fox News, 129–130, 131, 140
France, 101–102; *Charlie Hebdo* attack in,
    1–2, 83, 182
Francis, pope, 151, 177–179
Frankfurt School, 17
Franklin, Benjamin, 48, 179
Franz Josef, emperor, 133
Freeman, Morgan, 50–51, 52, 55–56, 69
Freud, Sigmund, 17, 21, 142
Friends of Abe, 151

Gadahn, Adam Yahiye ("Azzam the
    American"), 90, 95
Gaddafi, Muammar, 132, 162
Gallup poll, 176
Garner, Eric, 51, 64
Gates, Henry Louis, 51, 61–63, 141–142
Gay and lesbian rights: political
    correctness and, 120; public opinion
    and, 175–177; same-sex marriage and,
    14, 176–177

GE, 141
Generation of 1968. *See* Least Great
    Generation (*babacool*)
Germany, after World War II, 158–159
Gibson, Charlie, 58
Ginsberg, Allen, 6
Giuliani, Rudolph, 171–172
Global warming. *See* Climate change
Goldberg, Jonah, 141
Gore, Al, and climate change, 26, 31,
    32–33, 37, 43, 48
Gowdy, Trey, 138
Gray, Freddie, 52, 146
Greenpeace, 32, 35
Gruber, Jonathan, 22
Guardian, 178
Guevara, Che, 103, 149
Gun control, 50, 153–155, 186. *See also*
    Second Amendment
Gun violence, in 2015, 172

Hadith, 82
Halbrook, Stephen P., 154
Hamas, 151; Pelosi refers to as
    "humanitarian organization," 93
"Hands Up, Don't Shoot," 51, 56–57, 70
Harris, Sam, 142
Harris-Perry, Melissa, 157
"Harvey and Sheila" (Sherman), 181
Hayden, Tom, 6, 17
Hayes, Cylvia, 168
Hayes, Stephen F., 97–98
Healy, Patrick, 132–133
Herf, Jeffrey, 1–2
Herridge, Catherine, 131
Hillsdale College, 124
Hirsi Ali, Ayaan, 104, 135, 176
Hispanic Americans, 63–64, 173
Hitler, Adolf, 23, 92, 102, 153–154, 188; G.
    W. Bush compared to, 164
"Hockey stick" graph, of climate change,
    31
Hoffman, Abbie, 6
Holder, Eric, 51, 61, 63, 64–65, 148
Holocaust: denials of, 151, 187; gun
    control issues and, 153–154; Soros
    and, 165–167

Homocentrism, climate change and, 47–48

Horowitz, David, 183

"How America Was Misled on al Qaeda's Demise" (Hayes and Joscelyn), 97–98

"How the Nazis Used Gun Control" (Halbrook), 154

Hypercacher kosher market attack, 1–2, ˙50, 83

"I am best" versus "I know best" narcissism, 21–23

Ibsen, Henrik, 21–22

"Imagine" (Lennon), 188

Immelt, Jeffrey, 141

Immigrants, proposed voting rights for illegal, 170

Income inequality: black persons and, 52–53, 58–60; Piketty on, 104–105; redistribution, taxes, and "fairness," 59; state capitalism and, 169

Inconvenient Truth, An (Gore), 31

Indiana, 120

Inhofe, James, 26

Injustice: Exposing the Racial Agenda of the Obama Justice Department (Adams), 64–65

Internal Revenue Service (IRS): C. Hayes and, 168; Clinton Foundation and, 141; political use of, 114

IPCC (Intergovernmental Panel on Climate Change), of UN, 43, 48

Iran: al Qaeda and, 99; Islamic State and, 97; Netanyahu's speech to US Congress about nuclear pact with, 91, 92–93, 95–96, 99; nuclear weapons and, 174; Obama's foreign policy and, 87, 97, 100; Obama's world view and, 173; P5 + 1 nuclear pact with, 91–92, 95–96; treatment of women and gays, 177

Iraq, 13–14, 41, 78, 87, 99, 156, 164

ISIS. *See* Islamic State

Islam, 73–100, 159; climate change used as distraction from radical, 45; fear and, 74, 79, 85; G. W. Bush and, 78–79; jobs program proposal and,

84–85, 90; intentional ignorance of reality and history of, 74–77, 87, 89, 92–100; moral equivalency of religions and, 74–77, 82–83; nomenklatura's reluctance to criticize, 142–143; Obama's policies and growth of radical, 174–175; "submission" as meaning of, 74; threat from, ignored, 179; Western imperialism blamed for spread of radical, 73–77, 82–83, 89–90

Islamic State, 14, 82–83; Iran and, 97; nuclear weapons and, 174; Obama and, 75–76, 84–86, 172; present in all fifty US states, 170; treatment of women and gays by, 177; US failure in Libya and, 162–163; Western recruits to, 83, 90, 99–100

"Islamophobia," 74–75

Israel, 43, 92, 151, 154, 187; Obama's world view and, 77, 172. *See also* Netanyahu, Benjamin

It Is So If You Think So or *Right You Are (If You Think You Are)* (Pirandello), 23

Jack Kemp: The Bleeding- Heart Conservative Who Changed America (Kondracke and Barnes), 59

Jackson, Jesse, 56, 67

Japan, after World War II, 7, 158–159

Jarrett, Valerie, 87, 148

Jefferson, Thomas, 158

Jihadi John (Mohammed Emwazi), 90, 95

Johnson, Lyndon, 53

Joscelyn, Thomas, 97–98

Kazakhstan, 137–138, 139

Kemp, Jack, 59, 147

Kerry, John, 11, 92, 148; climate change and, 26, 44, 45; Islam and, 87, 92

Khalidi, Rashid, 77–78

Khomeini, Ayatollah, 18, 86

King, Martin Luther, 56, 57

King, Rodney, 145–146

Kitman (Islamic doctrine), 92

Kitzhaber, John, 168
Klein, Edward, 94
Kondracke, Morton, 59
Koran, 83–84, 86; jihad in, 82
Krauthammer, Charles, 140, 181
Kristof, Nicholas, 142–143
Kroft, Steve, 165–166
Krugman, Paul, 105
Kurtz, Stanley, 183

Laffer, Arthur, 59
Lamarck, Jean-Baptiste, 29
Language, leftists exploitation of, 115–117
Lasch, Christopher, 7, 8, 173
Lean, David, 102
Leary, Timothy, 6
Least Great Generation (*babacool*):
    moral narcissism and, 16–19;
    narcissism and, 5–9
Left-wing moral narcissism, 15–20
Lenin, Vladimir, 54, 111, 112, 119;
    pathological altruism and, 109–110;
    statue of, in Los Angeles, 103
Lennon, John, 6, 188
Lewinsky, Monica, 162
Lewis, Bernard, 73
Lewis, John, 56, 69–70
Lewis, Reggie, 62
Libertarian neocons, 191–192
Libertarianism, 14, 116, 135, 136–137, 147,
    192; gay and lesbian rights and, 176;
    technology and, 105–106
Libya: Blumenthal and protection
    of Clintons, 93, 162–163; Coptic
    Christian beheaded in, 84; US
    embassy in Benghazi attacked, 98–99,
    132, 138, 162
Lima Climate Change Conference
    (2015), 25
Lindzen, Richard, 42–43
Lomborg, Dr. Bjorn, 178
Los Angeles, CA: crime in 2015, 172;
    riots in, 145–146
Los Angeles Times, 77–78, 130, 131
Lynton, Michael, 141
Lyons, Eugene, 107

Lysenko, Trofim, 29

Madison, James, 120, 121, 143, 179
Maher, Bill, 142, 182
Mailer, Norman, 177
Mamet, David, 114, 183
Mandatory voting, proposed, 112
Mann, Michael, 31
Mao Zedong, 13, 15–17, 103, 109
Marcuse, Herbert, 17–18, 104, 139
Martin, Trayvon, 51, 63–64, 129
Marx, Karl, 15, 106, 117
Marxism, nostalgia for, 17, 101–125, 149;
    Affordable Care Act and, 110–112;
    drift toward totalitarianism and,
    101–103, 110–113, 115; exploitation of
    language and, 115–117; "fairness" and,
    109–110, 114–115, 117; Hillary Clinton
    and, 105–107, 109; indoctrination
    into American nomenklatura and,
    119–125; mandatory voting proposal
    and, 112; in media, 102, 104–105; net
    neutrality and, 113–115; in universities,
    102–104, 121–123
Matthews, Herbert, 149
"Mattress girl," 174
"Maunder Minimum," of solar activity,
    47–48
McCarthy, Andrew, 74, 84
Media: campus rape "epidemic" and,
    127–129; climate change and, 31;
    coverage of 2016 election cycle, 132–
    133, 136; lack of in-depth journalism
    from, 131; left and right media and
    supposed "impartiality" of, 129–134;
    nostalgia for Marxism and, 102,
    104–105; racism narrative and, 49–52,
    55, 64, 69
Media Matters, 110, 162, 163, 183
Metamorphoses (Ovid), 150
Microaggressions, 13, 53; indoctrination
    into American nomenklatura and,
    121, 122–123; racism narrative and, 71;
    restrictions on free speech and, 150,
    170, 189–190
Mohammed: Benghazi attack and

video about, 98, 138; Koran and, 84; slaughter of enemies by, 85

Money: Blumenthal, Clintons, and self-enrichment, 161–163; personal and political behavior divergence and, 163–167; silencing of critics and, 169–170; socialism and, 167. *See also* Capitalism

Moore, Michael, 19, 37

Moore, Patrick, 32

Moral narcissism, 9, 20; defined, 11–12; as enemy of change and democracy, 181–183, 184; "healthy" narcissism contrasted, 21–22; insecurity of elites and, 22–23; left-and right-wing, 13–20; self-regard and, 12–14; unchanging opinions and, 1–2, 12

Morsi, Mohamed, 80, 81, 94, 95

Mosby, Marilyn J., 52

MoveOn.org, 164

Moynihan, Daniel Patrick, 70

Moyo, Dambisa, 110

MSNBC, 157, 183

Mubarak, Hosni, 80

Multiculturalism, 16, 122

Muslim Brotherhood, 2, 76, 80–81, 86, 93–95, 174

Muslim Sisterhood, 94

Narcissism, Least Great Generation and, 5–9. *See also* Moral narcissism

NASA, climate change and, 41–42, 44–45

Nation building, moral values and, 158–159

National Endowment for the Arts, 114

National Environmental Policy Act (1970), 36

National Oceanic and Atmospheric Administration (NOAA), climate change and, 31, 41–42, 44–45

National Review Online, 154

Natural law: culture and, 159; US founders and, 158

NBC network, 129–130

Netanyahu, Benjamin, 91, 92–93, 95–96, 99

Net-neutrality, 113–115

New Republic, 128–129

New York, NY, 46–47; crime in 2015, 171–172

New York Review of Books, 73, 105

New York Times, 14, 43, 129, 137; coverage of 2016 election cycle, 132–133; Duranty and, 130, 149; liberal bias as "impartiality" and, 129–134, 140; Petraeus and, 164; Piketty and, 105

Newsweek, 28

Nixon, Richard, 36

Nomenklatura: business community and, 140–141; Clintons and, 137–140; defined, 119; drift toward totalitarianism and, 149–151; political correctness and indoctrination into, 119–125, 134–136, 143; self-preservation, stasis, and power of, 137, 140, 145–152; shame and, 141–142

Nye, Bill, 26

Obama, Barack, 2, 8; climate change and, 19, 28, 39, 44–45; Egypt and, 79–80, 81, 95; "fairness" and, 58–59, 117; gun control and, 136, 186; "hope and change" and, 57, 61, 79–80, 139; illusory change and underclass, 147–148; Iranian nuclear pact and, 91–92, 95–96; Islamic background of, 82, 87; Khalidi and, 77–78; leftist background of, 96; mandatory voting idea of, 112; moral equivalency of religions and, 75–76, 82–83, 87, 89; net-neutrality and, 113–115; shame and Islam, 86–87; understanding and support of Islam, 79–84; views of and effects on domestic and foreign policy, 172–174; worsening of race relations and, 50, 52–53, 57–63

Obama, Michelle, 113

Obamacare. *See* Affordable Care Act

Okrent, Daniel, 130

O'Malley, Martin, 146–147, 148

O'Neill, Tip, 177

Open Source Foundation, 163

Operation Iraqi Freedom, 13–14
O'Reilly, Bill, 30
Orientalism (Said), 73–74, 90
Origins of Totalitarianism, The (Arendt), 183
Orwell, George, 31, 75, 182
Ostrakismos (ostracism), 97
Ovid, 150

P5 + 1 nuclear pact with Iran, 91–92, 95–96
Pachauri, Rajendra, 48
"Pathological altruism," Lenin and, 109–110
Paul, Rand, 59, 147
Pelosi, Nancy, 22, 92–93
"Penthouse Bolsheviks." *See* Marxism, nostalgia for
Perry, Rick, 155
Petraeus, David, 164
Pew polls, 157, 175, 176
Philadelphia, PA, Black Panther Party and voting in, 51, 61
Piketty, Thomas, 104–105
Pirandello, Luigi, 23
Pity Party, The (Voegeli), 18
Please Stop Helping Us: How Liberals Make It Harder for Blacks to Succeed (Riley), 60
Police, racism narrative and, 51–52, 60, 64–66, 146, 173, 175
Political correctness: indoctrination into American nomenklatura and, 119–125, 134–136, 143; Islam and moral equivalency, 78–79; Islamic radicalism and, 174; need to ridicule, 182; nostalgia for Marxism and, 104; racism narrative and, 71; and shift toward totalitarianism, 149
Port Huron Statement (1962), 17
Powers, Kirsten, 169–170
Prager, Dennis, 124, 158
Prager University, 124
Pre-boomers. *See* Least Great Generation (*babacool*)
Presley, Elvis, 189

Putin, Vladimir, 137–138, 139

Qutb, Sayyid, 81, 85–86

Racism, 49–71; civil rights movement and, 53–54, 56; failure of liberal social programs, 54–55, 57–58, 60–61, 67–68, 112; media and incidents of, 49–52, 55, 64, 69; microaggression and, 122–123; nostalgia for, to bring back without solving problems of, 55–57; Obama and worsening of race relations and lives of blacks, 50, 52–53, 57–63; victimology and preservation of, 61–65, 67–71, 177
Rangel, Charlie, 39
Rape "epidemic" on campuses, 127–129, 146, 174
Rather, Dan, 128
Raza, La, 164
Reagan, Ronald, 139–140, 181
Real Time (television program), 142
"Red bourgeoisie," 116
Redford, Robert, 128
Reds (film), 102
Regnery Publishing, 170
Religion, US culture and drift away from, 151, 157–159
Religious Freedom Restoration Act, 120
"Repressive tolerance" theory, 17–18, 103, 183
Republican Party: election of 2016 and, 71, 132–133; nomenklatura and, 120–121, 147; same-sex marriage and, 175–176
Revelle, Roger, 32
Rice, Condoleezza, 103, 104, 135
Rice, Susan, 98
Right-wing moral narcissism, 13–14
Riley, Jason, 60
Rivera, Geraldo, 185
Rodriguez Maradiaga, Cardinal Oscar, 178
Rolling Stone, 127–129, 131
Romney, Mitt, 169
Roof, Dylann Storm, 49–50, 186–190

Rubio, Marco, 132–133
Rules for Radicals (Alinsky), 106–107, 139
Runnymede Trust, 74
Rutgers University, 103, 104

Sadat, Anwar, 84
Sagan, Mrs. Carl, 26
Said, Edward, 73–74, 76–77, 90, 92
Same-sex marriage, 14; public opinion and, 135–137, 175–176
Sanders, Bernie, 43–44; socialism and moral narcissism, 15–16
Sandor, Richard, 41
Schmidt, Gavin, 44–45
Schulz, Ed, 183
Schweizer, Peter, 137, 138–139
Scowcroft, Brent, 79
Second Amendment, 136, 153–155. *See also* Gun control
Seinfeld, Jerry, 182
Self-belief, loss of societal, 158–159
Self-regard, moral narcissism and, 12–14
Sergant, Yosi, 114
Shame: nomenklatura and, 141–142; Obama and Islam and, 86–87
Sharpton, Al, 51, 67, 68–69, 148
Shaw & Company Research, 95–96
Sherman, Allen, 181
Siege of Vienna (1529), 76, 89
Silencing, The (Powers), 169–170
Silent Spring (Carson), 35
Simpson, O. J., 55, 57
Singleton, Chris, 186
Sisi, Abdel Fattah al-, 80, 84, 95
60 Minutes, 50–51, 131, 165–166
Slate, 37
Slavery: black victimhood and, 173; seen as America's original sin, 70–71
Smith, Lee, 86
Soave, Robby, 189
Socialism: Sanders and, 15–16; Soros and, 167; state capitalism and, 169
Socialized medicine, nostalgia for Marxism and, 110–112
Socrates, 157
Solar activity, climate change and, 47–48

Solyndra, 116, 168
Sopoaga, Enele, 40
Soros, George, 109–110; leftist causes and crony capitalism of, 163–167
South Korea, 159
Southern Poverty Law Center, 164
Sowell, Thomas, 68, 112
Spencer, Robert, 76
Stalin and Stalinism, 15–17, 29, 107, 111, 119, 130, 149
Staten Island, NY, 51, 64–65
Steele, Shelby, 68
Steinem, Gloria, 6
Stephanopoulos, George, 138
Stephens, Bret, 20
Stevens, Christopher, 132
Stewart, Jon, 157
Steyer, Tom, 32, 168
Stone, Oliver, 17
"Stop and frisk" policies, in New York City, 171
Strong, Maurice, 41
Students for a Democratic Society, 17, 115
Sustainability, indoctrination into American nomenklatura and, 121–122
Sweden, 15–16
Syria, 43, 97
Szatowski, Gary, 46

Taqiyya (Islamic doctrine), 92
Tea Party, 69, 143
Telegraph of London, 28, 40
Ten Commandments, absence of God in culture and, 158
Thatcher, Margaret, 16
Thiel, Peter, 105
Tides Foundation, 164
Till, Emmett, 65
Time magazine, 28, 41, 128
Times of Israel, 1–2
Title IX statute, 140
Totalitarianism: Arendt on, 183; nomenklatura and drift toward, 149–151; nostalgia for Marxism and drift toward, 101–103, 110–113, 115; political correctness and drift toward,

149; Western imperialism blamed
for, 172

Trigger warnings, 8, 13, 135, 150, 152, 170, 174

Trotsky, Leon, 110

Trump, Donald, 147

Truth (film), 128

Turning Right at Hollywood and Vine (Simon), 184

Tuvalu, climate change and, 39–40

Ukraine, Stalin's starvation of population in, 16, 107, 130, 149

Unemployment, blacks and, 59–60

United Nations: anti-Semitism and, 187; IPCC of, 43, 48; Strong and scandals at, 41

Universities and colleges: campus rape "epidemic" and, 127–129, 146, 174; microaggressions and, 53; nostalgia for Marxism and, 102–104, 121–123; political correctness and indoctrination into nomenklatura, 121–123, 134–136, 150; victim culture and, 173–174

"University of California's Insane Speech Police, The" (*Daily Beast*), 189

University of Virginia, 127–129

Untold History of the United States (television series), 17

Uranium, Russia and, 137–138, 139

Vaihinger, Hans, 102

Values, lack of religion and confusion about, 157–159

Vencore Weather, 47–48

Vesey, Denmark, 49

Victimology: college students and, 173–174; preservation of racism and, 61–65, 67–71, 177

Villon, François, 101

Voegeli, William, 18

Voting rights: Black Panther Party in Philadelphia and, 51, 61; illegal immigrants and, 170; mandatory voting proposed, 112

Vox, 174

Walker, Scott, 132

Wall Street Journal, 97–98, 129–130, 131, 138, 161, 168

Wallace, Mike, 50–51

Warhol, Andy, 103

Warren, Elizabeth, 104

Washington, Booker T., 67–68

Washington Free Beacon, 168

Washington Post, 26, 120, 127–128, 131, 140, 141, 146

Watermelons: The Green Movement's True Colors (Delingpole), 42

Waters, Maxine, 67

WattsUpWithThat (website), 28

Weeks, Buffy, 114

Wenner, Jann, 127, 129

Western imperialism: blamed for poverty and totalitarianism, 172; blamed for spread of Islam, 73–77, 82–83, 89–90

"What I Believe" (Forster), 182

"White Negro, The" (Mailer), 177

Whitehouse, Sheldon, 26, 29

Willey, Kathleen, 162

"Willful blindness," about Islam, 74, 84, 94–95

Williams, Brian, 99

Wilson, Darren, 64

World Economic Forum (2015), 37

Wright, Jeremiah, 61, 81–82

Wynn, Barry, 133

Zero to One: Notes on Startups, or How to Build the Future (Thiel), 105

Zimmerman, George, 51, 63, 64